I FOUND THE KEY TO THE HEART OF GOD

Australia: Evangelical Sisterhood of Mary
P.O. BOX 430, Camden NSW 2570

Canada: Evangelical Sisterhood of Mary
R.R. 1, Millet, Alberta TOC 1ZO

Germany: Evangelical Sisterhood of Mary
P.O. BOX 13 01 29, 64241 Darmstadt

UK: Evangelical Sisterhood of Mary
17 Gills Hill Lane, Radlett, Herts. WD7 8DE

USA: Evangelical Sisterhood of Mary
P.O. BOX 30022, Phoenix, AZ 85046-0022

www.kanaan.org

I FOUND THE KEY TO THE HEART OF GOD

M. Basilea Schlink

Evangelical Sisterhood of Mary
Darmstadt, Germany

Original title: Wie ich Gott erlebte: Sein Weg mit mir durch sieben Jahrzehnte
First German edition 1975
First American edition 1975: I Found the Key to the Heart of God
First British edition 1975: A Foretaste of Heaven
Revised German edition 2017
Revised English-language edition 2023
ISBN 978-3-87209-596-1 hardcover
ISBN 978-3-87209-010-2 eBook

Printed in Germany.

This book is gratefully dedicated to Mother Martyria, who so faithfully stood by me over the years. Without her, I could never have fulfilled the commission God entrusted to me in the Sisterhood of Mary. Her wholehearted support was invaluable in each new venture of faith, especially as we acquired our Land of Canaan. She selflessly shared the burden, releasing me for all the other tasks to which the Lord called me. May the Lord reward her abundantly.

I praise His name of YES AND AMEN,
for paths ordained for me to walk in,
for blessings yielded by the night
and choicest fruit in darkest places.
I praise His name of YES AND AMEN,
His will of loving-kindness leading
onward, upward to the goal of heaven.

I praise Him for His guidance,
the wisdom of His counsels,
for His calling on my life
and the testing of my soul
in Mount Moriah's crucible;
for the glory that will dawn
when the darkness He dispels.

I praise His name of YES AND AMEN.
What He begins, He will complete
in ways too wonderful to comprehend.
Fruit and blessing in abundance
at the end of all His leadings.
Sing, my soul, sing His praises evermore.
Who is like God on high,
my ever-loving Father!

CONTENTS

PART 1: WHEN GOD CALLS

PART 2: WONDERFUL IN COUNSEL

Journeys for Reconciliation and Unity: Fruits of Times Apart with Jesus, 1953–1955

Canaan – A Foreshadowing of Jesus' Kingdom, 1955–1957

A Year of Death and Resurrection, 1958–1959

A Life Restored and New Commissions Granted, 1959–1964

Mount Sinai – The Climax of My Life, 1963–1969

PART 1:
WHEN GOD CALLS

ALMOST ALWAYS VERY HAPPY

CHILDHOOD AND EARLY YOUTH IN BRUNSWICK, 1904–1920

Gauss Street, in the north German town of Brunswick, was a quiet residential road with a few family homes set in gardens, and an inviting circle of chestnut trees. Yet at times the street was bursting with life. It seemed the neighbourhood was home to many children. A whole band of eight- to twelve-year-olds would make forays into the gardens, led, as it happened, by a little girl. Number 31, Gauss Street – the house where I lived with my parents and elder brother for so many years. What childhood memories the name brings back!

I considered Brunswick my home, though I was actually born in Darmstadt, on October 21, 1904. My father accepted a post as professor of mechanics at Brunswick Technical University when I was eighteen months old. That was when we moved to the house on Gauss Street, with its garden, the summer house and even a fountain with goldfish. My childhood domain included a room of my own in the home I loved.

Life at my parents' house was eventful and stimulating, as we participated in the intellectual life of the technical university, a seven-minute walk away. There my father, respected by all his students and naturally admired by his little daughter, was rector for many years. My parents followed the affairs of the nation with keen interest, which was intensified by the events of WWI. As a fourteen-year-old I was acutely aware of the collapse of Imperial Germany. This event caused my family to flee temporarily from Brunswick, as revolutionary elements planned to take my father hostage.

Not that any of this significantly affected my inner life. The strong ethical convictions of my parents made a far greater impression, as my journal discloses. As a thirteen-year-old I wrote:

L. and B. [two school friends] don't think lying matters. But I do.

January 25, 1918

Although I was encouraged to think deeply and had God-fearing parents who prayed with me as a little girl, I grew up without any real spiritual guidance. In those days my parents rarely went to church and had no contact with believers. They didn't yet know Jesus as their personal Saviour. For all my childhood joys, I missed out on true joy, for I couldn't sing from the heart, "I am Jesus' little lamb." Though cheerful by nature, I was also shy, reserved and fearful. In Scripture classes I heard Bible stories about Jesus, but my heart was not touched. So I had no one to turn to when I was troubled by a deep sorrow my parents were bearing, and often I arrived at school in the morning with eyes swollen from crying.

Soon, however, I would be my usual high-spirited self again, fun-loving and rather boisterous. Despite various troubles in my childhood years, I was often bubbling over with the sheer joy of living. I wrote in my journal:

I am almost always very happy. The world is just too heavenly.

January 25, 1918

Since I could be extremely lively at times, it was a mercy that I had a mother who brought me up wisely, making it plain I had to change. Indeed, I took her words to heart, convinced I was the worst child in the world. Repeatedly, I would take stock of my faults: "noisy, uncooperative, moody, quick-tempered ..." But what was the point? As a thirteen-year-old I wrote in my journal:

I do want to be good, but sometimes it's terribly difficult. I will try very hard now and earnestly ask God to help me and show me how to go about it. I can't do it by myself. I'm just too bad. June 22, 1918

Like most mothers in those days, mine wished for a domestically inclined daughter, who would sit quietly sewing beside her. However, I had no desire to sit still. Indoors, only the kitchen held a certain attraction, as I enjoyed trying out new recipes. But most of the time I longed to be out of doors where the children were waiting for new exploits with their little ringleader.

Being surrounded by a whole band of children naturally made me even more high-spirited, and my father would teasingly call me "little Miss Frisky". Instead of a well-behaved daughter, my mother had a scamp. She saw my liveliness and strong-mindedness with motherly concern and recognized where restraint was needed. Under her watchful eye, that side of my nature was curbed. Despite the many tears I shed, I thank God for giving me such a mother. It was His gracious hand that checked the shooting up of this aspiring little plant, pruning its branches. All this taught me to seek His help at an early age.

At fifteen I took dancing-classes, as was the custom, and experienced a similar "pruning process". Once again I found myself in my element, for dancing and music were my passion. As one of the most popular dancers, I had no lack of partners, and I enjoyed the company of others at the various homes where we met. But there was only one boy I really cared about. I loved him with all my heart. For a year and a half my thoughts and emotions revolved round him, and my one desire was to know whether he cared for me too. But in God's wisdom I was denied any such response. Once more it was His hand disciplining me in grace. Before the foundation of the world, He had chosen me to be His own. With this *no* from God my branches were cut back radically.

Soon my pleasure in dances and youthful fun was spoilt. It was the same on every occasion – this one boy I cared about seemed oblivious to me. In my distress I was driven to God. About that time I wrote in my journal:

> *What is the point of life? Only God can provide comfort in these situations. Without it I could not live with this heartache.*
>
> July 11, 1920

At that age, I took my troubles for real suffering, but they brought me closer to God. I was taking my first lessons in saying, "Whatever our God does is good; His will is best for me", as the hymn goes. I had come up against some of the limitations imposed by this life when we seek to enjoy it to the full. Nothing in this life is perfect – least of all human nature, my own included. "I think I still have my childhood faith" was an entry in my journal at that time. It was a faith in God, in Christ, though as yet I didn't know Him as my personal Saviour. But by the time I reached sixteen, even this faith began to disintegrate. I wrote:

> *Of course I don't believe everything in the Old Testament, e.g. the story of creation. How can anyone know how God created the world, etc.? Still, I can't understand how people can become atheists. I could never be an atheist or a materialist.*
>
> July 1, 1920

This last remark stemmed from my parents' positive influence: complacency and self-sufficiency did not tally with their idealistic way of thinking. They were against atheism and materialism, and this striving after a high ethical standard was also ingrained in me. I went on to write:

> *Anyone who doesn't believe in God is incapable of loving here on earth. There's no effort to achieve perfection or to work on their personality: they live only for self, and when they die it's all over. That's why they try to make their lives on earth as pleasant as possible, regardless of who else they may be hurting.*
>
> *Oh, I'm still so bad. So envious, jealous; above all, so defiant and moody – ugh! I really need to improve. I've resolved to test*

myself in the small things of daily life until I can get a grip on myself and overcome all that's bad in me. I really want to bring sunshine to others. July 1, 1920

Once I had completed my dancing lessons, a new chapter began in my life – confirmation classes. I had now stumbled into the area of religious controversy. I was sixteen, and an over-emphasis on the intellect, the ability to reason and evaluate, was awakened: the legacy of my forebears. At the time I did not realize how much trouble my intellect would cause me later in life. Nor did I suspect how deeply I was in bondage to my strongly critical nature. We had a pastor who brought many good and important points to our attention. But despite the fact that he believed in God, he did not seem to have a personal faith in Jesus as his Saviour. Much of what he taught us was mere idealism. He challenged us to keep up the fight against evil, but his enthusiasm was on a human level. At the time I wrote in my journal:

Pastor X said that we human beings can belong to eternity here and now. We don't have to wait until we die, as some believe. Do I belong to time or eternity? I want to belong to eternity, and I want to work on my personality and conquer my weak points, my Achilles' heel. With God's help I want to become a person of integrity.
October 30, 1920

Pastor X asked, "What would you do if you knew that you were going to die in twenty-four hours?" Probably you would fight wholeheartedly against your shortcomings and do all the good you could, for soon you would be standing before God's judgment seat. We should always bear this in mind, for no one knows how soon that may come. Certainly, the will to improve is strong, but the flesh is weak. If only I wasn't so terribly moody!
November 27, 1920

I concluded:

My life can't go on the way it is. I'll follow the example of the American Benjamin Franklin and examine myself every day, keeping track of my improvement with a chart. First I need to list my faults. At home that would be: stubbornness, untidiness, unkind remarks, a quick temper. When all is said and done, so often I've been downright selfish. November 27, 1920

The confirmation classes may well have served to strengthen my ethical strivings, but they also showed me that I was still very far from Christ and had no real contact with God – a new realization for me.

I'm beginning to think I've made an idol of X [the boy from the dancing classes]. All my thoughts and love are so focussed on him that I forget God. I'm not sure, but I don't think I'm very close to God, for I don't feel Christ is with me when I pray. I am too wrapped up in this world: any close contact with God would be strange to me. I can't quite express it – all I know is that I haven't found the right way yet.

When I hear that Christ must come into our hearts, that we should be conscious of Him accompanying us and that we should always be devoted to Him, it sounds like a foreign language to me. I wish my life was like that, but where to begin? How do you get there? I'm still too taken up by earthly things: love, school, having fun. I simply can't understand how great men of God can feel His presence and hear His voice. In my opinion, they must sense subconsciously that one thing or another will happen, or that they are supposed to do this or that. Almost without knowing it, I search all the books I can lay my hands on, looking for something I can identify with – though what it is, I can't say. All I know is that I can't find it anywhere.

December 30, 1920

The realization that I was missing something in my spiritual life was a gift of God, for the truth sets us free. From that point of view the confirmation classes did bring me closer to the heart of Jesus, even though they caused me more doubts.

The pastor preparing me for confirmation almost gave up on me. His wife told my parents that more than once he arrived home exasperated. "Any more like Klara Schlink, and I could pack my bags!" I raised so many sceptical questions, probably in an overconfident and high-spirited manner, that it must have been disruptive to the whole class. Finally, he quoted the Bible verse at me, "The message about Christ's death on the cross is nonsense to those who are being lost." With that, I was supposed to note that with my intellectual attitude I was liable to end up among the lost. Later, during the confirmation service, he gave me the same verse – this time with the other half as well: "... but for us who are being saved it is God's power" (1 Corinthians 1:18 GNT).

Several years later as a Bible college sister I visited this same pastor. By that time I was serving Jesus and witnessing to the power of the message of the cross. He could only exclaim, "Wonders never cease!"

In my childhood and youth, a familiar pattern was beginning to emerge. Every time my sinful nature craved satisfaction, God sent me a cross so that something in me was put to death. And each time, God brought something new to life in me.

During my childhood I learnt to pray to God for help, because my careful upbringing made me painfully aware of my faults. My big disappointment at dancing classes showed me that I had made an idol of someone else: my thoughts and feelings revolved round him so much that I forgot God.

It was during confirmation classes that I woke up to the negative side of my intellectualism and sceptical attitude when I saw how this was upsetting my pastor. Indeed, he frequently felt obliged to warn me of the consequences. Painful though this experience was, it was ultimately God who stood in my path, curbing the growth of my scepticism as He dealt with my over-emphasis on reason. His aim was to show me my need of a Saviour. It was a while before I capitulated, however, and in the next year or two I was to suffer increasingly under my intellectualism and strong-willed nature.

The yearning to draw near to God was born of these hidden troubles of my childhood and youth, and I was given a foretaste of the glory that all affliction brings. Our smallest cross, even the cross of our sinful nature, brings us closer to Jesus.

SELF-EFFORT FAILS – MY ENCOUNTER WITH GOD

DARMSTADT, EASTER 1921 – EASTER 1923

When I was sixteen-and-a-half my parents moved back to Darmstadt, my father having accepted a post at the technical university there. Since my school began four weeks earlier, I arrived in Darmstadt ahead of my parents and stayed with my aunt. If I was high-spirited and bubbly, full of plans for new escapades as a child, I was even more exuberant and fun-loving as a teenager. Often I didn't know what to do with all my energy. My fresh field of activity was my new class, where I soon caused chaos. During gym classes I would teach the girls the latest dances. In other lessons, too, I was quite a handful for my teachers, since I had an answer to everything. And though I was class representative, I had one order mark after another, and left school with a low grade in conduct. When my parents arrived in Darmstadt, they were greeted on all sides with tales of their daughter's pranks.

Yet my heart was filled with unanswered questions and a deep longing for God. Not that I let anyone suspect this. I was constantly at loggerheads with our Scripture teacher, who, as I strongly sensed, did not believe in Jesus. Outwardly self-assured, inwardly I was unsure of myself and seeking, as my journal shows:

> *Oh, if only I were still a child and could simply believe everything and be happy! But what can I do if my intellect raises objections and I just can't accept it all? No one can give me the answer: books can't help either.* May 22, 1921

I often ask myself if we have a free will at all. In my opinion, no, for God creates people with good or bad, strong or weak characters. Can a person help it if they have bad personality traits and are too weak to resist their sinful inclinations? Yet others find it easy to overcome their weaknesses. It just makes no sense to me ...

Christ died for us, we are told, so that we can conquer sin. But has anyone ever conquered sin completely? I am longing to know the answer to these questions but haven't found it anywhere. What is the good of all the beautiful sermons in the world when I doubt the basic principles? I read Schopenhauer on religion, but found he has a strong tendency towards atheism. Still, these philosophers are really interesting. May 23, 1921

This is what was going on inside me. I longed for someone to lead me to God but knew no one who could. Influenced by my brother Edmund, who was later to study philosophy, I turned to works by Schopenhauer and others in my pursuit of truth. None of this helped me to draw closer to Jesus. I still recall touring the bookshops of Darmstadt with my brother, in quest of books discussing ideological matters. But I was just as interested in the classics. By the time I was fifteen I had a small collection of art postcards and paid more attention to the history of art and of music than to my school subjects. My spirit was hungry and sought nourishment everywhere until I found the fullness of knowledge in Jesus.

But I had not found the Lord yet, and when I was seventeen I wrote in my journal:

Why can't I enjoy life like others in dancing and superficiality and having fun? November 7, 1921

Christmastime is really splendid, but the inner peace is lacking – I am still searching. Although I no longer act out of conviction, I still hold to the principles which were instilled in me in the past and which I'm unwilling to discard altogether. In my heart

I can't deny the intrinsic goodness of human beings, even though my common sense tells me otherwise. I have a belief in the basic dignity of humanity. Both believers and atheists act out of conviction, whereas I have nothing. This is the worst possible state. Oh, if only I had some sort of revelation, or could meet someone who could convince me! This uncertainty is terrible.

December 17, 1921

Why were we born? How can we have a free will when moods come over us which we can do nothing about? Yet if we put on a friendly face when we feel different inside, it's nothing but a mask: it's self-deception. Only a higher power can heal us with time. January 18, 1922

God, in His amazing grace, saw me through these agonizing periods of doubt and inner conflict. He shattered my wilful strivings and lifeless knowledge by thrusting me into new difficulties, as in my childhood and early youth. I found myself at a dead end. True to my religion (to strive for self-improvement) I was determined to overcome my weaknesses. But the more I strove, the more I realized I was making no headway.

Everything progresses, only I remain at a standstill. Every day I struggle with myself, and every day I am defeated. Afterwards I see the situation in a new light, taking a broader view, and feel ashamed at having got upset over trifles. June 2, 1922

A specific situation brought my frustration to a head. After completing school, I took lessons from my mother in home economics. I was thrilled when a good friend from Brunswick came to join me. Then the unforeseeable happened. Much to my distress, I developed an aversion to this friend. Living at close quarters with her, I suddenly found her unbearable: her whole personality and her mannerisms annoyed me intensely. What should I do? If I showed her my dislike, she would be very hurt, and I wanted to spare her that. Yet I was too frank by nature to hide my feelings. In this situation self-control and self-effort were useless. I was faced with my utter helplessness and wrote in my journal:

The situation can't remain the way it is, but what to do? I call R. my best friend and yet I take offence at the most trivial things in everyday life. Communication breaks down and we are hopelessly at odds. I could shake myself!

If one didn't have the hope of further development in the next world, one could almost seek death out of contempt for the wretchedness of human life. How imperfect and limited are the human will and emotions. But while I have the will and my sense of responsibility demands it, I will do everything possible to resolve the problem and get our friendship back on track – in keeping with my principle: love never fails. June 10, 1922

In this case self-control is pretty useless: my own will-power gets me nowhere. I've reached my limit. As a mere human I've got to the point where I can only humble myself before God and accept His grace with thanksgiving. July 10, 1922

Yet I still didn't find the way to Jesus. Indeed, how can we recognize Him unless He Himself opens our eyes? In the midst of these struggles I made the following entry in my journal:

I believe and trust in God and Christ. However, I am having such troubles, doubts and struggles, and so far no one has been able to deliver me from them. First I will write down my creed, to systemize what I do believe. I believe in the nobility of man. Ever since I was intellectually awakened, my instincts and conscience have told me that this was the most justifiable standpoint. And I cannot believe the words of Christ, "No one comes to the Father except through me" [John 14:6]. July 10, 1922

Then, in August 1922, came the big moment when at last I could make the words of a German hymn my own: "I have found a firm foundation" – that is, Jesus Christ as my Saviour. How did it happen? On two separate counts I had come to the end of my own resources. All my efforts to live in harmony with my friend had failed. Equally, my search for truth in the books I read had proved fruitless. I began to plead with God that if Jesus really was His Son, the Saviour of the world, who died on the cross and became for us the Way to the Father, He would reveal this to me somehow.

And God answered. I was ill and took to my bed for several days. And one night I was permitted to behold Jesus inwardly as the crucified Lord. Next morning, when I awoke, joy flooded my heart – "I know that my Redeemer lives!" I rejoiced to know that Jesus, the crucified Lord, is the Way to the Father, that He had redeemed me, and that I could follow Him. What amazing grace!

I did not confide my secret to a soul. Nor was I sure of the next step now that I had found Jesus, for I didn't know any other believers. However, God Himself guided me. My parents, who took an interest in a wide range of intellectual and religious matters, possessed books on various religions, including a number of biographies. Among these, unbeknown to me, was the autobiography of the Christian author Jung-Stilling. While I was sick in bed – actually, the day after that memorable night when I found Jesus – my mother brought me this book. Eagerly, I began to read, and found myself devouring the contents.

Now I could write in my journal:

I'm so happy and thankful that I have found my Saviour and that He lives within me. Now my heart will conquer all the intellectual torment. I know that my Saviour lives in me and that His love will grow in me. Oh, if only I too could be pure love one day! How I long to sing and compose songs about love, for what could be greater than Christian love?

September 2, 1922

Now I understand that everything depends on grace – a concept that never made any sense to me. I see now how I was on the wrong track before my confirmation when I kept tabs on myself. Every day I made entries in a booklet to see how far I had improved. How little I was able to accomplish by self-effort.

If I'd had any idea of the meaning of "Christ for us", I wouldn't have agonized so much. I'd have been happy at the end of the day to know I was forgiven for Christ's sake and would have asked for new strength and love. Where love prevails, weaknesses naturally retreat. Of course, we still have to work on our characters, read God's Word and pray. Then this attempt at practical sanctification will have God's blessing, even if we aren't instantly transformed. Without a prayer life we aren't Christians – but I didn't even know what a prayer life was before. How much I've missed! I was so alone. Now I need to do a lot of reading, to keep it all alive. October 8, 1922

Other than that, I had no spiritual guidance at all. I felt I must learn to pray and grow in love. But who was to point out the right way to me? I knew nothing about claiming the saving blood of Jesus in faith – and real prayer was quite unknown to me.

The Lord, however, had already prepared the way. Several months earlier when I tried to choose a career for myself, I decided on kindergarten teaching, for then I could work with people. In a magazine I found an advertisement for a Protestant Froebel Academy. This advertisement smiled at me like a greeting from heaven, for didn't "Protestant" mean "Christian"? At the time I thought so. I had to pass through many disappointments before I realized that not everything that is called "Christian" necessarily implies belief in Jesus as the Saviour. Nevertheless, God had set my heart on fire for this Protestant academy in Kassel, for there I was to meet Erika Madauss, who was later to found the Evangelical Sisterhood of Mary together with me. She introduced me to the local Girls' Bible Class (MBK), which helped me to grow in the Word of God. The course at the Froebel Academy was due to begin at Easter 1923.

During that last half year in Darmstadt I took my first steps as "a new-born babe in Christ" without any proper guidance –

though, in fact, I was not without guidance, since Jesus Himself led me.

As usual, during the winter season, I accepted invitations to student balls, since I loved dancing. But now I could not enjoy these dances so freely, for I felt they drew me away from Jesus and grieved the Holy Spirit. At that time I wrote in my journal:

> *So often I am unable to disentangle myself from trivial things and come to God.* November 11, 1922

> *Now I know for sure I have to go to Kassel. It's either Christ or the world. If I continue to go to dances, my thought world will belong to Satan. Thoughts of dresses, the desire to be beautiful and popular continually whirl in my head. And I can't pray when I come back home at four-thirty in the morning, carried away with the music, the dancing, and the exhilarating atmosphere – even though my fun was harmless. Afterwards, I have difficulty in shaking off all the impressions, and God's Word loses its power. My soul is so taken up with other thoughts that thoughts of God and spiritual things get crowded out. So I'll be glad when I go to Kassel.* December 18, 1922

This journal entry marked the end of my dancing days. The Lord made this denial very easy for me, for shortly afterwards I left Darmstadt.

SEARCHING FOR THE WAY

FROEBEL ACADEMY, KASSEL
EASTER 1923 – AUTUMN 1924

Kassel's Protestant Froebel Academy for women was a large house set in spacious grounds on the outskirts of the city. With youthful enthusiasm all 120 boarders would gather in the garden on summer evenings for folk dances and the old romantic folk songs to the accompaniment of the lute. Here the youth movement, though already on the wane, still exerted its best influence. A cheerful, natural, yet disciplined atmosphere prevailed. There was a strong sense of camaraderie. I was glad to be welcomed into this group of lively eighteen-year-olds, enjoying their friendship as we studied, sang and had fun together.

The staff placed great emphasis on this team spirit. They considered it their duty to train these young women – the future teachers of our nation's youth – to be caring, responsible and willing to serve. We were encouraged to look beyond our secluded boarding-school life and take an active interest in the national crises of the time.

I will never forget the moment on November 9, 1923, when the news broke of the Munich Putsch, Hitler's failed attempt to seize power in Bavaria. As inflation cast its shadow over us, we did not hesitate to share our devalued pocket money with each other. Among other things, it had to cover our daily bread ration. This was all part of our training, for our teachers set great store by such high ideals.

They were tireless in their efforts to instil in us a sense of duty, discretion and consideration for others. Didn't they aim to lead their students to our Saviour Jesus Christ? Reading the advertisement for the Protestant Froebel Academy, I had assumed so. Our Principal was a woman of high ideals, but for her, as for the pastor who gave us religious instruction, Jesus was merely a great example to be followed, rather than the crucified Lord and Saviour. While receiving an excellent and invaluable grounding in ethics, I failed to find the spiritual nourishment I longed for. God let me wait several years before leading me to a Bible college where I discovered my heart's desire: a Christian fellowship where I could hear about Jesus and be shown the path of discipleship.

Yet during my time at the Froebel Academy God provided everything I needed for my spiritual development. Through the good training we received He gave me a growing insight into my heart, and little by little He convicted me of my sins. God had a specific goal in mind. His intention was not for me just to enjoy the classes and recreation, the fellowship and celebrations. He took care to bring me into a group where I found it harder than usual to make friends.

In this educational system the 120 boarders were grouped in family units. Each unit had a teacher for "mother" and occupied a separate floor of the building. After several weeks had passed, boarders were due to be nominated for election as "senior" in the new term. The mother and senior of our family asked to speak to me and explained that although I had the right gifts, they felt unable to nominate me. They gave me to understand that such a position would not be good for me, since I was overconfident and placed too much emphasis on the intellect. This news came as a blow, for I would have loved to be chosen. A senior carried responsibility, taking part in organizing the life of the college, and in helping and caring for the other members of their "family". But there was another reason that this came as a real blow: the verdict "overconfident" was completely new to me. After this disclosure, I wrote in my journal:

The candidates for senior were announced, and I was not to be one. All at once my world fell apart. Then I heard why. Because I'm overconfident and place too much emphasis on the intellect … Now I know that I lack the greatest virtue of all – humility. Every day I will ask for humility and much love. I thank God for letting this happen. He can help me. Actually, I should be grateful to God; I can only benefit from coming to know myself better. If God has brought me into this situation, then He will also give me the strength to get over it. August 13, 1923

In His great love God revealed my weak point, showing me that nothing stands in His way so much as an overconfident and proud nature, and that He values humility above all else. Up till then I had taken my popularity for granted. Being the centre of attention came naturally to me: it was part of who I was. Now, for the first time, I realized that this had a negative, sinful root – pride and the desire for attention. God in His goodness had denied me the popularity and status I had come to expect.

I wonder what God's intention is for me, letting me go through all this without sparing me – laying bare my greatest weakness. More and more I feel the pain of ungratified ambition and pride. I'm way too dependent on the recognition of others, as the past few days have well and truly taught me …

If I'm jealous of someone, I can combat that with love. But what if the problem is more general – such as the need for admiration? Now I need to show the others all the more love. I have to keep praying that Jesus will help me fight this sinful streak. If I want to be a true child of God, my next step is to accept this humiliation. That is the whole point and probably why God has put me here. O Lord, help me! August 27, 1923

Being humbled and corrected was sheer grace. Troubles and dashed hopes are worth their weight in gold because of the immeasurable wealth of blessing they bring. By denying me admiration and status, God gave me something infinitely more precious:

a genuine realization of my sin. As a result I was driven to Jesus: I met Him in a completely new way. He did not leave me to wallow in hurt pride, but aimed a blow at my self-centred nature. I gave God my *yes*, accepting His discipline and determined to humble myself, as my journal frequently mentions.

Yet I still had no real mentor to disciple and guide me in following the Lord. What grace that God Himself took care of my soul! He showed me how important it was to listen when others challenged me – and then not to withdraw into myself but take the next step. In this case it meant accepting the reproof and going on to serve others in love as opportunities arose. From then on I did this as best I could.

After a number of weeks the mother and senior of our family told me that they had decided to nominate me after all, since I had not been offended and had been so willing to submit to others and to serve them.

Having come through this experience, I was elected in a later term to represent all boarders as head student. This position revealed new weaknesses in my character, showing me that I was in danger of letting the task of leadership, the organizing and the flurry of activities, preoccupy me just as dancing used to. Soon I sensed that something had to change. And in mid May 1924 I wrote in my journal:

> *As head student at the academy I am so taken up with worries about people's lives and other matters that I don't feel I'm living like a child of God. Instead of letting it absorb me, I should be abiding in God, dealing with everything in His strength. Because I haven't been resting in Him, I have often become over-involved, trying to work things out with my limited understanding.*
>
> *All this preoccupies me so much that I can no longer find the way to God. Oh, I beg God to change my life in this respect. I yearn to live in Him alone so that I can be a vessel of His blessing. But how can I be a blessing with all my impetuous remarks and witticisms, poking fun at people and things?*

The Lord increased my longing to be freed from busyness, and through my friendship with Erika Madauss He led me to spiritual sources. Erika took me with her to Höxter, to the big Pentecost conference of the Girls' Bible Classes (MBK) in 1924 – a very special experience for me. From all over Germany hundreds of dedicated Christian girls came to hear the challenge of the living Christ to wholehearted discipleship. This was the message I had been longing to hear all that time. The Spirit of God was moving in this conference. He set my heart on fire to be all out for Jesus, wholly dependent upon Him and independent of people and the things of this world.

That August I was able to spend a short holiday with my mother at a Christian retreat centre. (My parents had come to a living faith the previous year during an evangelistic outreach.) There the Lord spoke to me graciously, and gradually I began to see my position as head student in His light. In my journal I noted:

I have made a clear decision to serve the Lord with all my life and to dedicate myself completely to Him. I long for the day when I can leave the Froebel Academy: although God is acknowledged there, Christ is little more than a moral teacher.

August 31, 1924

Inspired by a biography of Sadhu Sundar Singh that I had bought on the way to Höxter, I longed with all my heart to live for God alone. Yet what powerful elements in my personality still stood in the way of leading such a life! This the Lord disclosed to me little by little.

Give me something of Your infinite love. Often I am so unfeeling and abrupt, with not a glimmer of human sympathy stirring in me. At times I can be so cold and unloving towards others. I know how terribly petty-minded and bad I am, but I am trusting in Your grace. In my overconfidence I keep finding fault with others, although they may have put their "talent" to better use than I have mine, however ethical I may seem. Oh, forgive me the sharpness of my critical thoughts. I am still so ambitious and pleased with myself, taken up with the things of this world. I care too much about what people say because I am dependent on them instead of You.

O my Saviour, make me wholly Yours. Show me all my sins without sparing me. Fill me with Your light and truth. Help me to believe in the power of Your grace to make me more like You. I am praying that my sinful self will at last be dethroned; that Your love will shine out of me and others will know I'm Your disciple. September 25, 1924

As an eighteen- and nineteen-year-old I had but a glimpse into the innermost recesses of my soul. Yet the Lord revealed more to me after I had finished my training in Kassel late in 1924. With high hopes I began my studies in Berlin, at the Home Mission's Women's College for Social Welfare Training. I had learnt of the college through Erika, who intended to become a Christian social worker. It was a two-year course designed to build on the one I had taken at the Froebel Academy. I would gain qualifications as a social worker and religious instructor.

What drew me, however, was not a desire for further education, let alone a career as a social worker. To this very day I remember how it came about. Erika and I were polishing our shoes together when she told me that she was going to Berlin next. There she would train for the Lord's service and then go on to a Christian job. That fired my imagination.

With these same expectations I had enrolled for the course in Kassel, only to be disappointed. But now, according to Erika, this college in Berlin with its religious education faculty was the perfect solution. Thrilled, I said, "That's the place for me!" And my parents gave their permission. The following journal entry, prior to Berlin, shows where I stood spiritually:

O Lord, thank You that now I can love You so much. Guard this inner life, but take away any self-congratulation. All that

I have comes from You and anything good in me is Your work. That I know very well.

Thank You for Your immeasurable love. How I long for You to reveal Yourself to others too – those who don't yet know You. This I pray with all my heart, having seen Your glory. Help me not to be unfaithful to You any more, but to fight resolutely against my lukewarmness so that I never let You go. Abiding in You is what counts, for then we're strong and can make progress. Help my unbelief! Help me when I suffer intellectual doubts. Help me to overcome my love for the world, to surrender the desire for marriage. Let me be wholly Yours, reflecting Your nature and winning others for Your kingdom. Bless my work, Lord. Thank You for Your infinite love. Help me to grow in You and bring You fruit. Amen.

The book by Countess Waldersee has taught me a lot. Now I see how faithless I've been. I hadn't taken Christ and His cause seriously enough. Now I have examined myself thoroughly and have found the root causes of my mistakes. I won't give up the struggle, for the Sermon on the Mount shows how much God expects of His children if they are to inherit the kingdom of heaven. Clearly I am lost if I bear so little resemblance to Jesus in spite of all my head knowledge. So I'm determined to wrestle in prayer that I may abide in Jesus and never forsake Him. I have promised myself that for the rest of my life I'll spend half an hour with Him each morning, and then go about my activities with Him. September 1924

MY WINGS ARE CLIPPED

WOMEN'S COLLEGE FOR SOCIAL WELFARE TRAINING, 1924–1925

I arrived in Berlin in October 1924, when I was turning twenty. What were my impressions of the metropolis? It brought to light all my hidden longings for the world. After a few days I wrote in my journal:

> *Now I've arrived in the big city! At first I was struck with such a desire for the world, for excitement and pleasure, that I would have loved to plunge into city life.*

At the earliest opportunity Erika Madauss and I boarded the open-roofed double-decker buses, keen to see the sights of Berlin, such as the boulevard *Unter den Linden*, the cathedral and the old museum with its famous works of art. Each day we took a different tour of the city. This was all in keeping with the aims of the college, whose hostel was located in the west end. A broad-minded outlook was actively cultivated. We were encouraged to engage with the intellectual, social and cultural trends of the times, attending lectures and visiting concerts and the theatre. At the same time we were to be well-grounded in the Bible and in Christ. Full of enthusiasm, I threw myself into all that was offered in the classes, as well as taking advantage of the intellectual and cultural activities.

In His grace, God set up limits on all sides, "clipping my wings". Who knows, I might otherwise have found fulfilment in these experiences and in a particularly precious friendship. As in all the earlier chapters of my life it was God's *no*, the cross He sent into my life, that was the saving of me. In each case the cross was a bridge that led me into a new and previously unknown land of His love and brought me His nearness and the revelation of His glory. In retrospect there is nothing in my life that I can praise more highly than the crosses the Lord sent me at every stage – each time in a new and different form. Either He denied me the desires of my heart, or He took away what I most treasured and valued at that time. The loss nearly broke my heart. But in each case pain gave rise to newness of life and undreamt-of blessedness in Jesus. Whenever He took, He gave, true to His word: "If you try to hang on to your life, you will lose it. But if you give up your life for my sake, you will save it" (Matthew 16:25 NLT).

In those first few weeks after arriving in Berlin, I was unconsciously seeking to "hang on to my life". Unaware that anything was amiss, I was trying to satisfy the cravings of my soul and mind. But I was soon to discover that this openness and love for the world and my keen interest in intellectual matters did not bring me the expected joy and enrichment, but rather distress. The desire to marry – a natural enough inclination – began to get the better of me; and through the intellectual approach in the lectures, especially the textual criticism, I once again found myself questioning my faith. I was in deep inner turmoil. After those first few weeks I wrote:

I'm having a terrible struggle to resist both intellectual doubts and worldly desires. O Jesus Christ, help me and my unbelief! Time and again I tell myself that this is my thorn in the flesh. You have to give each of us a thorn to bear, according to our individual needs, so that we will strive to win the kingdom of God and never lapse into complacency, which is spiritual death… The authenticity of even more Bible passages was questioned in class. That hurts deep down inside, for my faith is everything to me. It's not that I would ever let Jesus be taken away from me, but obviously my faith can't be very strong if it suffers under these gnawing intellectual doubts. So I cry out to You, Lord, give me books to read where I can sense Your Spirit at work.

In You alone can we find true salvation and peace. Help me to conquer my doubts, for You are greater than our limited human understanding. November 9, 1924

How disappointed I was that the classes caused me such inner conflict. Here, too, I had failed to find my heart's desire. I had come to Berlin with the wrong expectations, envisaging some sort of Bible college that would lead me deeper into the Word of God and closer to Jesus. I was hoping to be equipped for Christian service. Instead, I found myself at a college for social welfare training with religious studies for church workers as an optional extra.

Subsequently, I was grateful for all the stimuli I received as I studied social sciences and the humanities, in addition to theological material, for they broadened my outlook. I am especially grateful for the teaching of Elisabeth Nietzsche, who went on to become principal of the college. At the time, however, I simply had a sense of not being in the right place for my spiritual development. Unlike most of the other girls, I didn't come from a Christian background. As a young believer I thirsted for true spiritual life, teaching inspired by the Holy Spirit. For much that was offered, I lacked the spiritual maturity: doubts took hold all the more easily.

Soon I became very unhappy. The big city lost its charm. It was a trial for me to have to pore over my books with intellectual doubts threatening to rob me of my faith and even of Jesus Himself. When I first took possession of my little room, I felt like royalty: now my "palace" seemed like a prison. Not a single garden, shrub or tree in sight! How different this hostel was from the Froebel Academy in Kassel where an active community life based on a family system was integral to our training, and where the boarders were encouraged to share each other's joys and sorrows. Here in Berlin there was a good Christian atmosphere under the leadership of the highly respected principal, Countess von der Schulenburg, but it was more like the life of university students. Apart from sharing a floor of the hostel, we led our separate lives, and I felt lonely. And I missed the field of activity I had enjoyed in Kassel as head student. Here in the social welfare training college I was one of the youngest; no one took much notice of me and I was left to my own devices. As a result, I focussed on a particular friendship with another girl. This friendship was like an island in the stormy seas for me. It was my refuge. Doing things together was a joy: we understood each other so well.

But once again God in His wisdom said *no*. First my enjoyment of academic life was marred by the tormenting doubts. He knew it would have proved a snare to me. Now He prevented me from losing myself in an all-consuming friendship – an even more intense disappointment. My friend, who had shared all my joys and sorrows, was suddenly taken up by another friendship. Disillusionment and jealousy ate away at me: the sense of humiliation was acute. Something deep within me fractured, and darkness crept into my soul.

Alone in my little room, I shed many tears. Any desire for excursions in Berlin was gone. My wings were clipped and I let them hang low. Nor was there anyone to whom I could have confided my troubles and inner conflict. It was as if the heavens were shut, and Jesus dead. And I hardly knew what my next step should be, for by studying at this college I had set out on a path I had never intended to take.

In my journal I poured out my heart to God, and He answered me in His infinite mercy. He answered me wisely, as only a firm and caring Father can, disciplining His child in love. He showed me how to unravel this knot of confusion, sorrow and tears. He showed me the solution, the one true solution, whatever problem I faced. This I was to discover throughout my life and later for the Sisterhood of Mary. He pointed out to me that my sin was the root of my distress. Because my love for Jesus was still so weak, my world collapsed at the loss of human love and friendship, making me miserable and clouding my soul. Besides, my pride and jealousy were piqued that someone else was preferred to me. This I suddenly realized.

Forgive me for being so small-minded, proud and jealous, and for letting something like this get me down. If only I can be made fit for Your kingdom, and weep for the things that really matter ... I know that I can't yet love in spirit only: I simply can't, for I'm still too dependent on her friendship. Cleanse me, Jesus, and instil Your love in me. January 25, 1925

Several weeks later:

Quite different things make me sad now ... I'm appalled at myself. Now I see how terribly petty-minded I was, so very human, dependent on others, clinging to their love. How that hinders God's working. March 28, 1925

This knowledge of my sin was a blessing, for it brought me to repentance, which is a never-ending, hidden source of new life. Looking back, I am awed at the way the Holy Spirit opened my eyes. Otherwise, bitterness and tension would have built up in my soul. The troubles of our daily lives are there to help us see our sin: repentance sets us free and brings us joy. Then we no longer fall into the trap of blaming God for laying burdens on us, for robbing us of our happiness or spoiling our plans. We also stop blaming others who let us down. Our eyes are opened to see where we ourselves are to blame, and we learn to thank God that He uses these troubles to bring us release and lead us into intimacy with Himself.

After those months of struggling in the wilderness, I went on holiday with my parents at Easter. There I was blessed with a new and deeper love for Jesus. Finally, intellectual and cultural interests lost their hold on me as I learnt to give them to the Lord.

So much has changed: God has given me clarity about various things, and He has set my heart aflame. All I want is Jesus. My one desire is to honour and serve Him. I can see just how petty-minded I was – so very human. How wholesome and necessary this disappointment has been for me. Now that this time is over, Christ is especially close to me. The sense of His presence is so strong. Now I see so clearly how my heart clung to people and things, how dependent I was on the praise of others, and how all this hindered God's work in me.

Now I know that it is Satan who tries to persuade us to place too high a value on academic achievement and intellectual debate. But when we see how much this hinders the Spirit of God, then we know it is not His will. So many souls are waiting to be shown the way to Him; that should be our priority. It's not about being so well-informed that we can engage with people. It's about God's Spirit shining out of us powerfully. About people sensing: here is something special, a touch of God. My sole desire is to serve Christ. I long for the day when I will be completely dependent on Him, living for Him alone. I'm praying He will enlist me in His service, refine me through suffering and draw me closer to Him. But whether I am to become a deaconess or lead some sort of secluded life, I don't know yet. April 8, 1925

O Lord Jesus, once more I have resolved to spend my life for You, to live for Your glory and consciously renounce all earthly things. O Lord Jesus, give me the strength not to be so dependent on things like clothes, food, living conditions. Make me content with the bare necessities. Above all, set me free from the desire for recognition. Make me immune to all that would foster my self-love and need for attention. Let me seek only Your honour.

Oh, give me the strength for the rest of my time in Berlin ... Even if it means pain, as before Easter, I will gladly bear it. All I want is to come closer to You, refined by suffering. Please forgive me for complaining about suffering. Lord Jesus Christ, I love You more than anything in the world. Make me completely free, humble through and through, fit to live and work for Your glory.

April 16, 1925

Dear Lord Jesus Christ, You know my heart. I can hardly contain the love burning within me. There is no limit to Your goodness and greatness. No one could ever praise You enough. Lord Jesus, if only I could demonstrate my overflowing gratitude to You! Oh, let me suffer, let me be held in contempt, if it seems good to You; if it serves to purify me and enable me to honour You all the more. Lord Jesus, use me as Your instrument so that I may bring You glory. I want to proclaim Your almighty love and power, lead souls to You and make them happy ...

I don't know whether I can bear it yet, but I long to suffer for Your sake. May Your love be so deeply rooted in my heart that it stands the test of suffering. Oh, if I only have You, I can bear everything. May 1, 1925

The cross threatening to smother the life out of me during those winter months brought me unspeakable glory and unimagined bliss in Jesus' love. It brought me a heart full of adoration, renewed dedication and a greater intimacy with Jesus. I was privileged to know the blessings that flow as we accept our cross as coming from the hands of our heavenly Father, to purify us.

As another token of His love, He showed me the next stage in my studies: a Bible college where the longings of my heart would finally be satisfied after all those years. There Jesus was preached in the power of the Holy Spirit as the risen Lord who is alive and active today, a God of miracles.

One day in May 1925 a fellow student at Berlin happened to show me a picture postcard. "This is a Bible college not far from here. I'm going to visit a friend of mine who is studying there." At the words "Bible college" my heart leapt and my old yearnings were reawakened. Perhaps this was the place I had searched for so long, a place where I could train for the Lord's service? So one day I set out to see this Bible college for myself and find out what was taught there.

In a valley near Bad Freienwalde I found a cluster of buildings, nestled against the woods and bordered by meadows. Set apart in the tranquillity of nature, it seemed like paradise to me after Berlin. As I approached the main building, I could hear the strains of harmonium music and singing coming from various houses.

I sensed the presence of God resting on this valley. Here were people who were sure of their call to serve the Lord with their whole life, many in overseas missions.

The friend of my Berlin acquaintance showed me over the house and brought me to a large, bright classroom where the co-founder and spiritual leader of the college, Jeanne Wasserzug, was lecturing. I was fired with enthusiasm. This was life and spirit! This was not a Jesus confined to the past. This was the risen Christ, alive and active today, convicting of sin and setting hearts aflame, calling people into His service. Intellectual doubts were swept away by the reality of His presence. He was truly there – Jesus Christ, the living Lord! I was overflowing with joy. At last I had found the object of my quest. After the class, I took a few steps into the woods and threw myself down in the grass, my heart bursting for sheer joy. What a wonderful Lord! If I had a thousand lives, I would give them all to Jesus for love of Him.

At that moment I dedicated my life once and for all to Jesus and to His service.

My heart sang as I returned to Berlin. I had made up my mind. In the autumn I would discontinue my studies there and go to Malche Bible College.

Visiting my parents during the Pentecost break, I told them of my decision. Understandably, my father wasn't convinced. He was adamant that I should first complete my training in Berlin and qualify as a social worker and church worker. But my mother, sensing how much this step meant to me spiritually, spoke up for me. And the day came when my father relented. We were sitting together on the terrace when he suddenly asked from behind his newspaper, "What are the fees for that place?"

What a joyful return that was to my small room in Berlin! No longer did it seem like a prison cell, for now the door had swung open and soon I would fly out to the land of my heart's desire – to Bible college. Life, not theory, was what I sought. My whole desire was that this year at Bible college would help me to come to know Jesus more intimately and pattern my life on His. Working with a church youth group in Berlin had brought home to me the importance of living out the Gospel. In my journal I wrote:

Now that I am leading a youth group it has become so clear to me that Bible studies [by that, I meant theory] are not the way to share Christ with girls who do not yet know Him personally. To reach them you have to be passionate for Jesus, radiant with His love – not someone bad like me. First it means being gradually weaned from all else and focussed on Him, dying to self, seeking Him in prayer when you feel lonely. If Jesus is to shine out of us, and if we are not to lose Him in the busyness of everyday life, we need to be one with Him, firmly anchored in His love. Help me, Lord, and make me humble and single-hearted. Give me the simplicity of a child. Only then can I enter Your holy service. Forgive me where I have failed. May 16, 1925

In July and August 1925 I transferred to Darmstadt to do my social work internship for the college in Berlin. My job entailed escorting groups of children to holiday camps, and on the return journeys I would read the biographies of Mathilda Wrede, George Müller, Charles Finney and others. Stirred by their example, I longed to be fully surrendered to Jesus and give up everything for Him. The fire burning in my heart grew in intensity. Sometimes the greatness and glory of Jesus overwhelmed me.

Lord Jesus, how great and wonderful You are! How can we ever express all our gratitude! O Lord Jesus Christ, to think how often You have visited me in all Your glory. To abide in You is sheer bliss. What a privilege, what holy joy! Sometimes it is just too wonderful to comprehend; almost too much glory for sinners like us to bear. Lord Jesus, fit me for eternity. Make me the kind of person You want me to be.

Yet so many millions don't know You. They are living in spiritual darkness. How incredibly sad. Only You know why that should be and why so few know You. Lord Jesus, send us Your help. Raise up a Finney and a George Müller for this generation, so that our nation may turn to You, and Your kingdom may advance. Call people to work for Your kingdom.

With all my heart I thank You, Lord Jesus, for the amazing privilege of being Your child. Such grace fills me with awe. Sometimes I love You so much that I could burst for sheer joy. All I can do is praise You. And yet there have been long stretches when I was so cold towards You, Jesus. Forgive me, Lord.

I want to spend my life in loving You. And when I am not fully abiding in You, bring me back through humbling experiences. Make me all Yours, free of worldly, human interests. Grant me the grace of glorifying Your name wherever You place me. Oh, may You shine out of me. Then those who don't yet know You will realize this can only be Your doing. Take my life and use me; I want to live for You. All I am and have is Yours. Bless my start at Bible college. May I be clothed with Your love and humility.

July 25, 1925

On September 23, 1925, at almost twenty-one, I arrived at Malche Bible College.

OVERFLOWING LIFE DISCOVERED

MALCHE BIBLE COLLEGE
AUTUMN 1925 – SUMMER 1926

The cheerful atmosphere and fellowship I had enjoyed on a human level at the Froebel Academy, I now found at Malche Bible College on a spiritual level. Once again we were split into groups. They put us "young ones" together, for, unlike the Froebel Academy, the students spanned quite an age range. In my year comprising sixty "Sisters", the average age was thirty to forty, so I was one of the youngest.

Instead of exploring the busy streets of Berlin in search of life, we sought the quietness of the woods after all the spiritual stimulation during class. Indeed, when Jeanne Wasserzug finished her lectures, I usually found it hard to stay indoors. I couldn't wait to get out to the woods – running, skipping, singing for joy, my heart full of all that I had heard about the greatness and glory of Jesus and His marvellous purposes for the whole world. Or else I would have times of sharing with the friends whom God in His love had given me that year. How grateful I was for our mutual understanding and oneness in Christ. Altogether that year was sheer bliss, bringing me my heart's desire, for Jesus had become greater to me – more real and more precious.

The power and majesty of God thrills me to the depths of my being. My heart is aflame with the greatness and love of my Saviour. Daily I am blessed with His presence and glimpses of His glory. And to think that this Lord is my Saviour and my God! All I can do is rejoice and dedicate my life afresh to Him.

Lord, keep me single-minded and focussed on the goal, that I may attain to the first resurrection.

O my Lord and my God, I scarcely know how to bear the greatness of Your glory, now that Romans 6:8 has been opened up to me. O Lord, how great You are! I can only bow down in worship before You and rejoice that I am Yours. Crucified and buried, my old self no longer lives to usurp Your rightful place. Now it is You living in me! Teach me to reckon with You and Your power at all times – the power by which You created and rule over the heavens, the earth and the sea.

O Lord Jesus, what a wonderful Lord You are. I want to show my gratitude by spending myself completely for You. Keep me focussed, ever pressing on to the goal. I want to be someone You can count on – solid and dependable like a pillar. April 1926

I was drinking in the Word of God in my longing for Jesus to be magnified in my life. But hearing His Word was not enough: I had to be convicted by it. Jesus can reveal Himself to us only in so far as God's Word brings us to the end of ourselves and we kneel before Him as a sinner in need of forgiveness.

This had been my experience in Berlin and earlier in Kassel. With awareness of sin, with contrition and repentance, comes newness of life. Forgiveness leads us deeper into God and sets us ablaze with love for Jesus. Yet the greater my determination, the weaker I felt. The more I struggled, the more conscious I was of sin in my life. So what was the fruit of my battle against sin? As never before I came to know Jesus in His power to save and transform us from glory to glory. A new creation in Christ! This was to be my discovery as I encountered the power of God's Word for the first time. At Bible college, truths were brought home to me in a fresh way: *Jesus is alive, Jesus answers prayer, Jesus brings release, and as we take our stand on God's Word, we will see His promises come true.*

On the day I arrived at Malche Bible College I covenanted with Jesus:

I am writing this down, Lord, so that later I can praise and thank You for the miracle of Your grace. Then I will see, and others too, that with God, nothing is impossible.

Just now I'm still so locked into my character, still so dependent on praise and recognition, still so pleased with myself. It's part of who I am. I enjoy being asked for my opinion and made to feel needed. I like others to know I am clever, gifted, yes, and popular too. I am happy when I am on good terms with everyone, when I can share my heart, when I can shine. But, Lord Jesus, You came to serve. Today I surrender my longing to be a somebody. I renounce all pleasure in being important. I've made up my mind not to be sad in situations when I feel insignificant, unnoticed, a nobody. I won't try to think of ways to change that, or to make people recognize my potential.

Lord Jesus, every time I feel put down, help me to accept this as coming from You and to follow gladly in Your footsteps, rejoicing simply in knowing and being known by You. Give me the strength to keep going when it hurts. Help me to keep on praying until I can joyfully embrace the challenge of humiliation. Lord Jesus, from now on I want to put this into practice. Here people don't know me. In their eyes I may seem a mere child and maybe won't count for much. Help me to walk this path with You – starting from today. By the time I leave Bible college, I want to be able to write beneath this entry that You have freed me from this deeply ingrained sin. This year, make me small and humble. 23 September, 1925

In His grace, God answered this prayer. That year a definite beginning was made, though the purifying process was to continue at a deeper level over the course of my life. In June 1926 I wrote:

My Lord and my God, I want to thank You with all my heart. How great You are! You did indeed hear my prayer by the end of my time here – just as I had asked ... And now, with only a few weeks to go, I can affirm that You have made a beginning and that You keep Your promises. You have taken away my pleasure in being able to shine, for through the working of the Holy Spirit I have felt a bitter sting whenever I received praise or recognition from others. It no longer gives me pure, unmixed pleasure: there's almost a tinge of sadness and apprehension. I know that You will continue to wean me from this desire for recognition as I walk painful paths. I do feel good when I'm praised, but anything that is not pleasing to You isn't pleasing to me. O Lord, what You've done in my heart is the biggest miracle of all. Teach me more and more not to take pleasure in the things that aren't pleasing to You.

A special blessing was learning about the saving power of Jesus' blood in Jeanne Wasserzug's classes. Now I was taught the way to victory: claiming the power of His blood over my sinful nature. Previously I had known little of this.

The nine months sped by quickly. Parched with thirst for so long, I now drank deeply at the fount of living waters. I couldn't get enough. Admittedly, after the disappointment of Kassel and Berlin, I saw everything at Bible college through rose-tinted glasses: I was just so thrilled to have found the pearl of great price.

Despite the many blessings that year brought me, one nagging issue troubled me during my course at Malche Bible College. At the time it was not resolved. In fact, many years were to pass before I found the answer; but when I did, it unlocked the door to a wonderful treasure house. My problem concerned world-renunciation and world-affirmation. It was partly related to the issue of law or freedom. As a committed Christian, how involved should we be in cultural activities?

I would reason with myself: Being all out for Jesus is like being called up to war. Peace-time activities, however permissible, are just not on. In wartime a soldier has to be completely focussed: the future of a nation hangs in the balance. Yet even more is at stake in the battle between the kingdom of darkness and the kingdom of light. It is about rescuing souls from the brink of hell. Shouldn't I focus exclusively on the kingdom of God, laying all else aside?

Even so, I was not convinced. It just didn't add up. There was another side to the argument. Why did God create us with an appreciation for beauty in art and nature, for instance? Didn't God design and create everything with love? If we turn our backs on God's good gifts like ascetics, isn't there something unnatural about our lives? We are denying and rejecting the very things God has created in love. I was unable to reconcile these conflicting viewpoints.

In my distress I turned to a teacher I greatly respected. She had a relaxed, open-minded approach to life. I asked her about Gerhard Tersteegen's SELECTED BIOGRAPHIES OF HOLY SOULS. To my way of thinking, the people he described were ascetically inclined. Could it be that they were right after all? They were so obviously anointed, living in tune with God and reflecting Jesus in their lives and words. Perhaps she saw a personal danger for me; at any rate, she strongly advised me against such a path. This, she explained, was mysticism, which she felt could be a pitfall. She said that wherever the Lord led me I should enjoy complete freedom as a child of God but always remain fully committed to Jesus. This was precisely my problem! How this theory was to work out in practice she did not say. How was I to spend my time? Pray? Or visit an art gallery? Pursue intellectual interests? Engage in discussions, chat and socialize?

Spiritually I missed out by heeding the advice of this teacher. And yet I still struggled with these issues, as the following entry shows:

O Jesus, once more I commit to You my last ten weeks here. Help me not to waste a single hour doing anything outside Your will. All I want is to be wholly dependent upon You, always there for You.

You know how receptive my mind and soul are to the world You created – people, the fine arts, psychology, contemporary issues. You're the one who put me here as a child of Yours, and

I have to live in the real world with both feet on the ground. Continue to show me hour by hour, minute by minute, whether I should become involved when the opportunity arises, or whether I should draw apart in order to seek You, study Your Word, attend to Your business.

Legalism will never solve this problem, but You are Spirit and Life. Give me Your Holy Spirit so that I can decide from case to case what to do. Lord, I want to follow wherever You lead. Keep me from deviating or being side-tracked: You are to be my all. Change me, make me like You. Keep me from being emotionally or intellectually taken up with the world. I want to be completely available to You. Help me always to recognize Your truth in this world, but keep me from ever becoming legalistic.

April 22, 1926

Loving Jesus was the answer, only I didn't know that yet. My love for Him was still so weak. So after the Bible course ended, I carried this unresolved problem over into my new work. It would cause me many dark moments, though at first the privilege of working for God's kingdom eclipsed everything else. Jeanne Wasserzug's words were burning in my heart: "There is no greater honour than being called by God into His service."

During my first holidays from Bible college in 1925, I was spending Christmas with my parents in Darmstadt when the preacher from the Darmstadt City Mission came for a visit. Hearing that I was training at Malche Bible College, he spontaneously asked if I would like to start youth work in the Darmstadt City Mission after I finished my course. My parents and I felt this was God's leading and the Board at the Bible College agreed to commission me for this ministry as one of their sisters, commencing in August 1926. I was then twenty-one years old.

However, before beginning my ministry, I found myself in severe inner conflict. It was the same problem that had troubled me at Bible college due to my time in Berlin. The whole issue flared up again. I was staying at a Christian retreat centre that stressed the importance of "the community of true believers". According to this teaching, they comprised the elect, the truly born-again. It was all about dying to self. The Bible studies in themselves were powerful, and I was richly blessed. Yet the emphasis was on going through life with sorrow in our hearts, as this was a flawed and suffering world.

Yet in my heart the words of my teacher Jeanne Wasserzug still echoed. In contrast to this stern teaching, she spoke naturally and joyfully about the love of God. She was trying to create in us an awareness of a loving, caring Father in heaven, who delights in blessing His children with good gifts, even if He also has to discipline us for our good. But here there was a constant emphasis on God wanting us to die to self. Christians who thought differently were considered immature – converted, yet not truly born again. The group also maintained that women should not proclaim the Word of God, even to other women or to young people. They were convinced that there could be no blessing on such a ministry.

A high-school teacher who adhered to this teaching gave me an earnest talking-to, appealing to my conscience not to accept my new post for this reason. In a state of great turmoil I wrote in my journal:

My Lord and my God, You see my pain. You see my bewilderment at all the different paths followed by Your children, each maintaining that theirs alone is right. Lord, I am indeed willing to renounce everything if only You would show me clearly that this really is Your way. Give me a sign, some sort of answer, for I don't know what to do. I'd rather You put a spoke in my plans than let me be disobedient and set out on a path that is not of You.

Lord, see my tears. You know how troubled I am by what Mr. X keeps on saying. Show me what is right. Help me to hear Your voice. Keep me from being squeezed into a mould. Don't let me fall into legalism again. On the other hand, don't let me become so broad-minded that I lose sight of "the one thing needed" [cf. Luke 10:42]. *Show me what to do with statements like: "Those who are born again are the elect. No amount of searching or striving can help the others." Something else they say here is that a woman who speaks in church forfeits a great deal of grace and glory, because she is acting against the will of God and therefore lacks one of the traits of a true child of God. Is this to imply that Jeanne Wasserzug doesn't belong to the community of true believers if she can't subscribe totally to this viewpoint?*

Oh, Lord, they are all Your children. It is not for us to judge who is born again and who isn't yet. Surely, being one of the chosen doesn't depend on how far we accept this teaching as the counsel of God. It can only depend on the fullness of the Spirit and the degree of our devotion and love for Jesus.

Then everything else follows naturally: fruitfulness, the right attitude to the world and everything else. Do I allow the Spirit to govern my thoughts, words and actions? How passionate am I about this? That will always be the main point. I feel it is bordering on legalism to put people in boxes: this one born-again, that one converted, the third spiritually alive...

July 16, 1926

This first taste of disunity in the Body of Christ filled me with a sense of foreboding. Later, as part of my lifework, I would live for healing within His Body. I would seek to counter the infighting among God's children, each convinced that they and they alone are right.

Even now, in this time of testing, God gave me a glimpse of the solution that leads to fruitfulness and unity. As we focus on Jesus, our attitudes to people and things fall into place. But I still had a rough ride ahead. The Lord had to deal with me at a deeper level before I knew in practice that love for Jesus was the only solution to the divisions within His Body, the Church. By the time I took up my new post, I had battled through and now had peace that I was acting rightly:

> *Thank You for the assurance that being fully dedicated does not imply legalism. Sticking to the guiding principles in Scripture, we have complete freedom in the Spirit, women included.*
>
> July 25, 1926

MY BATTLE: WORLD-DENIAL OR WORLD-AFFIRMATION?

YOUTH WORK IN DARMSTADT SUMMER 1926 – SUMMER 1928

In August 1926 I was publicly installed as the new youth worker during a ceremony at Darmstadt City Mission. From the outset of my ministry the preacher assured me I would have free rein, and he generously kept his word throughout my time there. His main concern was that I would build up a new youth group for girls. We enjoyed a harmonious working relationship in this joint ministry, in so far as it could be called joint. Young and inexperienced though I was, basically I was on my own, both in shaping the work and in providing spiritual direction and pastoral care.

A recent tent mission in Darmstadt had resulted in the conversion of a number of girls whose parents belonged to the City Mission. I visited these girls, prayed with them and tried to help them in the various issues they faced. With them I started a youth group, which soon grew to forty girls, half of whom were older than I was.

Yet despite this good beginning, I was soon deeply unhappy. I had set myself too high a goal. At the age of twenty-two I was under the misguided impression that needy people would experience swift and extensive release and transformation through faith in Jesus. So I was convinced that victory, joy and dedication would soon be evident in their daily life as proof of Jesus' saving power. But my counselling did not seem to have this effect. It came as a shock to me that the Body of Christ sometimes appears the opposite of what it should be, making Nietzche's criticism understandable: "Believers will have to look more redeemed if I am to believe in their Redeemer."

After all the time I had invested in my girls, talking and praying with them, they would relapse into this or that sin. Although they were believers, there were areas of their lives they were withholding from the Lord. Desperately I battled for the girls, almost crushed by the force of their struggles, which became my own, for I loved them dearly. I simply couldn't understand why they weren't being set free. In the end I couldn't take any more. The burden was too heavy for me.

My parents, sensing I was working too intensely, tried to win me back to a more relaxed way of life. So I faced a battle on both fronts with no one to support me spiritually. Time and again I came to the conclusion that I was too young, too ill-equipped for this work. I felt helpless, as if I was up against the power of Satan and all the suffering of this world. Darkness engulfed my soul. The joy I had known at Bible college evaporated in the face of these real-life issues. In my journal I wrote:

L. is on the verge of despair. H. didn't come; she has lost all hope and courage. You're simply not helping her. Oh, please show her why. Let her see where she has gone wrong. K. is in crisis again. And at the meeting with the girls yesterday I couldn't get the message across. You could have cut the atmosphere with a knife. Mrs. B. is almost hysterical in her struggles and sorrows – unable to find peace, unable to believe it was Your love that allowed her husband to be taken from her … Oh, Lord, Lord, where are You? Have mercy on them. You love them. Lord, please help! You are mercy itself! Please send help for Your name's sake, for You are so great and powerful … Help me to believe for others. I need Your help for the youth work tomorrow. Spiritually I am under so much pressure, in such darkness, and so far away from You. I can't possibly deliver a message in this state. But in You we have everything we need.

Lord Jesus, I'm not going to complain or despair. You are my Strength, my Joy, and everything will work out to Your glory. I trust in You. In humbling me, You exalt me. I give thanks to You. Oh, don't let the others suffer any harm. Overrule and bless them in spite of everything. Amen. November 1, 1926

Lord, why have You forsaken me? I can't go on living like this. Lord, I'm just too young. Oh, if only I didn't have to speak and do counselling when I am so inadequate myself. Sometimes I think I'd rather help out with simple, everyday tasks if only I could glorify You. And yet it is all grace to be in Your service at all, and so I will serve You gladly. November 28, 1926

Why was it so dark in my soul? Apart from my youth and inexperience, there was another reason, a personal one, which had to do with my sin. Although I was not in any way emotionally attached to the girls I led, I was so passionate about their souls that I was desperate to extricate them from their life-controlling problems. All my energy went into this. Whatever the demands or expectations, nothing was too much for me.

In Darmstadt I had my own room with a private entrance to welcome the girls whenever they came to me with their needs. They were at home in my room, where we had our many counselling sessions and prayer battles. I loved my girls in all their weaknesses, and they loved me too. I was so taken up with the group of girls entrusted to my care that others noticed. An aunt visiting my parents remarked how quiet and unresponsive I was until she asked me about my work. Suddenly it was like talking to a totally different person, as I enthused about my girls. But my concern for them stood in need of a refining process: it was still on a human level. As a result, the cries for help in my journal at that time often sounded more like accusations, as if it was God's fault for not helping.

Why can't people believe? Why is life so awful? And now L. is plagued by doubt and rebelling against You. Soon I will have reached the limit. It is so terribly difficult. Lord, my God, I can't take any more. Give me faith. Give me the strength to overcome the feelings of despair, the agonizing Why as I see these struggling, seeking souls ... You're just not helping or revealing Yourself to them. April 5, 1927

It just breaks my heart to see others going through agonies – J., Mrs. H., L. and so many others. They want to believe, they want to be victorious – but just can't. Why all these emotional ups and downs? Is it disposition, heredity? Lord, I want to stop asking Why? I will trust You, because You are truly just and holy. There must be a solution, though we probably won't see it until we get to heaven. May 26, 1927

There was a solution, though I was looking for it in the wrong places. I thought I needed to pray my way through to a deeper faith. That was good and necessary. It was also excellent training for later when I would build up and lead an entire organization, the Sisterhood of Mary, by faith. Painfully aware of my inadequacy in these seemingly hopeless struggles, I battled through again and again to the place of faith.

So this is the real world – and yet I'm supposed to preach and preach again about Your victory, though all around I see defeat. But even if I saw nothing but wrecked lives, and had to live on in torment, my work in ruins, still I would trust in You and Your victory. Lord Jesus Christ, You are the living One. Your power is greater than sin. Life may make no sense and Your dealings with others may leave me bewildered. Even so, I place my trust in the One who is in me. April 5, 1927

But the real problem lay deeper, rooted in my personality, my sinful self. I was engulfed in spiritual night because I was on the wrong track. I cared more about the pain of human souls than Jesus' pain because of them. They filled my heart more than Jesus. I didn't see what we do to Him when we are unwilling, resistant and faithless. Instead of grieving for the wounds we inflict on

Jesus, I felt sorry for the girls, who weren't experiencing victory and release. Knowing so little of His heart, the very source of love, I couldn't relate to His pain. Although I didn't yet realize it, this had thrown my spiritual life out of kilter. Allowing myself to be dragged into the depths and the fluctuations of human souls, I lost my joy and peace in the Lord and the assurance of victory. The souls of these girls were the centre of my attention, just as individual people had been previously.

During my year in Berlin, darkness had engulfed me because my life revolved more around a friendship than Jesus Himself. At that time I quickly spotted the root of my sadness, but now in my youth ministry it was much harder to discern. It was years before I realized that we can be zealous in ministry, but focus on the people we seek to serve, and not on Jesus.

God in His goodness must surely have wanted to open my eyes even in those days, but as yet I did not respond. It wasn't until later, when the prayer battle for specific people thrust me deeper still into spiritual night, that He gave me light. Nearly breaking under the strain of wrestling in prayer for unresponsive souls, I finally recognized the sinful root in my heart. He showed me that I was not trusting implicitly in His love, but was harbouring a spirit of grumbling against Him. In our ministry Jesus has to be the focal point. Moved by the pain in His heart, by His love and pleading, we will abide in love, true joy and peace. The emphasis shifts away from people and onto God.

In the course of those two years of ministry things did start to look brighter. God blessed us with a small revival and the youth work flourished, developing into several lively groups. A special joy was a core group of supportive girls who shared the responsibility and spent many hours with me in prayer. We were one in the Lord. He had brought us together as prayer warriors for the advance of His kingdom. During our prayer meetings my small room resembled an army camp with girls sitting on all the available floor space and targeting souls with prayer. We wanted to set the whole city ablaze for Jesus. In the momentum my inner struggles and unresolved problems faded into the background. During my second year I wrote in my journal:

> *My Lord Jesus, thank You for showing me the precious side to this ministry. I can only rejoice in the privilege of serving You. I think this ministry is the most precious thing in my life.*
>
> April 3, 1928

> *Where is a God like You? Lord, in You is such an abundance of riches, such overwhelming joy, that sometimes my heart can't take it all in. "How inexpressible is the prompting of Your wonderful love!" Unto You I lift my song of praise: "By the grace of God I am what I am: a bride of the King, betrothed to the Lamb. Rejoicing I bow down in awe"* [E.G.Woltersdorf].
>
> June 30, 1928

Looking back, I see how great was the goodness of God. Young in faith as I was, and very young for this work, He never allowed me to be tested beyond my strength. He showed me His love by blessing my ministry and encouraging my faith. At the same time, the Lord continued to work in me. Again and again He tackled my weak spot, my tendency to despair or blame Him for the failure of those I prayed for. He showed me that something was fundamentally wrong. Not until later, in the Sisterhood of Mary, did I truly grasp the solution I sought when I wrote as a twenty-two-year-old, "There must be an answer." It lay in understanding the concerns of Jesus' heart, feeling His pain.

World-affirmation as opposed to world-denial was the other issue that continued to burden me. I was torn between fear of compromising my dedication to Jesus and fear of legalism. In vain I searched for someone to advise and guide me. In my ministry I was very much on my own, though for a while I was blessed with a prayer partner, a deaconess in charge of the women's work in the Darmstadt City Mission. We were on the same wavelength when it came to advancing God's kingdom. But my problems were not hers, since she did not share my cultural and intellectual background. So I continued my lonely struggle with these problems.

Not only did I suffer under a sense of isolation in my work in Darmstadt, where I longed for a kindred spirit: I was deeply troubled on a further count. It concerned Erika Madauss. Ever since our Froebel days when she led me closer to Jesus, we had stayed in touch, even though outwardly her life had taken a different direction from mine. Now our paths diverged spiritually as well. She was so taken up with art and cultural interests that Jesus no longer had first priority in her life. That was very painful for me.

Yet I couldn't overlook Erika's unerring instinct for what was genuine or false as far as I or anyone else was concerned. When we met or corresponded, she would challenge my "greenhouse piety". She had a way of penetrating my defences. I had to admit she was often right, and in love I tried to understand her. Still, her approach to discipleship didn't seem right either. My journal mirrors my distress.

> *I just don't know what to do. How utterly miserable I am! Lord, what is the way out of this maze? Is Erika's faith fundamentally different, or has it just taken another form? Sometimes I am so at one with her and understand her fully when she says that a Christian's place is in the midst of life in all its diversity. At other times her way of life seems so foreign to me, so completely different, that I feel we can't walk together. Still, I don't want to pass judgment. As for me, I would hardly dare to use this freedom, but perhaps it's right for Erika.* December 21, 1926

Puzzling over all this in my mind, I made a vital discovery. Up till then my ideal was a certain brand of Christianity – single-minded and devout. That was what I was familiar with. Sadly, in my ministry I found that believers who embraced this type of piety, or used the attending jargon, often produced lifeless sermons and prayers.

One little incident served as a pointer. I'll never forget visiting a woman who was seriously ill. I could tell at a glance that she took a broad view of life as a Christian. Yet she made Jesus more real to me than all the sermons and prayers I had recently heard. A single remark revealed her humility and complete yieldedness to God, her utter surrender to His will. In her I encountered the living Lord, the One I longed to live for and bear witness to. This woman gave me a copy of Albrecht Dürer's woodcuts of the Passion. Remarkably, God spoke to me through this work of art with an immediacy I had missed in the prayers and sermons of the fellowship where I worshipped. Shortly afterwards I noted in my journal:

According to Pastor X, everything here on earth is to be shunned, because it's under a curse. And so we have to go through life with sorrow in our hearts. To have an experience with God we have to be radically one-sided. Christ can be found only in the Word and as "Christ in us". But that means renouncing the whole of life – a depressing thought.

Bypassing life is not being real. Yet if I seek God in all that life has to offer, fully involved as a Christian, I'm afraid I'll end up being a half-hearted disciple. All truly fruitful men and women of God, like Paul and the holy souls described in Tersteegen's book, were radical in their commitment. For them, it was all or nothing. Or were there others?

Lord Jesus, help me to understand Your Gospel. It seems so contradictory to me. On the one hand it stresses total commitment to the point of legalistic self-denial; on the other hand it proclaims tremendous freedom ...

Show me the right way and set me free from legalism. You know how inflexible I can be. I almost have a guilty conscience when I do something that is not directly related to Your service. If once in a while I read art books or purely literary works, I'm afraid that I'm not making the best use of my time in this short life, for You and Your cause. Oh, what is the right way?

January 4, 1927

This question is probably the cross of my life. January 20, 1927

Coming to the conclusion that it was possible to have an encounter with God in the diversity of life, I rejoiced:

> *Lord, thank You for revealing Yourself to me in nature, people and art. Thank You that I can live for You and at the same time enjoy all these things with a clear conscience, as they only increase my love for You ... Thank You for freeing me from the demands of the law.* January 6, 1927

Yet a few weeks later I felt I was not on the right track. I wrote:

> *I always have the feeling I'm not doing enough. It all seems so futile and empty. O Lord, at all costs I want to spend my life completely for You and Your cause – on fire with Your love. Keep me from becoming a half-hearted worker for the kingdom of God, spiritually more dead than alive, and with no streams of living water flowing from me.* January 26, 1927

Tossed to and fro, I agonized over this question. Still the answer eluded me. As I now realize, there was a purpose to this inner conflict: God intended me to discover the answer not in theory but in practice. Later, I was to found and lead a religious order, and the future sisters would need wise leadership to keep them from falling into one of two extremes. On the one hand, a legalistic, world-denying Christianity producing spiritual cripples and self-righteous Pharisees. On the other, a lukewarm, powerless Christianity, lacking the "salt" of wholehearted dedication.

Only from personal experience would I be able to point out the right way to my spiritual daughters. As children of the heavenly Father we are to accept His good gifts gladly and naturally, enjoying them with thanksgiving whenever He chooses to give them. At the same time, as a bride of Jesus we are to lose our life. We are called to follow Him on the way of the cross, fully surrendered and denying self as the Spirit leads.

In my writings I would later call others to the path of true discipleship, which is anything but legalistic asceticism. The key was love. Not a general love, but a personal love for Jesus, a love for God the Father, for the Holy Trinity. All this I had yet to discover. So where did I find the secret of discipleship inspired by love for Jesus and free from legalistic narrow-mindedness? Not through any specific Christian tradition. Rather, it was a process. In the following years I was exposed to many different views as I worked with Christians from various backgrounds and fellowships. Gradually the Lord helped me to understand what His Word says about Law and Gospel.

During my youth ministry I struggled with one aspect of evangelicalism that I found problematic. I still recall my first Christmas in the City Mission as a sister fresh from Bible college. In a large, plain, dimly lit hall about four hundred people – members with their families – sat at long tables for coffee and cake. Poems were recited and choirs sang. Somehow I found it all too shallow and too loud. Coffee and cake seemed so important. My heart sank. Where was Jesus in all this? In my journal I wrote:

> *O Lord, I don't think I can work here any longer. I don't fit this mould ... Everything is so blatant and empty – down to the prayers and general presentation.* December 28, 1926

Was this what the fathers of the revival intended? I could see little resemblance to their original vision. Malche Bible College had grown out of the Pietist movement, and I had been thrilled to be there, but here I felt a flatness, a keen sense of disappointment. I know the atmosphere in many other Bible-believing circles is different. But no doubt God allowed me this experience to teach me to look beyond the outer forms of any tradition and get at the true centre. And that can only be Jesus.

I came to see that being converted doesn't necessarily imply we are following Jesus. As evangelicals we often use the phrase "I'm saved" as a cushion to rest on or as a shield to hide from the light of truth. The danger of hypocrisy and Pharisaism is very real. Sure of our own rightness, we look down on others, sometimes even being reluctant to take communion with "mere churchgoers". We write them off as belonging to the world because they still attend lectures and concerts. We totally overlook the fact that some of these churchgoers are more pleasing to God than us, like the tax-collector in the parable who prayed, "God be merciful to me, a sinner."

Still, I couldn't help noticing the indifference prevalent in liberal churches: the missionary zeal characteristic of evangelicals was often sadly missing.

One thing became evident to me, and later I was to recognize it even more. In any Christian tradition there are half-hearted followers as well as genuine disciples. So what is the secret of true discipleship? A contrite and broken heart. The Lord made this increasingly clear to me in His Word, often underlining it through His leadings in my own life. The humble can admit their failings and accept reproof – "Yes, I've sinned against God and others." A pardoned and forgiven sinner will then love Jesus wholeheartedly (Luke 7:37–50). And this love brings true freedom, sorting out problems and resolving thorny issues. Yet I had a long way to go before I found the key.

As the next step, the Lord led me into an environment poles apart from the City Mission: among Christians who were open to the world. I found myself back in Berlin at the Women's College for Social Welfare Training. But I didn't go with flying colours, as I had four years earlier. This time, I went in obedience to God, though it crossed through my dearest wishes.

Why the return to Berlin? This move had to do with my struggles in the youth work. My parents felt I had become too one-sided, totally absorbed with counselling to the exclusion of other interests. Convinced that it was vital I should leave this work, they consulted various Christian leaders who happened to visit us, as well as writing to the Malche Bible College Board. From all sides came the same advice. "If you don't want to end up as a legalist and spiritual cripple, you need to leave such a narrow field of work and engage with the world again."

I was strongly advised to complete the course at the Women's College for Social Welfare Training and grapple with social and intellectual issues. Returning to Berlin was a bitter prospect, but I knew the Lord wanted it.

WHY THIS DETOUR?

BACK AT THE WOMEN'S COLLEGE FOR SOCIAL WELFARE TRAINING, BERLIN, 1928

It was autumn again when I returned to Berlin in 1928. I was nearly twenty-four. Again I was given a small room in the hostel facing the other side of the building across the courtyard. But everything was so different. The city with its sights no longer enticed me. Now living in a closer relationship with Jesus, I sensed the darkness of my urban surroundings. I felt walled in, and the atmosphere oppressed me. For the first time I noticed the kind of girls standing in the doorways near our hostel. I sensed the dark goings-on behind the façades of these grand Berlin apartment buildings. Counselling work had made me sensitive. My heart was seared by the misery caused by sin.

This time I sat in my room grappling with all the problems of a student whose studies were interrupted three years earlier and who now has to follow a new curriculum, partly under new teachers. With so many new laws to learn by heart, I had to catch up on almost the whole of the first-year course. My journal reflects my state of mind:

> *Laws, laws and more laws to drum into my head ... Horrors! Oh, this dreadful city! The atmosphere is almost stifling me. These stone walls. Berlin: dead in all its life, soulless in its frenetic activity. This is what faces me wherever I go ... and to think I have to live here for a whole year! I often clutch at my head*

and ask myself, "Why did you do it?" To acquire greater understanding of social concerns? To be better equipped to help people in real-life situations? It's tempting to blame my stupidity for having taken this step, but I overcome these feelings with the assurance that I was only acting in obedience to an inner prompting. So You have to help me, Lord! October 17, 1928

Indeed I might ask why I was back in the college I had left on my own initiative. Rationally I had no explanation. Still, I was convinced God had a plan, which would unfold in due course even if at the time I did not understand it.

August had brought a moving farewell from my girls in Darmstadt, and I felt very homesick when I thought of my youth work there. I longed for a pastoral ministry in God's kingdom. For years, however, God denied me the fulfilment of this wish. He saw the dangers of such a ministry for me, even if I didn't. My heart was on fire for the advance of His kingdom. But without my realizing it, ministry had become more important to me than Jesus Himself, whose desire was to be my only love. I was completely taken up in wrestling for souls in prayer. I hadn't yet realized that the spiritual can be mixed with the emotional, and love for Jesus with love for our ministry.

But God is a jealous God, desiring a pure and undivided love. He wants to be loved for His own sake. My longing to minister to people seemed spiritual, but in reality it fed my emotional needs. And so He began a refining work in my soul, leading me into desolate and waste places where for many years my heart's yearning was unfulfilled. But a crown of glory awaits us at the end of the pathway of the cross. Today I would gladly endure even tougher stretches in the desert to win such a crown. A great mystery was revealed to me as I walked this pathway of the cross: the secret of "Christ within us". We learn to love Him with the love of a bride, and this is heaven on earth, bringing us Jesus Himself.

At the time the whys and wherefores of this detour to Berlin and of later desert roads were hidden from me. I was firmly convinced that when my year in Berlin was over the way would open for a ministry in the kingdom of God. For the time being I was content to know I was where God wanted me. I was here in obedience to an inner prompting. Soon I was fully participating in all my classes and even enjoying studying the humanities and the theological material. Unlike my first year in Berlin, nothing – not even biblical criticism – caused me doubts.

Together with another Christian student I arranged for Bible discussion sessions for our class. Since I was taking this second year in Berlin to explore contemporary social and intellectual issues, I made a point of attending extracurricular lectures and concerts. History of art had always interested me, and I took the opportunity of visiting art galleries and museums. Yet, as I noted in my journal:

My constant longing is to be free again for Your kingdom purposes. Although there is so much here that is beautiful and stimulating, it is a self-centred life. "Your kingdom come" – that's the prayer that spurs me on. February 11, 1929

All the time, God was refining this urge to spend myself for His kingdom. That was the purpose of this year in Berlin. Firstly, God gave me no opportunity for Christian service. Secondly, I received constructive criticism from those who lived and worked alongside me. Something was amiss in my personality and attitude. I realized God was speaking when various people made similar comments:

Today L. told me again that I lack vitality. She said I am too tense, too serious – not natural and relaxed. I seem to have forgotten how to be fun-loving. I depress other people.
April 20, 1929

Unhappy about this state of affairs, I wrote:

I can't go on like this. I don't want to inhibit and depress others. How awful! Probably all the distress I faced in my youth ministry has made me so solemn.

Indeed, recalling my bubbly personality as a child and teenager, I realized I must have changed considerably. All the struggles had brought out the more serious side of my nature. And in those days I still fought my battles very legalistically. If Christ is the fulfilment of the law (Romans 10:4), we will not be spared this phase of legalism. Those tough years had left their mark on me: the more serious strands of my personality came to the fore. This caused me real distress.

Darkness surrounds me. O Lord, show me Your way. What is right? I really don't know. My goal – was it wrong?

Why is everything so unspeakably confusing and complicated? Lord, I know it's You challenging me when everyone says how tense and uptight I am, making others feel frivolous when I'm around. They say I have an overdeveloped sense of duty. But how can I help it? If only I weren't continually faced with people's distress, the sheer misery of the human condition. Am I supposed to ignore all this? How can I possibly just live for my own enjoyment and the fulfilment of my potential?

H. did seem to be standing up for me when she said dedicated Christian service involves sacrificing, in some measure, our intrinsic selves. There are enough people living to develop all that's good and beautiful in human nature. Shouldn't I be able to surrender this for Christ? Only, I really don't want to depress others. April 22, 1929

After all this heart-searching I concluded: It's Jesus I want to live for, spending myself for Him alone.

Make me childlike: then I'll be free from this tenseness which people find depressing. April 28, 1929

Something was definitely wrong with my tense and legalistic brand of Christianity, as this second period in Berlin showed me. That was the grace of God, for "the truth will set you free" (John 8:32). How wise of God to remove me from my ministry in Darmstadt where I no doubt came across as a deeply devout

Christian. On a human level my return to Berlin was pointless, as I never became a social worker. But, as a teacher at Bible college was fond of saying, the Lord is more concerned about us personally than our work for Him. He wants us to become more like Him and fit for heaven. Continuing with my ministry in Darmstadt would have been spiritually damaging to me. I would have become like a greenhouse plant, just as Erika Madauss had warned: "At this rate you'll soon be a saint, but you'll scare people off with your piety." By which I took her to mean I wasn't natural, free and happy – the signs of true love and humility.

It was not an easy time for me: yearning to emerge from the chrysalis as a butterfly, yet lacking the wings of love to fly into freedom. But God had already prepared the way for me: further refining lay ahead.

THE REFINING FIRE

TEACHING AT MALCHE BIBLE COLLEGE AUTUMN 1929 – AUTUMN 1930

The year in Berlin was over, but I did not return to the youth ministry. On completing my course, I took up the invitation of Malche Bible College to join their staff. Returning to the college where I had spent such a happy year was an attractive prospect, although teaching was not really my inclination. At heart I still yearned for a youth group to mentor and lead deeper into the Word of God. I had only a hazy idea of what lecturing at Bible college involved, but when asked to serve there, I knew I should accept. So in October 1929 I arrived at the Bible college for the second time in four years.

Little did I realize how different life would be as a lecturer rather than one of the students. Though living in the same building, I missed the companionship of fellow students, which I had so enjoyed. This time I had a small room to myself, which soon felt like a prison cell – just like my first room in Berlin.

What did my life now comprise? I held classes in the missionary teachers' course, the Bible course, and the advanced course for church workers. I was teaching, among other subjects, German, psychology and church history. Not being part of the student body, I had no further contact with them. And so there were only two alternatives when I finished classes: either to return to my room or take a lonely walk. I should have found my place among the rest of the staff, but I did not fit in there either. At twenty-five I was actually closer in age to the students. In the next room I could often hear the hum of conversation when some of the staff who were old acquaintances gathered together. However, since they did not know me, I was never invited to join them. Probably my reserve made it difficult for them. Some may relish being alone, but I found it began to weigh me down.

Yet loneliness was not the real reason why my second stay at Bible college was so different and hard for me. I was now older and more mature. Four years earlier my joy at being at Bible college had partly been due to youthful enthusiasm, which had naturally abated. Once again I became aware of something that had troubled me while working in Darmstadt. As older Christians we easily assume a certain religious tone and mode of behaviour which can be oppressive. Often it is a sign of unresolved issues that we are trying to mask. I was disappointed to discover these same symptoms here. And wasn't it my own reflection I now saw in others? After gaining a little more spiritual experience, I realized I was becoming prone to the same malady.

In Berlin, God in His grace had relentlessly shown me my nature. Now, in His grace, He was alerting me to the dangers of becoming rigid and inflexible. Again, it was sheer grace that my emotional desires withered and died when denied the active, creative, hands-on role I longed for in Christian service. In Berlin at least there had been variety, intellectual stimulation and the company of other students – but here? I had no opportunity for one-to-one ministry, and very little fellowship.

They [my colleagues] are so different from me. No sparkle, no passion, no sense of fun. And oh, this teaching routine! – when I'm dying to get things going and try my hand at something new. I want to be involved fully in people's lives, sharing their journeys and caring for the whole person, not just their intellectual needs.

November 8, 1929

Life at Bible college, once a joy, now became a burden. In addition – though I may have imagined it – the other lecturers seemed to keep their distance. Probably they noticed that I didn't fit their spiritual mould, at least not at first glance. I felt trapped like a bird in a cage.

Nor was this my only problem. Various works of psychology that were required reading in preparation for classes caused me considerable inner conflict. The God-encounters of great Christian men and women down through the ages were interpreted on a purely human and psychological level. Denied the youth work I longed for after the year in Berlin, I found myself "buried alive" in barren wastes. Yet all this paled in comparison with a grief which brought me close to the brink of despair. God was taking me through a further refining process. He was dealing with the part of my nature that had caused me so many problems during my work in Darmstadt: a false zeal for souls.

This time it concerned Erika Madauss. She had drifted further and further from Jesus, and her many doubts were causing her deep distress. My heart almost broke. Watching others suffer was much harder than accepting pain in my own life. Basically I could say yes to God's will when it only involved myself. But it was a huge struggle to put my trust in God's love when I agonized over those dear to me. Why was it such a struggle? Actually, I was grumbling against God's leadings. In my journal I wrote:

Oh, why is it so hard for me to believe in God's love? In everything that affects me personally – whether the loss of my job in Darmstadt or now being stuck in a lonely, unfulfilling occupation – I know this is the only way that blessing can come. And though I may be very sad, I never despair, because I can see the hand of God in all this. I only want to go where He leads, even if it means dying to self. But the issue at hand is far more serious. I simply cannot stand by and watch what happens when someone doesn't follow through with their commitment. It's not only the turmoil and brokenness they suffer here and now. There are implications for eternity.

O Lord, when will You answer my prayers? Why do You save so few people? The thought torments me ... Lord Jesus Christ, demonstrate Your power and teach me to believe in Your love. Forgive me! Amen.

November 16, 1929

I was going through a deep spiritual night. The Word of God did not speak to me. Prayer in the power of faith was beyond me. There was no one to confide in. God no longer seemed to answer: He seemed distant, lifeless. Day after day I sat in my room; tears were my food, anguished thoughts preyed on me. Someone dear to me had drifted far from God.

How the Lord brought me through, I don't know. But all the time it was as though Jesus were asking, *Will you stay with Me? Will you live for Me alone? Am I enough for you even when I almost seem dead, giving you no reassurances, no loving proofs of My presence? Am I still enough for you when I don't give you a satisfying ministry in My vineyard ... even if I don't seem to hear your prayers for loved ones engulfed in darkness ... even if I don't answer your questions about a Christian's place in the world?*

And the Lord did help me; otherwise my response would have been sadder still. As in that difficult first year in Berlin, He used my distress to reveal the sin in my heart. Kneeling at His feet in contrition, we will not lose Jesus. The Saviour and the pardoned sinner belong together. During my intense struggle I wrote:

> *More and more clearly I see that my Christian life is utterly powerless. Otherwise, how could I have despaired at the very time I was supposed to be trusting You for someone else? Lord, give me faith.* November 4, 1929

> *I don't know – my life seems so impoverished and fruitless. What does my Christian life consist of? Am I too preoccupied with myself and my misery? ... Help me to slam the door shut on all self-pity ... the agonizing question "Why?" – which surely has no place in a life that has known God's love.* November 7, 1929

> *Lord, You know how I've been struggling these past few weeks to believe – and how I've failed. But unbelief is nothing but grumbling against You! Armed with prayer and all the promises in Your Word, I'll fight it ... Why is my faith so dead? How dare I challenge God for allowing such distress? "My thoughts*

are not your thoughts." [Isaiah 55:8] *When will I finally surrender and bow to Your sovereignty?* January 25, 1930

How differently my journal entries read after the Lord brought about a breakthrough:

The scales have fallen from my eyes and I can behold Your glory again. I am overflowing with joy for what You have done for Erika! Now I see all my unbelief, bitterness, even defiance towards You, my spiritual deadness, my slackness in prayer, my lovelessness, my self-absorption to the neglect of others. I can only weep in shame over this winter. May 19, 1930

Thank You, Lord, for taking me to task, but also showing me that prayer is the way to life. Pray, pray, pray – that's what I want to do. And I know You will rekindle in me the spirit of prayer. Oh, if only I had turned to You more often! June 12, 1930

In His loving-kindness God took me by the hand as His child. He heard my cries from the depths.

May each hour of darkness and death to the soul give rise to a love that hopes and bears all things – in thanksgiving that You've always brought me through in the past.

December 4, 1929

I have but one desire in life, one heartfelt plea to God. Wherever He places me, I want to respond with love, love, and more love – even in the face of hostility. December 16, 1929

God pays special attention to prayers from an anguished heart, crushed and stricken by Him, bereft of any power to believe, and yet daring to hope against hope. Not one of my prayers went unanswered.

Humanly speaking, my soul seemed to be burnt out in the furnace of affliction. Not a spark of love, joy or faith remained in me. I had reached the end of myself. God wanted to expose my true nature so that I would see myself as a sinner, poor and needy, yet pardoned by Him. He bestows His riches on the poor and shows mercy to the afflicted.

The year at Bible college drew to a close, bringing with it a special answer to prayer. Erika, for whose soul I had wrestled, found her way back to Jesus. My heart brimmed over with joy and thanksgiving, my unbelief put to shame. The end of the college year also marked the end of my time there – for me a welcome release. Yet where would my path take me next?

The senior classes of the Bible college were supervised by Dr. Gertrud Traeder – later Dr. Wasserzug-Traeder, Beatenberg – who had formerly been prominent in the Women's Division of the German Student Christian Movement. I had only been lecturing a few months at Malche Bible College when both she and Jeanne Wasserzug, formerly a Bible teacher in Tunisia, felt I should work as a spiritual counsellor for women students. Dedicated Christian workers in this field were in short supply. Foreign students would be my main focus. To suit me for work among students, I needed to study myself. But how? I lacked the necessary qualifications, having left school at sixteen.

In Berlin, however, it was possible to take an aptitude test, provided you had recommendations from public figures. Receiving these recommendations, being accepted for the test, and actually passing it – I took none of this for granted. But evidently it was all part of God's plan for my life.

During my youth work in Darmstadt I had attended a seminar on psychology by Professor Paul Luchtenberg, later to become Minister of Education and Culture for North Rhine and Westphalia (1956–1958). On the basis of his recommendation I was admitted to the aptitude test. After the written examination it seemed doubtful whether I would pass. Then came the oral examination. At the Ministry of Education on Berlin's famous boulevard *Unter den Linden*, I had to take my place alone at a long table, facing a row of professors and other influential people. They tested my intelligence and aptitude in a whole range of subjects. And by the grace of God I passed.

Now the way was clear for me to go to university, taking philosophy and history of art alongside psychology, my main subject. However, my studies were only meant to be a bridge, enabling me to reach students with the Gospel.

EMBARKING ON A NEW MINISTRY

BERLIN UNIVERSITY
AUTUMN 1930 – AUTUMN 1931

A year after leaving the Women's College for Social Welfare Training, I was back in Berlin again – for the third time now – and feeling even more lost. Everything was so different. For a start, there was the time factor. Soon I realized there was no way I could pursue my own studies as well as build up a new ministry among foreign students. The distances were so great that a single visit often took half the day.

After the first few weeks, during which I arranged two public meetings for foreign students, it was clear that under these circumstances it would be impossible to complete my studies in the normal space of time. So I made the decision to finish my studies first in preparation for the planned ministry. A few weeks later the Berlin branch of the Women's Division of the German Student Christian Movement (DCSB) asked me to work with them. I agreed, as combining this with my studies seemed feasible and I was hungry for fellowship with other believers among the students.

My studies weighed upon me like a cross. True, I had always taken an interest in intellectual matters. Even as a young girl when my mother was training me in housekeeping, and later during my youth work in Darmstadt, I had attended lectures on psychology, philosophy and history of art. But I never had the inclination to spend many hours over books. When I was a child, half an hour of reading was enough and I would be up and about again. I was anything but a bookworm. Yet now for weeks, months and years I had nothing else to do but pore over books – books on psychology, philosophy, history of art and also theology, which I had chosen as a first-year option.

For my main subject, psychology, I attended the lectures of the brilliant founder of a new school, Professor Eduard Spranger, one of my examiners at the aptitude test. His broad-minded treatment of psychological issues from the scientific aspect opened up many new perspectives. The professors of theology, with their lively presentation, taught me to enjoy the subject. Textual criticism could no longer unsettle me personally, though I was distressed to see young students doubting their faith. Usually it was extremely hard to help them.

From my base in Berlin I often met up on Sundays with Erika Madauss, who had returned the previous year from England and now held a position as a social worker in Hamburg. Real spiritual fellowship between us was restored: a gift of God for me. Being one again in the Lord was to prove significant. Later we would walk the same spiritual path and go on to found the Sisterhood of Mary together.

UNFULFILLED UNDER "CHEAP GRACE"

UNIVERSITY AND TRAVELLING MINISTRY
HAMBURG, AUTUMN 1931 – AUTUMN 1935

Beginning with my second year, in autumn 1931, I studied in Hamburg, living with Erika and her family. Spiritually, this marked a new chapter for both of us. In the course of my life there had been several crossroads when I made decisions in obedience to a clear inner prompting. That was the case when I interrupted my course in Berlin to attend Malche Bible College, and later when I gave up my ministry in Darmstadt to complete my social welfare training in Berlin. A similar inner compulsion played a special role when it came to the question of marriage. The thought of marriage appealed to me, for I would have loved to have children of my own. But it was clear to me that God was calling me to be single. Every time the question arose, I felt I must say no. I knew I was called to dedicate my life exclusively to Jesus and His service.

While studying in Hamburg, I felt a similar inner prompting to live a common life with Erika, with shared finances and belongings. It was during this period that I received another marriage proposal – this time from a pastor who asked with great sincerity. Serving in a local church was an attractive prospect. Yet I knew I had to decline because of God's calling on my life. I had the assurance that Erika Madauss and I were set apart for a joint ministry. At the time we were ill-prepared, but eventually His plan would materialize. We read many theological works, especially those of Martin Luther and Karl Barth, as well as histories of Christian missions; and compared with my last year at Bible college I was happy. But was I really happy in Jesus?

On a human level, life was good. Things were so different now. The two previous years had been lonely ones, fraught with trials and temptations and various problems. But now I found myself in a warm nest. No longer did I live alone in student lodgings, but with a family, who cared for me lovingly. After the year in the urban desert of Berlin, I was very grateful for the change.

This was a leafy, residential area of Hamburg, full of parks and gardens. It was a short walk to the riverbank of the Alster. Hamburg was truly a lovely city, and it won my heart immediately. The small university, surrounded by lawns, was within walking distance. It was close to the *Dammtor,* site of the old city gate. How relieved I was that I didn't have to take the underground railway to lectures. I felt I had left the unnatural existence of the previous years and settled down to a more normal way of life. Body and soul rejoiced in the light and sunshine.

While I was lecturing at Bible college or studying in Berlin, books had more or less been my only companions. In Hamburg I enjoyed Erika's company; she had the same interests and shared my joys and sorrows, and I was at home in her family.

Together we did the art tours necessary for my studies, visiting the Netherlands, France and Italy. During these travels we discovered the wealth of art and nature. No longer did I have to study alone in my room, for Erika, who had always been interested in art and psychology, even shared in my studies. Late in the afternoon when her work was over, she would either join me at the university for some of the lectures, or we would meet on the banks of the beautiful Alster. On glorious summer days boats would skim across the water, sails billowing, with the venerable towers of the Hanseatic city rising in the background.

With Erika typing my doctoral thesis and testing me on the material, studying for my PhD was made easy for me during that last summer at Hamburg University. I had chosen a religio-psychological theme, THE SIGNIFICANCE OF THE CONVICTION OF SIN IN THE RELIGIOUS CONFLICTS OF FEMALE ADOLESCENTS, based on some four hundred letters I had received from the girls in my youth work in Darmstadt.

In 1933 I had presented this thesis to the well-known psychologist Professor William Stern. In contrast to those of Spranger, his lectures took an empirical slant, influencing my approach. However, owing to the political upheaval of 1933 I was not able to complete my doctoral studies under him but had to change professors – in all three subjects. Professor Stern was Jewish, as were the other professors under whom I mainly studied: Ernst Cassirer (philosophy) and Erwin Panofsky (history of art). All three were highly respected and distinguished in their fields. To my deep regret, and that of many other students, they were dismissed that same year, soon after Hitler came to power. Consequently I was examined by new tutors, and it was no matter of course to be awarded my doctorate with a good grade.

Even though God in His loving-kindness made my studies as easy and pleasant as possible, at heart I still yearned for a real ministry like the youth work I had in Darmstadt. Academic life left me basically unsatisfied. True, my increasing involvement in the work of the German Student Christian Movement (DCSB) was some compensation. I became president of the Hamburg branch of the women's division, later regional and then national president. What grieved me, though, was that the seed of God's Word did not find much fertile ground among the students. It was choked by the thorns of the many intellectual and theological debates. Further complicating the issue, my activities from 1933 to 1935 coincided with the onset of the Nazi regime. Genuine Christian work was greatly hampered by the German Christians – a racist, anti-Semitic movement that subscribed to the absolute authority of the Führer. Every Christian student group was split in two. Wherever I went, there were disputes and a sharp clash of opinion.

I still recall a stormy night session in Hanover in February 1934. The question was whether or not we, as a Christian student organization, should comply and implement the Aryan Paragraph. The motion to do so was rejected. That meant students from a

Jewish background would continue to be welcome at our meetings. It also meant we were in danger of disbandment, which actually happened in 1938. As national president I wrote to all DCSB branches on January 16, 1934. After mentioning the Board's rejection of the Aryan Paragraph, I went on to say:

> *In many universities we are now faced with serious decisions because of the prohibition of dual membership. It is a question of remaining in the DCSB or of switching over to the ANST [National Socialist Women's Student Committee]. I realize that for some this has already caused considerable fear and anxiety, especially in those places where the ANST is hostile towards the DCSB. Your success in exams may be jeopardized, so too your career opportunities. Such thoughts are inevitable if we face the situation realistically. As Christians we need to counter this reality with the reality of Christ. Before His power and majesty all else fades into nothing. People and things are merely instruments in the hand of the Maker of heaven and earth. Sovereignly, He fulfils His purposes for those who belong to Him. So I urge you to "ponder anew what the Almighty can do".*
>
> *Now is the time to stand up and be counted; now is the time to commit to His cause, regardless of the cost. This is a highly significant time, a time of decision. We are faced with a unique opportunity: let us not miss it. When God calls, let us respond with the profession of our faith: "Christ is my Lord. In life and in death I belong to Him."*
>
> *May the Lord find the DCSB alert in this time of decision, so that His promise may be fulfilled: "The Spirit of glory and of God rests on you"* (1 Peter 4:14).
>
> *Let us now close ranks and uphold each other, so that no one leaves the movement out of weakness. Let us be one in professing Christ our Lord and courageously put our trust in Him: His is the kingdom and the power!*

In May 1934 the Confessing Church emerged, born of the effort to resist state interference in church matters. I soon became a registered member and led the DCSB in this spirit. However, I was not in favour of Christian student fellowships as a whole joining the Confessing Church. These fellowships were supposed to be evangelistic. Enquirers who knew nothing of this conflict would be unable to join, as they were not registered members of the Confessing Church. They would miss an opportunity to hear the Gospel and come to Christ.

Many found my position hard to understand. So I not only had students from the ranks of the German Christians to contend with, but also students from the Confessing Church. The latter were demanding that the DCSB as a whole join the Confessing Church. In the midst of this controversy I stood by sadly. My deepest concern, to introduce students to Jesus, was almost always frustrated by these theological debates. Often they were not conducted in the right spirit. Even during Bible studies my fellow students tended to respond on a purely academic level.

From 1933 until completing my doctorate in 1934, I was honorary national president of the DCSB. From 1934 onwards I was national president and travelling secretary combined. Systematically I visited local DCSB groups in the various university towns. Grateful though I am for the inspiration, insight, correction and fellowship I experienced, I look back with regret, feeling I failed the students and graduates. I myself sensed that my ministry was ineffectual. I lacked the spiritual authority to reach people's hearts. This couldn't be attributed solely to contemporary events or an academic environment: there had to be a deeper reason.

Back then the reason was not clear to me; in retrospect I see what it was. During those years in Hamburg I was not walking the path of the cross. Since God had given me a new and deeper fellowship with Erika, I no longer stood alone. She helped me shoulder many a burden that would otherwise have weighed me down – political concerns, or difficulties in the DCSB or in my studies. In addition, we had rich times of sharing. The agonizing conflicts over matters of conscience came to rest, even if the issue of world-affirmation versus world-denial was yet to be fully resolved.

The real reason for my powerless ministry was that my love for Jesus had grown lukewarm. Life was pleasant and, without noticing it, I had become conformed to the world. I was no longer challenged by Jesus' words: "Whoever wants to be my disciple must deny themselves and take up their cross and follow me" (Matthew 16:24). The truth was that I didn't want to bear my cross. While travelling for the DCSB, I would complain of the strain and the discomfort. I was not serving gladly. Was it any wonder that my ministry was not fruitful?

The way Erika and I spent our Sundays was typical of our spiritual life. All week long we looked forward to Sunday when we would make an excursion to Wedel, a small village on the other side of Blankenese. There we had a wonderful view of the Elbe as we wandered over the dykes for an hour, wending our way through lonely pastures where cows were grazing.

To be sure, we always made an early start in order to reach Wedel in time for church, for the Word of God was important to us. But the real emphasis of our Sundays was the enjoyment of the beautiful countryside. In spacious pastures, under wide skies, we would relax while Erica painted her lovely watercolours. Usually we read spiritual books, but even so our real focus wasn't on Jesus. Our main purpose was not spending Sundays in quietness to meet Him in prayer: it was acquiring theological knowledge.

Our workdays were similar. We never missed our daily quiet time and evening devotions, nor the weekly Bible study. But where was the determination to fight sin in our lives, the passion to see God's kingdom grow, the sacrificial zeal to reach others? Where was the wrestling for souls in prayer? Where was the spirit of worship or that sense of awe at the magnitude of God's love? I had slipped into a half-hearted, conventional Christianity, though in the eyes of the students I was the radical one, with my insistence on uncompromising discipleship.

For all the riches I gained from fellowship with Erika and the intellectually stimulating life of those years, I was impoverished. Because I rarely wept over my sins, my soul could not rejoice in Jesus my Saviour. I lacked the power of the Holy Spirit to help the students see Jesus in His glory as King and Saviour and hear the call to love Him.

If those years only diverted me from the true purpose of my life, then why did God lead me to university? That was a question I frequently asked myself in the difficult years following 1935. Today I realize that the period in Hamburg was a significant part of God's wise and loving plan for my life. My studies served to strengthen my keen psychological attitude towards life and in particular all religious experience. In myself and in others I learnt to discern what was purely spiritual and what was influenced by the personality and the ego.

God was guiding me in His wisdom, for later I was to discover a wonderful gift of grace: loving Jesus with the love of a bride. Through my writings, I was to share this message of first love for Jesus with many others. But years of studying psychology and psychoanalysis alerted me to potential dangers. It is vital to discern any soulish elements or repressed emotional needs camouflaged as spirituality. I soon realized that legalism – or, at the other end of the spectrum, over-enthusiasm – can usually be traced back to repression. Bridal love, in contrast, is soundly rooted in the truth. It lies in seeing and regretting our sins, experiencing a change of heart, turning from sin. Bridal love for Jesus grows out of the experience of forgiveness, as seen in the love of the great sinner in Luke chapter 7.

As the Holy Spirit uncovered my sins in His all-revealing light, I was privileged to receive this gift of grace. Repentance was the way to greater intimacy. In Jesus I found fulfilment for my life, the fullness of joy. The Bridegroom of my soul drew near, revealing His heart to me, just as He had revealed Himself to me as the crucified Saviour when I was seventeen years old. As a sign that this love was genuine and Spirit-given, He granted me a new love for my cross and new grace to overcome. From now on no sacrifice was too hard, for "Christ's love compels us" (2 Corinthians 5:14). For His sake I could say, "I do not account my life of any value nor as precious to myself" (Acts 20:24 RSV).

It is a fact, you can't lead others where you haven't been yourself. There is a price to be paid before you can share the message of love for Jesus – or any message. First you have to work it through in your own mind and life, and battle through the issues. Then you can stand firm on the insights gained and guarantee that it's the right way. Only if you know the pitfalls can you help others avoid them.

In yet another way the years in Hamburg proved significant. After disappointments in people who stressed their conversion, Martin Luther was a fresh discovery for me. Reading his works and those of Karl Barth drove home to Erika and me the blessings of justification by faith. I found myself reacting against the legalism I had been caught up in – that striving for sanctification which had such a dampening effect on others. Luther's teaching provided a balance, though now I was in danger of succumbing to "cheap grace". But for the time being Erika and I simply rejoiced in the assurance that we were saved by grace and that God pardons and justifies the ungodly, those who stand condemned as guilty sinners.

Grappling with the works of Luther and Barth, we also gained a new understanding of the importance of daily repentance. This too would be significant in leading the Sisterhood of Mary. Until then I had been familiar with the path of conversion, regeneration and sanctification. This was the basis of my spiritual life. But in His grace the Lord led me into various real-life situations where I was faced with specific sinful attitudes. Repentance opened the door to a deeper knowledge of God and closer fellowship with Him. Reading these works together, Erika and I now acquired the theological grounding for the insights the Lord had given.

We made a vital discovery about salvation. It's not just about a one-time experience at conversion: *I am a sinner who has fallen short of the glory of God, but I'm justified by grace.* It's about an ongoing process in the life of every Christian. Daily we sin, daily we fall under God's judgment, daily we receive forgiveness by faith in Jesus – and daily we experience His grace. Only daily repentance can keep us from judgmentalism and hypocrisy – to which the religiously-minded are prone, as Jesus so often warned.

The seeds sown in those Hamburg years would bear fruit later as difficult situations brought us to our knees. What we had accepted theoretically we would then experience in reality. All have sinned and fallen short of the glory of God – ourselves included. A painful realization. Yet the place at the foot of the cross is the place where Jesus wins our hearts as we respond in gratitude to His forgiveness.

It was God's grace that led us into this new understanding. All along, He had in mind the future Sisterhood of Mary, where we are called to live and proclaim a life of bridal love for Jesus. "Sinners justified by faith alone" was the sound teaching that would keep us grounded in reality, instead of soaring into mystical realms and losing ourselves in a piety and holiness of our own invention. With good reason Erika, later known as Mother Martyria, would focus on Paul's letter to the Romans when teaching her spiritual daughters. She wanted to give them a firm foundation for their spiritual life and this was the wholesome diet she chose.

And so even in the Hamburg years, when other interests vied for first place in our lives, God was at work. He was preparing us for what lay ahead. Soon He would draw us into a deeper level of commitment, something far more radical than anything I had imagined during my years of legalistic striving for sanctification. At the same time He would lead us out of law into the naturalness of a child of God inspired by love for Jesus. But first God had to lead us out of the outwardly pleasant years of Hamburg into the desert, in direct preparation for the Sisterhood of Mary.

ALL IN VAIN?

BIBLE COURSES AT STEINBERG HOUSE DARMSTADT, 1935–1938

At the end of my time in Hamburg God planted the seed of a new commission in my heart. For this I had the unmistakable assurance, even though the contours were still hazy. The Lord seemed to be saying He wanted a place that would be a "beacon of light" making known the great deeds He does today as in biblical times, to the glory of His name. People would be called to Him and He would be exalted.

In 1935, almost thirty-one years of age, I moved to my parents' home in Darmstadt – this time with Erika. The next step was shown to me. We were to start three-month and six-month Bible courses for young women, in particular for future clergy wives. The purpose was to lead them more deeply into the Word of God before they started training for a career or serving in a congregation as a pastor's wife.

With the way ahead shrouded in darkness, I prayed for a confirmation. I wanted to be certain this wasn't a self-chosen path. I had been so sure this mission was from God, but I was fully prepared to give it back to Him. If the Board at Malche Bible College asked me to serve there, I would give up our planned ministry in Darmstadt. In earlier years the principal, Jeanne Wasserzug, had often mentioned that she would be glad to have me on the staff after I finished my studies. So it was highly probable that she would offer me the post. I prayed that God would direct her heart. If she did ask me, I would take it as a sign of God's will for me at this junction in my life.

In February 1935 I set out for Malche Bible College. But God held His hand over the situation, and I was not invited to teach. Half a year later the invitation came, but by then the die had been cast. Erika had already moved to Darmstadt with me. At a time of widespread unemployment she had given up her position as a social worker and the security of a good pension in order to serve Jesus. And I had resigned as national president of the DCSB, although they were reluctant for me to go and actually asked me to stay on. There was no turning back now.

In obedience to a call of God we moved from Hamburg to Darmstadt, feeling rather like Abraham setting out from Ur of the Chaldeans! We were embarking on a venture of faith, not knowing whether the mission would materialize or how it would be financed. Yet I was utterly convinced it would take shape, because it truly was a mission from God. So when the Bible College asked me to serve there, I wrote to the Board, "I believe God intends to do a great and significant work here in Darmstadt, and so I feel I should stay here."

But for now, nothing seem to come of it. In the winter of 1935–1936 Erika and I had lovingly prepared the upstairs apartment in my parents' home, Steinberg House, for the students who were to come and live there, as well as installing a basement kitchen and dining room. All these renovations came at a substantial cost. During that first year Erika and I lived at close quarters in the same room where we held Bible studies for women, as we were reserving the top floor for the coming students. My parents welcomed us warmly and provided furniture and bedding.

However, the beds remained empty and the rooms silent. After publishing a brochure advertising the Bible courses, we waited from week to week for applications. But they were few and far between. Those who did apply withdrew shortly before the course was due to begin. What a disappointment! During those first years the words "in vain" seemed to be stamped on all our preparations. In vain had the rooms been furnished. In vain had Erika spent all her savings from her social welfare work in Hamburg on the interior decoration of the rooms. In vain had she given up her government job. It had all been in vain.

Then came the voices of temptation. Had I been mistaken, as others were trying to tell me, in thinking that this was a God-given mission? Was I walking in disobedience to Him? How happy we had been to move into Steinberg House, 26 Hölderlin Way! But soon that large, friendly house, with its spacious garden, in a lovely residential area close to the woods, no longer smiled at us so kindly. What painful recollections we have of our walks through the woods when we discussed our situation. To this day it cuts us to the heart when we come across one of the benches where we sat in tears. Our hopes dashed, we were at a loss as to the next step. Darkness engulfed us.

The greatest comfort was that I now had someone to share the burden with. Together, Erika and I recognized more and more clearly the voice of God speaking through circumstances. Admittedly, the times were unfavourable for starting Bible courses. Young women had almost no opportunity of attending because of government and Labour Office regulations. Yet ultimately it was God who was saying *no* in this situation. He showed us unmistakably that He couldn't yet use us for this ministry. We could only humbly acknowledge, "Your ways, God, are holy" (Psalm 77:13). But step by step He did open the way for us to hold regular Bible studies at Steinberg House for thirty to forty women.

A few months later a teacher asked me to take over a local Girls' Bible Class (MBK). Nationwide the entire movement had disbanded in 1933 to avoid enforced conformity by the Nazi regime. I couldn't help feeling sad as I began this work, for nothing had come of the Bible courses for future clergy wives, which we thought would be our real ministry. Little did we realize that this Girls' Bible Class was a seed that would grow from year to year and one day blossom into the Sisterhood of Mary. That first Bible study with six girls aged between fourteen and eighteen was actually the birth of something new. It marked the beginning of God's hidden plan for the sisterhood. Significantly the text I chose after much prayer was, "Repent, for the kingdom of heaven has come near" (Matthew 3:2). That verse accompanied us right up to the founding of the sisterhood and beyond. It would become the theme of the dedication of the Herald Chapel and the watchword of our Land of Canaan and Canaan Friends.

How could we guess the significance of this first Bible study? All we could see was that our plans lay in ruins. God was saying *no* to us, not least through the constant reminders of others that such "self-chosen paths" were doomed to failure.

But in the darkness of that first year God caused a star to shine. It was a verse He had given Erika at a critical moment.

> For the vision is yet for an appointed time, but at the end it shall speak, and not lie: though it tarry, wait for it; because it will surely come, it will not tarry. Habakkuk 2:3 KJV

On this verse we took our stand in faith. What choice did we have but to live by faith? When it came to our material needs, there was no other way but to ask our heavenly Father for each item, for we had no regular income. We also had to walk in faith in view of our mission from God. For months on end, the empty apartment stared us in the face.

When the Bible courses failed to materialize, the furniture provided for that purpose was no longer available. And without it, there was no way to accept future students.

Those first years after the move from Hamburg were fraught with trials and temptations. It was a long, dark tunnel, and we almost despaired of ever seeing the light again. But in our hearts a new and different light appeared. What we had accepted mentally in Hamburg was now to be worked out in practice – the doctrine of justification of sinners. The *no* from God, the contempt and shame we bore, the challenges of living with others – all this helped us to move from intellectual assent to real-life experience. We came to see ourselves as sinners indeed, and learnt not to be dismissive of criticism but to accept that we were far from perfect. So we had cause both to weep over our sins and to give thanks as pardoned sinners. Through Jesus' sacrificial death and His forgiveness true justification was ours – not in theory but in practice.

All along God had in mind the Sisterhood of Mary. Even then the foundations of contrition and repentance were being laid – a prelude to the move of repentance that would sweep through the Girls' Bible Classes during the 1944–1945 revival. In 1936, at the end of that first challenging year, I wrote to Erika on the occasion of her birthday:

> *"Who is a God like you, who pardons sin …?"* (Micah 7:18) *We can praise and glorify God for many things, but no joy on earth can ever surpass the joy of sin forgiven. The jubilant song, "Bless the Lord, O my soul!" sounds forth here on earth, but also echoes beyond the skies, for there is "rejoicing in heaven over one sinner who repents"* (Luke 15:7). *And one day, when all our songs of praise for God's goodness in this life cease, another song will be raised by the heavenly hosts above – the song of the Lamb, who has taken away our sins.*
>
> *Does this song of thanksgiving still ring in our hearts: "Who is a God like you, who pardons sin?" Or is this note of praise missing in our prayers? If so, how will we join in the song of the Lamb at the throne of God? Erika, this time last year the song had faded in our hearts. Do you remember when we first found Jesus? For you, it was confirmation classes and the year at Kassel, and for me the time at Bible college. Among my favourite songs back then were "O bliss of the purified, bliss of the free"* [Francis Bottome] *and "There is a fountain filled with blood drawn from Emmanuel's veins, and sinners plunged beneath that flood lose all their guilty stains … Then in a nobler, sweeter song I'll sing Thy power to save …"* [William Cowper].
>
> *Yet in the long years of waiting that followed, while I was at university and you were doing social work, we grew indifferent and complacent. Weighed down by the things of this world, our hearts no longer sang for joy – "Who is a God like you, who pardons sin!" Victory eluded us in various areas of our lives,*

and we had slipped into resignation. Our failings no longer saddened us the way they used to.

We weren't crying out for release from sin. We weren't singing for joy over His forgiveness and deliverance. Down this road we continued, not noticing that it was taking us further and further away from Jesus.

But Erika, God never lost sight of His goal for us: to rekindle the song of the Lamb in our hearts – all in preparation for His great day above. So in His mercy He made us acutely aware of our sinful reactions. We saw this happen in the work situation over this past winter, but above all in our relationship with X last summer. It showed us just how incapable we are of responding to unfairness with love, forgiveness, humility and gentleness. How can we expect to join the ranks of the overcomers one day the way we are? "Without holiness no one will see the Lord." (Hebrews 12:14) *Oh, Erika, what a mercy that God helped us to recognize our sins this past year. He couldn't have given us a greater blessing. "Who is a God like you, who pardons sin!" There couldn't be a more fitting verse as we look back together on lost years.*

Erika, now we can share the good news of forgiveness of sin, with the song of jubilation ringing in us. We couldn't before, because we had neither the right nor the authority. We need to be able to sing from the heart, "He has washed away all my sins" [J.A.von Poseck] *and point with shining eyes to the Lamb, who paid the full price for us ...*

The past year revealed our bondage to sin and our need for God's forgiveness. This year, let us pledge ourselves to wrestle wholeheartedly in prayer to overcome sin in our lives. We won't let go until the victory comes. We will battle on, trusting in His word, "If the Son sets you free, you will be free indeed" (John 8:36).

In the previous years we had grown lukewarm in the battle against sin, because we were not under discipline, which would have shown up our sin. But as God now opened our eyes, the breakthrough came. Once again the jubilant song of salvation, the song of the Lamb, rang in our hearts. And this song of love for Jesus was to become the song of the Sisterhood of Mary. I still can't take in the goodness of the Lord in freeing me from the spiritual tepidness of the Hamburg years. Once again my heart sang for joy – the sign of a pardoned sinner.

As in my childhood and youth, my troubles were the saving of me. Without God's hand of discipline, I would have been the most pitiable Christian on earth – self-righteous, self-satisfied, lifeless and proud into the bargain, and either legalistic or worldly. But what blessings each pathway of the cross brought. I have become the happiest person imaginable. Embracing my cross brought me a dual perspective. I had a glimpse into the abyss of my sinful heart. At the same time God's heart of love and mercy was revealed to me. And the sight of the crucified Lord, pierced for my sins, set my heart aflame. With every cross He sent me, my love grew stronger, preparing my heart for the most precious revelation of all: the mystery of the Holy Trinity.

Discipleship of the cross would be integral to our sisterhood as part of its spiritual basis. God was training Erika and me as its future leaders.

After the uncertainties of that first year (autumn 1935–autumn 1936), an urgent request came from Malche Bible College. My highly respected teacher Jeanne Wasserzug was terminally ill and asked me to step in for her and teach her classes. I had nothing scheduled in Darmstadt at that time, and since Erika could easily take over the Bible classes for both girls and women, we decided I should go for three months. During that period my beloved teacher died and I was asked to stay on to bridge the gap. And so I continued to hold lectures till summer.

Erika stayed behind in Darmstadt, a strange city where she knew hardly a soul. She had no money, because from the very outset we felt clearly led not to accept any financial support from my parents, as long as we were certain that God had called us to Darmstadt. By means of occasional tutoring Erika managed to tide over this period. Unbeknown to anyone else, she was living in real poverty, though she did have the basic essentials of life.

It was a time of dying to self; a time when God gave us the grace of repentance and of fruit-bearing. How could we have begun the Lord's work as we were when we came from Hamburg – proud and unbroken? The Lord Himself was guiding us into the paths we would later embrace voluntarily in the sisterhood for love of Him. Pain and discipline were His tools. He was training us to live by faith, to do without and, as followers of the Lamb, not to insist on our rights or try to get even. Only when we had practised this ourselves could we later call sisters to walk in the same way.

First one year, then another, passed in this manner. Now we had an inkling of what it means to be poor and living by faith. During the winter when I helped out at Malche Bible College I had little more to wear than a skirt and pullover. Like poor folk, we were dependent on cast-off clothes from others. Money otherwise spent on clothes had long since been set aside for our future ministry to ensure its financial independence. My father kindly offered us the apartment rent-free, as well as other assistance. But in view of our mission from God we didn't feel it was right to accept. Poverty is a real cross, and God was obviously using it to train us. He wanted us to persevere in faith and trust Him for all our needs. Only then would He be glorified in the end for bringing us through. It would be clear for all to see that He had been guiding us. At the same time poverty was an effective cure for our pride.

What did grow in those dark times was the small Girls' Bible Class, which soon developed into several groups. Yet, as far as we were concerned, this was not what God was really calling us to do. By July 1937 we still didn't know where our path would take us. The course I had been teaching as a stand-in at Malche Bible College had come to an end.

Both Erika and I were subsequently invited by the Board to join the teaching staff full-time. Change was in the air. It seemed our path would take us away from Darmstadt and any future ministry there. At first we agreed, as this detour seemed to be from God, though I never lost the unshakeable conviction of God's mission for us in Darmstadt. Then I received a letter from the Bible college which showed me clearly that going there was not an option. So I cancelled, though only after an intensive struggle in prayer to be sure of God's will.

The upshot was that we remained at Darmstadt with no clear mission and no income. Often we had less than five German Marks between us. The Girls' Bible Classes continued to expand, but we held these on a voluntary basis. Only from the weekly women's Bible class and the occasional talk I was asked to give, for example, at a ladies group did we receive a small honorarium. Waiting for an invitation to serve was humiliating. Not that I ever doubted that God was allowing it for my own good. Bearing it for love of Jesus was all that mattered.

Less than a year after our move from Hamburg I noted in our work journal:

> *May the future be as God wills regarding our ministry. That the ministry will materialize we know. But what detours and crushing blows it takes! Christ must be glorified in every situation. May God enable us.* June 29, 1936

In the summer of 1938 some future clergy wives came to us for a Bible course – the first and last one we held. There were only three girls living in and one day-student. One of the girls had to leave us before the course was over because her wedding date was put forward. So it hardly counted as a Bible course.

When the course was over, our hopes crumbled. A second course failed to materialize. God continued to humble us through hardship and poverty, and we felt His holy hand disciplining us in love on that long desert road.

Humbling ourselves beneath His chastening hand, we came to see the truth about ourselves more clearly. We were so insistent on being right, so quick to feel indignant towards others. Against the backdrop of His discipline we became even more aware of His infinite love, and that made our faith grow, as our journal entries from 1937 to 1938 show. On October 21, 1937, Erika wrote:

Though we are having to grope in faith, His love is behind it all, leading us through a dark valley regarding our work. But into the darkness shines a bright light: the assurance that His call is still upon us. What a gift of God! He has not taken away our mission and mandate. As yet indiscernible to human eyes, it is clearly revealed to the eyes of faith.

Beneath this entry I wrote:

He will bring it to pass. God's Word is true and cannot lead us astray.

Soon afterwards our call was once more in danger. To all outward appearances we lacked full-time employment. At this very point Erika received an offer for a travelling lectureship with the Leipzig Missionary Society. On November 16, 1937, I wrote:

Lord, have mercy on us. The way is very dark. I believe Your promise in Habakkuk 2:3 for our ministry as of Easter.

On January 21, 1938, I wrote:

Humanly speaking, it is as black as night. But why does God continue to delay our ministry? He must have a purpose in this. Oh, I simply have to believe it. Free us from our insistence on being right and our resentment towards X. Do not let these sins stand in the way of Your ministry. You know this is our one great concern, our one plea.

On April 2, 1938, when we had only three applications for the Bible course:

Once more we face a task demanding all our time, energy and financial resources, yet it neither thrives nor dies. In actual fact, we don't really have a ministry at all. That goes especially for me, as I don't have the big youth ministry like Erika. It's so humiliating. But in it all we see God's hand and give Him thanks, for He humbles His children only in order to exalt them.

So during those first three years (1935–1938) God led us in great wisdom. Though we didn't realize it at the time, we were privileged to follow in the footsteps of Jesus. It was a path of poverty, humiliation and lowliness, where we walked in darkness, our faith constantly tested by impossibilities. What a blessing. God in His love took us there. With trembling but grateful hearts we followed, knowing that we were being led in love and that such humbling experiences did us proud sinners good. We learnt to value these paths because they were His ways and Jesus drew close to us there. They would later characterize our life as a community.

In September 1938 we reached our lowest point. That summer's course for future clergy wives was hardly a success; and, as already mentioned, no new applications came. Again we were standing at the edge of nothingness. It seemed we had no choice but to leave Darmstadt. The rent for the apartment was due – and no relief in sight. By October 1938 we were down to our last penny.

At this point the Leipzig Missionary Society renewed their offer to employ Erika as travelling lecturer. We asked ourselves whether this was God's leading. It seemed like the only viable option in that hopeless situation. He no longer seemed to be confirming our joint ministry in Darmstadt. But that meant facing the end of our mission from God. If we accepted this offer and Erika went to Leipzig, we would be separated and all hopes of any future joint ministry would be buried for good. However, God had the Sisterhood of Mary in view. We were to sacrifice our vision, but in spirit only, just as Abraham offered up Isaac. Even now, He held His hand over the work in Darmstadt.

Strangely, when God asked this sacrifice of us, He also inspired us with the faith that we would receive our "Isaac" – our mission in Darmstadt – back from the dead; that it would come into being after all. It was a gift from the Holy Spirit that we battled through in faith all those years, taking our stand on the verse:

> For the vision is yet for an appointed time, but at the end it shall speak, and not lie: though it tarry, wait for it; because it will surely come, it will not tarry. Habakkuk 2:3 KJV

Going into town to buy a suitcase for Erika's Leipzig-based ministry, we laid our shared life and mission on the altar. But on our return, we found a note in the letterbox, brief and to the point: "Don't leave Darmstadt. A group of friends will support the youth ministry."

God had intervened! What was the story behind the note? The senior pastor at the local deaconess house, who had always had a heart for youth work, had been following the growth of the Girls' Bible Classes with interest. When he heard of the renewed offer Erika had received from the Leipzig Missionary Society, he moved swiftly. Together with Pastor Wolf of St. Paul's Church (most of the girls lived in his parish), he made arrangements. A group of friends at St. Paul's committed themselves to club together each month and support the Girls' Bible Classes with a modest but fixed sum. Only a year earlier, in 1937, our Girls' Bible Classes had been formally affiliated with this church because of the political situation. Once more God was making it clear He wanted us in Darmstadt.

In two years the work that I had begun with six girls grew, under Erika's leadership, to a hundred. God had confirmed this ministry and it was flourishing despite the unfavourable conditions under the Nazi regime, which actively opposed all Christian youth work. At the time someone suggested that perhaps the mission God had shown us for Steinberg House might develop from the Girls' Bible Classes. That seemed inconceivable to us. But God's plan was far more wonderful than we had imagined. He had called the Girls' Bible Classes into existence, for they were later to give rise to the Sisterhood of Mary. Of this we had no inkling. God was still preparing us for our future ministry.

With the youth work Erika now had a ministry from God. Actually, I had begun this work and had longed for just such a youth ministry for years, since I enjoyed working with young people. Yet I clearly felt I was not called to share the leadership with Erika. Again, I was guided by an inner prompting. In the autumn of 1938, after our first and last clergy wives' Bible course, I had no work.

The Bible classes continued to grow, but I knew this was Erika's ministry, not mine. My attitude must have seemed rather strange, but I stood by my decision, much to Erika's concern. A year later it became evident that a plan of God stood behind this inner compulsion, but for the time being I had no field of activity. All I could do was wait for an invitation to give a lecture, hold a retreat for a ladies' group, or stand in as a substitute speaker.

My birthday in autumn 1938 was marked by tears and humiliation. It was a beautiful autumn day, and in the morning Erika and I went on a walk to Eberstadt, a residential suburb of Darmstadt. We went to pay a visit about an occasional opportunity to minister. It was very humiliating. Again the answer was *no*. On our way home after this disappointment, we sat down on a bench with a direct view of the place where our motherhouse now stands. But the future was hidden from our eyes and I wept bitterly, not knowing what fruit these tears would yield.

In the afternoon some relatives who came to pay a birthday visit told me that all my ways since my youth work in Darmstadt had been self-chosen and egoistic. My alleged call to start Bible courses and all my talk about divine guidance were nothing but tempting providence. Had I not learnt my lesson now that I was confronted with the collapse of all my plans and undertakings? When would I finally repent?

The next few weeks led me deeper into the vale of humiliation. Later, as I looked back on that half-year, I wrote in our work journal:

Lord, You know that I was only trying to obey You, seeking Your will alone at each junction. I've been willing to do whatever You say. So one day You will demonstrate before all the world that we have been following Your guidance. March 2, 1939

Here I was in my mid-thirties, with college and university qualifications and having held various leadership positions. And I had no choice but to hire myself out for housework and gardening at an hourly wage. At the time I wrote:

Feel very put down and useless. But knowing I'm under Your grace and in Your school is more important than being involved in active ministry and feeling happy. March 2, 1939

In what was to be a long purging process, the Lord was cutting back my soulish desires – the creative urge to initiate and organize in Christian ministry. Ever since leaving the youth work in Darmstadt as a twenty-two-year-old, I had been waiting for the Lord to fulfil my desire for a similar ministry. I remained under His hand of discipline for almost twenty years, right up to the founding of the sisterhood. I needed it. God was purifying the longings of my soul for a purpose. The sisterhood was His work, not mine, and He wanted to ensure that all my activities would be for love of Him and not for my personal satisfaction under a cloak of piety.

It hurt me to see my father distressed by such strange leadings. He urged me to apply for positions in keeping with my academic qualifications. I did write one letter, but felt unable to send it. Again, I was acting on an inner conviction. When the time was ripe, God would intervene; until then I simply had to bide my time in Darmstadt.

Out of the blue came an invitation, only weeks later, to take over the travelling lectureship of the Wiesbaden-based Mission to the Muslims. In some trepidation I went to the interview. Though thankful at the prospect of a ministry, I had to face the same spectre that had haunted me eighteen months earlier. Would this mark the end of the vision God had given me for Steinberg House ever since 1935?

During the interview I was to discover how wonderful God's thoughts and plans are. The usual requirement for staff to live at the mission centre was waived in my case. The reason given was that Erika and I were a team and God was clearly at work at Steinberg House in various ways. Dropping everything at once would obviously be difficult for me, so to start with, I could work from Darmstadt. In the end I travelled on behalf of the mission for seven years, beginning with Easter 1939, and Darmstadt remained my base throughout that time.

WIDENING HORIZONS – NEW CONTACTS

TRAVELLING LECTURESHIP FOR THE MISSION TO THE MUSLIMS, 1939–1946

What was the situation as this new phase began? The Bible courses we had envisaged for future clergy wives failed to materialize. They had morphed into Erika's work with the Girls' Bible Classes and my travelling lectureship on behalf of the Mission to the Muslims in Wiesbaden. Yet from these two roots grew a tree – the Sisterhood of Mary. How wonderful are the ways of God! I felt inwardly restrained from co-leading the Bible classes with Erika, though I knew nothing of God's ultimate purpose. He was reserving me for the travelling ministry. My acceptance of the post would ultimately lead to the founding of the sisterhood, but that lay hidden in the future. Since I was now employed by the Mission to the Muslims and Erika was fully occupied with the Bible classes, there seemed to be no hope left for our actual vision. On the day I took up the post, I made an entry in our work journal in blind faith:

> *"My thoughts are not your thoughts."* [Isaiah 55:8] *They are much higher and far more wonderful than ours. "All this also comes from the* Lord *Almighty, whose plan is wonderful, whose wisdom is magnificent."* [Isaiah 28:29]

My travelling ministry took me to the missionary society's support groups, to churches and fellowships, where I was asked to give missionary talks and, above all, Bible study courses. Due to physical weakness and wartime conditions, I did not find travelling easy. I still recall the cold winters of 1940 and 1941 when there was a serious coal shortage. Shivering day and night and unable to sleep, I travelled in sub-zero temperatures (minus 30° to 40° Celsius) for four weeks in East Prussia. Due to the blackout I often struggled to find my way, alone, through the city streets at night – I, who had always been fearful by nature. I found myself criss-crossing Germany from Hamburg to Munich and from Lörrach to the Rhineland or Westphalia. The atmosphere was stifling in the overcrowded trains, and often I heard the roaring of enemy bombers overhead. In my letters to Erika I described the situation:

May 23, 1943

After an hour-and-a-half of sleep, we were awakened by the air-raid warning. The anti-aircraft guns were shooting furiously, and we went down to the cellar. Although the raid was on another town, the doors rattled in their frames as the bombs fell. When we went back upstairs at three in the morning, I simply couldn't get back to sleep. I was terrified as I thought of the plight of the people in the town that was hit. So I tossed and turned all night long.

June 18, 1944

I have arrived safely, wonderfully protected by the angels and surrounded by the presence of Jesus Himself, His peace and joy. When I left Bielefeld this morning, the sirens were wailing. It was at the height of the alarm. And the train was crammed. You can't imagine how secure I now feel during all these travels – perfectly content as a child of His. I am really conscious of Jesus' love sweetening the hardships of the journeys I undertake for His sake. My heart overflows with thanksgiving.

"For You" – two little words that helped me through those difficult times. Praying, "All for You, all for You, Jesus" eases the burden. In contrast to my travelling days for the student organization DCSB, I was making a point of doing everything in love for Jesus. Now I could share more from the heart about the power of Jesus' blood, His victory and His return in glory.

My main themes were: *God's Plan of Salvation* (which covered the Second Coming of Jesus, God's redemptive purposes for Israel, and the City of God), *Heaven and Hell, The Blessing of Suffering,* and *How to Overcome.* My talks were very different from those I held as a twenty-two-year-old in my first youth ministry in Darmstadt. Not only was I working with young people, I was still so young myself. Immature and unproven, I wasn't really speaking from experience. Now I could vouch for what I was saying. It had been tested in the crucible of suffering. I had battled it through myself under God's hand of discipline. In particular, He was constantly challenging me to prove my love for Jesus by not insisting on my rights but choosing to walk in the way of the Lamb. This was a special emphasis He laid on my heart.

From 1939 to the outbreak of revival in 1944, we were able to pass on some of the fruits of the four preceding difficult years. At the same time we were being prepared for the Sisterhood of Mary, birthed by the revival. In the years from 1936 to 1940 I had found valuable insights in Johannes Gommel's LEBENDIGES WASSER [Living Water] and Dietrich Bonhoeffer's THE COST OF DISCIPLESHIP. Both books, though so different from each other, gave me a new incentive in the struggles Erika and I were going through. In the face of unjust accusations and demands we had to learn to walk the way of the Lamb and go the second mile. It meant accepting the Sermon on the Mount as binding. "If anyone wants to sue you and take your shirt, hand over your coat as well." – "Love your enemies, do good to those who hate you." (Matthew 5:40; Luke 6:27)

Even during my first youth ministry in Darmstadt (1926–1928) I had struggled with the issue. In my passion for justice I could sometimes be overzealous in the way I handled grievances against myself or others. My heart cried out for release. I longed to experience the saving power of Jesus in this area of my life. At that time I wrote in my journal:

> *Oh, I could almost hate X. She's making my life a misery and wearing me down. For Your sake, Lord Jesus, I want to humble myself before X.* September 30, 1928

> *I find it so hard to let love take precedence over my sense of justice. There's only one way, and that's to speak Your name, Jesus – then something melts in my heart. I am also helped by Romans 12:21 – "Overcome evil with good."* October 7, 1928

How hard I found it to show love when I had obviously been treated unjustly. The thought agonized me. Yet it was God's grace that even at that early stage He brought someone into my life who was so challenging for me. A diary entry during my second year of youth ministry in Darmstadt was to become my life-long prayer:

> *Grant me a love that is not easily provoked or resentful, a love that bears all things, hopes all things, believes all things, endures all things.* October 21, 1927

Now, ten years later, God took me into His school again – this time together with Erika, who suffered alongside me. All those years I had constantly prayed for His love to fill my heart. But with my nature it would be a long drawn-out process. This is why the hammer blows kept coming. My heart cried out because of all the injustices, but God did not hold back. Figuratively speaking, my heart was to be targeted with arrows till the hard spot was riddled with holes. Then contrition and repentance for my inability to love and forgive would overflow, making me receptive for the gift of His love.

My old self writhed. But the blood of the Lamb, which I kept claiming in faith, demonstrated its power. Bit by bit the hardness in my heart melted away and I was filled with compassion for those who had wronged me. And so I learnt to walk the way of the Lamb and go the second mile. The Lord was teaching me not to be defensive or dismissive of criticism, but to endure unjust reproach without trying to clear myself. This, I discovered, is what it means to follow Jesus. It was His pathway.

Again, God had a wise purpose in all this. Perfect love would later be a key theme in my writings. But how could I write on this topic if God had not taught me through suffering and painful discipline to claim this love in faith? "Walk in the way of love, just as Christ loved us." (Ephesians 5:2 NIV) Again and again His Word drove home to me the inadequacy of human love. When challenged to love our enemies, we soon reach our limit. But God was gracious. I have spent many years in His school. Now I can say from experience that when we are spiritually bankrupt, the moment of release is near. Coming to an utter end of our own righteousness, we will see the gates of His righteousness open for us. It is then that we are in Christ and He is in us, just as He says in John 17:26: "I have made you known to them, and will continue to make you known in order that the love you have for me may be in them and that I myself may be in them".

My struggle against sin in my life and my battle in faith to attain love resulted in a series of Bible talks on the theme of *How to Overcome.* Based on real-life experience, they spoke to people facing similar issues. At the suggestion of a pastor, the lectures were taken down in shorthand, typed and duplicated. Hundreds of copies were distributed, initially without my knowledge, and I was filled with thanksgiving to the Lord for opening doors for His Word. Little did I realize that this was the birthing of my writing ministry, which was to be one of my main tasks.

Letters dating back to that period showed my deep yearning to overcome in my personal life, especially in areas where victory seemed impossible. Dismay over my previous lukewarmness in the battle against sin now spurred me on.

In March 1942, while I was in Karlsruhe for a meeting, I wrote in a letter:

Watchwords when tempted to give up a seemingly hopeless struggle against sin

Tell yourself when you think it's all no good:

1. *It's my own fault that I've got into such bondage, held fast by the chains of sin. How long has it been since I truly regretted my sinning and repented? If I had seriously battled in faith, I would have seen victory. I neglected the battle, and now I am deeper than ever in bondage to sin. So I have to wait, in all humility, till God frees me. But no matter how long I have to wait, I will battle on till victory comes. I will not give up until I'm free.*

2. *God is training me in faith. He is teaching me to believe, just like the sisters of Lazarus at his death. He delays sending help so that I will learn to have faith before seeing any results. If I believe, I will see the glory of God. That is how the story of Lazarus ended and that is how my struggle will end.*

3. *God delays coming to the rescue and lets me feel my chains and human frailty so as to make me humble. When release comes, then He will get the credit, and I will give Him all the glory. So I want to learn humility even when I'm tempted to give up. I won't lose hope or rebel against God when my chains won't give way. Like the Syrophoenician woman I will keep on begging, refusing to take no for an answer when Jesus doesn't seem to help. The struggle is worth it if it makes me patient and humble. The longer the battle, the greater the victory, the more lasting the fruit. Maybe I will look back one day and see that these very troubles, however unwelcome, helped me to mature spiritually, making me more like Jesus. He is fitting me for heaven, preparing me to attain the first resurrection, which is for the overcomers and the humble of spirit.*

4. *I will give God thanks for revealing my sins. And, when tempted to despair, I will praise Him for the victory that will be mine. Jesus will be glorified, for when He sets us free, we are free indeed. So I will praise Him for trials and temptations. He*

is using them to purify me and free me from a range of sins now coming to light. He is teaching me how to overcome and gain the victor's crown. As His Word says, without holiness no one will see the Lord and those who overcome will inherit everything [Hebrews 12:14; Revelation 21:7].

After the war, when it became possible to publish Christian literature again, we had these talks printed – so great was the demand. How wonderful are the ways of God! There in my own little world, where God had placed me, I fought out my battles, claiming the power of Jesus' blood in faith. Amid suffering and painful discipline I persevered. And God used this testimony to help others to overcome in their trials and temptations, as we heard again and again. But even greater was the significance of such leadings in view of the future sisterhood and its calling. For love of Jesus we are called as Sisters of Mary to walk in the way of the Lamb. Rather than insisting on our rights, we are to walk in humility and to love as He did with a patient, forbearing love.

In another area I sensed the hand of God upon me in those years, redirecting the course of my everyday life. He was establishing His ownership over my life as never before, with every hour dedicated to Him and every penny placed at His disposal. In my heart I could hear Jesus pleading, *Spend more time in prayer and reading the Word. Give Me more room in your life, more of your gifts and possessions, however paltry they may seem.* Along with this challenge, the Lord also granted me a strong love for Him. Real love never does things by halves. For real love, it's all or nothing. Love is undivided in its devotion and loyalty. But there will inevitably be clashes when we work this out in everyday life, with other interests clamouring for our time, money and attention. Something will have to give way.

As I put this into practice, Erika initially found it hard to understand. Basically she was in agreement with me, but faced with the practical realities she raised rational objections. She asked whether this was self-effort and would stand in the way of grace.

By nature Erika had never been inclined to follow someone else's lead unless personally convinced. So it wasn't always plain sailing. There were issues to be resolved.

Once again, our shared ministry was called into question, although we still carried it deep in our hearts, believing it to be God-given. In the present state of affairs we could not serve the Lord together and build up and lead a joint ministry. Yet in my heart I knew I had to follow my conscience and obey this call of Jesus, even if it meant separation and the heartache of sacrificing our vision. Painfully we thrashed the matter out, as is evident from our correspondence in 1942 and 1943 while I was travelling. I wrote, for instance, in reply to Erika's objections:

Bad Oeynhausen, December 13, 1942

You write in such a dejected manner because you can't go along with my perspective. I'm not saying we shouldn't do anything that isn't directly concerned with the ministry. The point is: What drives me? If I'm inwardly driven to pray, read God's Word and visit people out of a desire to win souls for His kingdom, there will be little time left for personal interests. If a pastor's wife, for instance, takes the time to read all the latest Christian novels, it is a sign that something in her spiritual life is out of kilter. If she truly longed for souls to be saved, she would be busy virtually day and night in serving the church. If in our hearts we seek first the kingdom of God and accept everything else in so far as God chooses to give it, that's not being legalistic. It's being passionate about Jesus and saving souls.

Johann Christoph Blumhardt was so passionate about saving souls that he used to fast in obedience to what Jesus had shown him. That was not legalism. Otherwise, all Christian discipleship would be legalism. In true discipleship we surrender all – in obedience to Jesus. Think of Jesus' words, "Those of you who do not give up everything you have cannot be my disciples" [Luke 14:33]. *Nor is abstaining legalistic when I do it out of love for the souls of alcoholics. Let's pray that we'll be motivated by love for Jesus and for human souls, then everything else will take care of itself, and we will know what to do and what not to do.*

Two days later, on December 15, 1942, I wrote:

You feel that my wish to place every area of our lives completely under the dominion of Jesus is over the top. Actually, it's biblical. What you see as legalistic isn't legalism at all. It's about loving Jesus. Then it's only natural to surrender all and let Him have the say in my life. That's why I long to serve Him with all that I am and have, putting everything at His disposal.

Something else: can't you see that I had good reason to be sad at the results of our tithing? Giving so little for His kingdom is for me a sign that something must be wrong with our love for Jesus and His kingdom. Where is the passion to give Him everything? It's like being suddenly reminded it's a long time since we did something nice for a person we used to love very much and shower with gifts. We can only conclude we don't love them so much any more.

What you call legalism is to me an opportunity to show Jesus my love and devotion. After all, this can only be expressed in practical ways. How can we say, "I want to belong completely to Jesus" – "I want to be detached from the world" – "I surrender all", and then dismiss it as legalism the moment things get practical? All of a sudden we don't feel under any obligation.

Where is our commitment when Jesus shows us something He's asking us to give up? How do you define total commitment to Jesus? Commitment doesn't happen in a vacuum. Commitment means placing every area of our lives (money, time, etc.) at His disposal and under His dominion, so that we serve Him alone. Total surrender – this is what love is all about. All that I am and have is His. I hold back nothing for myself.

You believe certain things are indispensable. You say we need to take time to develop our cultural interests. Actually, the points you list are a sign of being under law. Love doesn't think like that. If we love Jesus wholeheartedly, first seeking Him and His kingdom, we can trust Him to let us have our share of cultural life. All that can be safely left to Him. Otherwise, we are not on the right track. We are so afraid of being legalistic that we fall short of total devotion to Jesus. This is one of the subtle wiles of the devil, who is determined to keep us from a life of joy and fruitfulness. So let us pray for a spirit of repentance in this matter, and God will hear our prayer. For me, there is no turning back. I must be true to God and His call on my life. Anything less would be disobedience. If you find you can't go along with this, it almost looks as if our ways must part. Actually, I can't see what's holding you back, as it is all about our souls' eternal well-being ...

Let's talk everything over in the light of Scripture. His Word will convict us as we pray and do what He says, losing our lives in practical ways. Surely it would be a bit cheap to expect revival and a move of the Spirit without responding where He is already moving in our lives. We have to begin somewhere and show our willingness to die to self.

As so often in my life, I was acting on an inner conviction when I wrote these lines. And the Spirit of God, whose purpose was to prepare us both for a shared ministry, gradually made us one in this matter too. What made it so remarkable was the fact that our unity did not come naturally to us – it was the work of the Holy Spirit. God's call to total dedication, so significant for me at the time, was to shape both the Sisterhood of Mary and my own life in particular.

Perhaps even more importantly, my travelling ministry brought us together with people who would be of great significance for the founding of the Sisterhood of Mary. Since 1939 it had been our daily prayer that God would bring people into our lives to lead us on spiritually. In addition, those seven years of travelling introduced me to a wide range of churches and fellowships. No doubt this was all part of God's plan for the sisterhood's future call to live for unity within the Body of Christ. He opened many doors, and soon I was not only speaking to the missionary society's circle of friends but responding to requests for Bible courses for other groups throughout the country. The missionary society generously gave me the freedom to plan my itinerary so as to include these other invitations.

God evidently wanted me to encounter the diversity among believers as I came into contact with many different types of Christian fellowships and learnt to love and respect each for the way it was. I was to learn to see Jesus in every Christian tradition where people loved the Lord and believed in Him. Jesus also wanted to show me something of His pain over His divided Body, though at the time I was little prepared for this.

One of my speaking engagements took me to Beerfelden, a small town in the Odenwald, where the pastor's wife introduced me to her best prayer warriors from the next village, the pillars of the church. There in a home Bible study group I encountered the gifts of the Spirit, as described in 1 Corinthians 12 and 14, which were being used in a biblically sound manner. I was also blessed by the uncompromising discipleship of a woman leading a fellowship in Kassel. She was a great intercessor and gifted counsellor.

Most significantly, I came to know Paul Riedinger, who lived in the southern town of Ansbach and was a district superintendent of the Methodist church. He was to become the spiritual father of the Sisterhood of Mary. This is how we met.

In the winter of 1942–1943 I was in Hof, holding a seminar on the theme of *Heaven and Hell.* Among those present was a pastor with whom I had a brief but significant conversation before he left for his train. Eternity was a topic close to both our hearts.

Soon afterwards came an invitation to join a small group meeting at a pastor's house in Egloffstein. Mainly clergy with roots in the Oxford Group, they did not shrink from humbly confessing specific sins before the whole group. But they did not stop there: conviction of sin gave rise to worship. We were deeply moved when Paul Riedinger, whom we met there for the first time, knelt down in spontaneous worship of God the Father, the Son and the Holy Spirit. Here were people who lived a life of true adoration. The Spirit's presence was almost tangible. He had given this group of believers new songs of worship, which we all sang together in great joy. Here we were challenged to a priestly way of life – following Jesus, the Lamb of God. This was the same path God had been leading us on: not to be indignant because of someone else's difficult personality, but to bear them with love, mindful of our own sins, and win them over in a spirit of repentance.

I was then requested to hold Bible courses in various church groups in the region, and so we became even more closely linked with these brothers and sisters in the Lord.

July 1944 stands out especially in our memory. Those were unforgettable days. In our hunger for deep spiritual fellowship we set out at six each morning, walking from the pastor's house in Affalterthal to the pastor's house in Egloffstein. Constant bomb attacks made it a hazardous journey, and due to the political pressure we took care not to meet in a room with a window facing the street. On the evening of July 20, 1944, we were shaken by the radio announcement of the failed assassination attempt on Hitler. Not only in intercessory prayer but also in worship, the desperate situation of our nation was always with us – as was the plight of the Jews and their prophetic significance in God's plans.

In the politically sinister climate God held His hand over my travelling ministry. Informers frequently infiltrated the meetings, and my Bible courses covered the election of the Jews and their leading role among the nations in the millennium. Twice I was reported to the Gestapo and interrogated for hours because of my challenge to follow Jesus, since in their opinion there was only "one true Führer". Oddly enough, I was not called to account for my talks on the God-given destiny of the Jews. And I was allowed to go.

The Bible courses I held during my travels I naturally repeated for the Girls' Bible Classes in Darmstadt. Even though I did not lead the classes myself, I cared for the girls deeply and welcomed the opportunity to introduce them to the lessons He had been teaching me. And so they heard the call to discipleship for love of Jesus. They were challenged to follow the way of the Lamb rather than insist on their rights. They learnt the way to victory, hating and forsaking sin. They heard the message of Jesus' second coming and of Israel's destiny. I always looked forward to these sessions upon my return, as they allowed me to participate more fully in the Bible Class ministry. Each girl was dear to me and I knew where she stood spiritually, almost as if they had been entrusted to me personally. Indeed, many of these girls would be later under my care as spiritual daughters in the Sisterhood of Mary.

During my travelling lectureship the work of the Girls' Bible Classes steadily grew. In addition to the groups for teenage girls, there were groups for children – including one for boys – as well as groups for housewives, college students and professional women. Through these Bible studies some 150 people heard the Word of God weekly. God graciously held His hand over this work during the Nazi era. Erika Madauss was already on the black list for daring to teach the Old Testament as well as the New, and for encouraging the girls to profess their faith openly. Inevitably this resulted in tension within the groups and some even left. Most of the girls, however, abstained from positions in the League of German Girls, the girls' wing of the Hitler Youth, as they were unwilling to give up their membership of the Girls' Bible Classes.

During those travelling years I was privileged to taste some of the fruits of the long paths of discipline. God still seemed to be saying *no* to my actual ministry in Darmstadt, but my hankering after a satisfying pastoral ministry with a regular and established group had come to rest. Now I could accept my travelling lectureship, for which I had no natural inclination, as coming from God. And, resting in His will, I could do it with joy. In His amazing love He set me free from the desire for human love and children of my own. To His glory I can say that I found all I needed in Jesus. About that time I wrote in my Bible as a testimony:

> God is the greatest, the dearest and noblest,
> Faithful and worthy, unchanging and true,
> Best of all treasures, the joy of my heart.
>
> PAUL GERHARDT

Love for Jesus was now the compelling incentive. I wanted to walk where He walked – in poverty, humble service, sheer faith – to His glory. God heard the cries of my heart during those dark times at Bible college in 1929, when I begged Him to lead me, at all costs, into a love relationship with Him. In this love I discovered that the whole world is mine, for it belongs to Him.

How different this was from my years in Hamburg. Now love for Jesus taught me to hold the goods and gifts of this world lightly, as merely on loan (1 Corinthians 7:29-31). With that, all false scruples were swept aside. I no longer had to worry about forgoing this or that. Love for Jesus now moved me to spend as much time as possible with Him on Sundays, for instance. I would immerse myself in the Word, communing with Him in prayer or singing of Him.

At the same time I had the freedom to enjoy God's gifts in nature, art and culture whenever He granted me them in His fatherly love. Jesus had made one of my favourite Bible verses come true: "If the Son sets you free, you will be free indeed" (John 8:36). Free from sinful bondage – and free for Him, day by day growing happier, more natural and childlike. Now I had the answer to what had troubled me ever since I had struggled with conflicting views as a twenty-one-year-old. Freedom or legalism? Total dedication or a broad approach? Naturalness or one-sidedness? The key is love for Jesus. With love binding us to His heart, we learn to use the things of this world in the right way, because we are one with Him.

GOD COMES WHEN ALL IS DARK

AIR RAID ON DARMSTADT
REVIVAL IN THE GIRLS' BIBLE CLASSES
FOUNDING OF THE SISTERHOOD OF MARY
1944–1947

The night of September 11–12, 1944, was God's hour of judgment for Darmstadt. Fire rained down from the sky. In eighteen minutes the city was almost entirely destroyed by an air raid. It became a sea of flames, leaving a mass of rubble. Only the houses in the outlying districts remained standing. The next morning thousands lay buried beneath an expanse of ruins; and the survivors, mostly bombed out, were evacuated to the surrounding countryside within a sixty-mile radius.

At the time I was in Wiesbaden, where I was holding a Bible seminar. Although greatly alarmed by the events of that night, I was unable to return immediately as I felt obliged to complete my assignment in Wiesbaden. Erika endured the night alone in Darmstadt. The next morning, as she searched the devastated city for the members of her Bible classes, the horrors of death stared her in the face everywhere. Charred corpses littered the streets, and the city was eerily empty, as if the inhabitants had been swept away from the face of the earth. Although most of the girls had miraculously escaped death, they had fled from their burning homes and left the city with their parents. Only a handful of girls stayed behind. The ministry of the Bible classes seemed to lie in ruins.

But to our amazement, five days after the air raid – on the first Sunday afternoon following that terrifying night – a whole troop of girls made their way to us. Most of them had cycled long distances from the Odenwald and the Bergstrasse, braving the increasing attacks from low-flying aircraft. New faces appeared daily at our door, as the girls came one after the other to see if we were alive. In their troubles they longed to pray with Erika. Never in past years would they have made such sacrifices to attend Bible studies and prayer meetings. Never before would they have given up a precious free Sunday for this purpose. The night of terror had become the hour of birth. Out of death came life. The seed of God's Word, sown over many years, now germinated, and our Bible classes took on a completely new character. Now we were like one big family, bound together in warm fellowship in Jesus.

By God's grace, Steinberg House at 26 Hölderlin Way was still standing, though heavily damaged, while some of the neighbouring houses were completely flattened. Rail services were widely disrupted as more and more cities were destroyed, and my travelling ministry came to a standstill and I was mostly at home. This was significant, for it meant I was there when revival broke out.

For years we had prayed for revival: at last it had come. For many of the girls, the night of judgment became the night of grace. These were good Christian girls, but in the face of death and eternity, with the fearful prospect of God's judgment, their self-righteousness crumbled and they wept in genuine repentance. Many of them came to confess their sins for the first time. That night had brought renewal. With the experience of forgiveness came the joy of salvation. During our Bible studies we would burst out in song again and again, "O bliss of the purified, bliss of the free! I plunge in the crimson tide opened for me." Overflowing joy gripped these young people, although outwardly they had little reason to be happy.

Town after town went up in flames under renewed air raids, with the death toll rising into thousands and everyone living in constant peril. The sheer human misery had assumed untold proportions. Most of the girls had lost their homes along with everything that had made life pleasant and comfortable for them. Some were also separated from their parents.

One name now lit up their bleak existence and put a song on their lips. It was the name of Jesus. He was their well-spring of joy. But didn't they already know Him? They did indeed – very well. Under the Nazi regime some had put their careers on the line and declined coveted positions and honours – all for His name's sake. But so far His name hadn't made their hearts sing for joy. Why not? Because they did not see themselves as sinners in need of grace. Now they wept in repentance over their sins and started putting things right in their lives. If there is joy in heaven when a sinner repents, then surely there should be a foretaste here on earth? In previous years Erika and I had often looked with sadness on the large, flourishing groups, which others felt were under God's blessing. In our hearts we thought, "You have a reputation of being alive, but you are dead" (Revelation 3:1).

Now they were infused with new life. There was a spirit of repentance, joy, prayer and mutual love. Repentance was triggered by conviction of personal sin but also a growing, painful awareness of our failure as Christians towards our nation in its hour of trial. When judgment was catching up with our nation, we were not gripped by God's holiness and on our knees praying and pleading for the thousands entering eternity night after night. Seldom, if ever, were we at hand to show what help we could when the Jews, the "apple of his eye" (Zechariah 2:8), were stripped of their rights, persecuted and deported.

Yet outwardly we had seemed so devout. Morning by morning we read God's Word; each week we attended Bible study and prayer meetings as the war rolled on. Now the scales fell from our eyes. How could we have been so blind! Struck by the gravity of our sin, we longed to make up by interceding and standing in the breach for our people (Ezekiel 22:30).

One Sunday in February 1945 we were gathered together for the Bible class at Steinberg House. The badly damaged roof had not yet been repaired. So this time we met in the Blue Room, where the rain did not come through as quickly as in the rooms upstairs. I spoke to the girls about our priestly calling of prayer and worship, and our failure to recognize this calling, let alone fulfil it. Pagan Nineveh repented in sackcloth and ashes at the mere threat of God's judgment (Jonah 3). Yet we, who were Christians, had not repented when judgment came upon us as a nation. All those years we had remained unmoved, sure of our own rightness, although judgment begins with the household of God (1 Peter 4:17).

Suddenly, in the middle of the Bible study, the grace of repentance fell upon the gathering like rain from heaven. Girls who had never prayed in front of others now spontaneously prayed aloud. Genuine tears of repentance flowed for all our sins and failures. In the previous months the girls had repented as individuals, mainly for personal sin, but as the awakening spread throughout the youth, the focus widened. Together we now grieved before the Lord, repenting of our apathy, spiritual death and the failure to take our priestly calling seriously in view of our national guilt and the plight of our people. Repentance revitalized our prayer life. Intercessory prayer and worship of Father, Son and Spirit reached a new level.

Erika and I were privileged to see our young people blessed with the same experience that had been ours in the previous years. Where there is conviction of sin and repentance, new life bursts forth. We were overjoyed! Our prayers all those years for a revival in the Bible classes had been wonderfully answered.

Our one prayer was that God would keep the grace of repentance alive in us and our youth groups. And He heard that prayer, right up to the founding of the sisterhood and beyond, to this very day. Lovingly He has continued to discipline us.

Painful but healing, such experiences ensured that the flame of love did not burn low or die out. Knowing ourselves better than we did then, we have grown to love Him even more. This is what has kept us walking in daily repentance and singing of His saving grace. Everyday life with all its challenges has shown us up – much more than we realized back then – as sinful through and through. Unloving attitudes, self-will, status-seeking, disobedience and self-indulgence are deeply rooted in the human heart. Our times of fellowship in the light are a special gift from the Lord. As sisters in Him, we encourage each other to see more clearly where sin has gained a hold. This helps us to take responsibility for specific wrong attitudes and actions, confessing them to God and apologizing to others wherever necessary.

In March 1945 we took some of the girls to a long-planned retreat in Falken-Gesäss in the Odenwald. It was a gift of God, who in His loving-kindness prepared us a table in the presence of our enemies (Psalm 23:5). With intensified attacks from low-flying aircraft it was risky to be seen in the streets. Any day Darmstadt could fall: the American troops were already approaching. Those politically implicated were fleeing the cities in large numbers. Tension ran high. The frightening events were all-absorbing. People could think of nothing else.

Although personally affected and in danger of our lives, we were as contented as children, quietly and happily resting in the Father's heart. We were overwhelmed by the amazing love of Jesus and the blessings He had granted us in our youth group during the past months.

Despite the hazards, Erika and I went through with the planned trip. Fifteen of the girls took part in those quiet days of preparation, focussing on our priestly ministry of prayer. There in Falken-Gesäss, in the home of friends, we were safe from prying eyes in those times of political oppression.

I had already gone ahead to hold a Bible seminar in nearby Beerfelden. So right up to the last moment Erika had to face the decision alone, whether or not to undertake the journey. It is unlikely she would have risked taking the girls if the Lord hadn't assured her in prayer that He would send His angels to protect them and that she would return them safely to their parents before the Americans marched into Darmstadt. She was particularly concerned about the last point: there was a real danger the demarcation line would run between Darmstadt and the Odenwald, preventing her from reuniting the girls with their families.

Rationally speaking, the trip did not make sense. We were simply acting on a strong conviction from God, as so often in our lives at key moments. Indeed, something significant for the future Sisterhood of Mary would happen during that time away: a sequel to the memorable hour of revival in the Blue Room in Steinberg House. This is why God led this small group of girls aside under such unthinkable circumstances. Between Erbach and Hetzbach their train was shelled and angelic protection became a reality. Screaming and wailing passengers rushed out of the train while the enemy aircraft, still circling above, shot down those who tried to escape. But in that moment of horror and death the girls had a deep sense of security and not one of them was harmed. Erika's inner assurance was wonderfully confirmed.

Higher up, in Beerfelden, I could hear the fierce shooting and knew their train was being targeted. For over an hour I headed in that direction, crawling more than walking, for the low-flying aircraft were still circling over the area. What a relief to find everyone safe and sound! After an extremely hazardous walk we finally found ourselves sitting in the small house in Falken-Gesäss, where we were warmly received. Our hearts were filled with thanksgiving to God.

Day and night planes roared over our heads. Yet in the face of such danger God was continuing to lay the hidden foundation for our future sisterhood. We spoke about our priestly ministry in the light of 1 Peter 2:9 – "you are a chosen people, a royal priesthood" – and considered the example of the Old Testament priesthood and the cleansing essential before service in the sanctuary. During those days as we prepared ourselves afresh for the ministry of prayer and worship, we needed first to undergo a cleansing of the heart, so that our prayers would not be superficial and ineffectual. This was the deep longing of the girls.

As we met again in the afternoon, the Spirit of God led us quite naturally – one after the other – to kneel down and confess our sins, in so far as this did not belong in private confession. It was a special hour when the Spirit of Truth moved among us and revealed what lay hidden. Seeds were being sown for the future. This was our first experience of fellowship in the light, which we would later practise in our sisterhood.

Greater than the danger from the aircraft circling above us, greater than some of the girls' fears and apprehensions, was the reality of God. Through His Word and presence He blessed us with the grace of repentance and a spirit of love and worship. The joy that the Lord had kindled in the hearts of our young people during the previous months was fanned into flame. This was the blessedness of pardoned sinners tasting the first love for Jesus. As the Bridegroom of our souls, Jesus was there among us, asking us to love Him with the single-hearted devotion of a bride. At the time we had no way of knowing that there was to be a Sisterhood of Mary, and that we would wear a ring as a symbol of bridal love.

Before leaving for my ministry in Beerfelden, I had received a letter from a pastor friend of ours, hand-delivered by a soldier as the postal service was disrupted. Inside was a Lenten meditation. I read it, profoundly moved. With the image of the Man of Sorrows etched on my heart, I longed for our girls to see in spirit Jesus treading His lonely path of the cross, utterly forsaken. It was as if our heavenly Bridegroom was appealing to us: *Who will walk where I walked – in lowliness, poverty, obedience, even facing scorn?* In that moment many silently gave Jesus their *yes* for love of Him, echoing the words of Ruth, "Where You go, I will go". Some were to renew their pledge later, on the day they entered the sisterhood. They chose this way of life in their desire to tread closely in His steps as true followers.

On our last day in Falken-Gesäss I held a Bible study for the girls on the City of God. The Holy Spirit worked in us an overwhelming sense of joy as we looked forward to the day when we will enter the heavenly Jerusalem and see Jesus face to face. This glimpse of the heavenly glory awakened in us the one great longing: that Jesus would prepare us for the ultimate goal of heaven and the Marriage Supper of the Lamb. No price was to be too high.

When we finally left for home, not even the horrors of war could diminish that taste of heaven's glory. Arriving at the railway station in Hetzbach, we learnt that the trains had stopped running four days earlier. We had taken the last train from Darmstadt! We had no other option but to continue our journey on foot.

After the experiences of the past few days, we felt borne along and when, after seven hours of walking, we did grow weary, a truck picked us up. Disbanded troops and refugees streamed towards us and when we enquired about Darmstadt, they shouted back, "You won't get into Darmstadt. It's already occupied by the Americans."

Undaunted, we sang hymns for the rest of our journey through the night, greeting soldiers and refugees with the love of God. Arriving at two in the morning, we found Darmstadt still free of American troops, and we were able to return the girls safely to their parents, just as the Lord had assured Erika before the trip. That very afternoon the Americans marched in. A German general had delayed their advance by one day; otherwise we would not have been able to return home.

The Nazi regime was over. All restrictions imposed on Christian organizations were lifted. The Girls' Bible Classes, soon to develop into the Sisterhood of Mary, could flourish freely; and the revival could grow unhindered.

The first thing that Erika and I did was to rebuild a wall in the upstairs apartment of Steinberg House that had fallen in during the bombing. For years this apartment had waited in vain for Bible students. Now the large room suddenly came alive with young people. Instead of a handful of Bible students, now forty to fifty high school and college girls would gather for a full day each week. They arrived early in the morning and left in the evening when the curfew introduced by the occupying forces was briefly lifted.

Singing, thanksgiving and worship filled the air in response to Jesus' loving forgiveness with every new sin brought into the light. It was a miracle of God's grace. After the long, dark years of agonizing in faith without seeing any fulfilment, Erika and I were now witnessing our God-given life-work taking shape. The apartment had become a home for our youth. Even in those days we had a form of community life, later to become more defined and comprehensive in the Sisterhood of Mary.

Since schools and universities were still closed that year, there was nothing to prevent our meetings taking place on a weekday. Once a week we spent the whole day together. Many of the young people had to cycle long distances to reach Darmstadt – as much as thirty miles – and some stayed for meals and spent the night with us. Food was scarce, and we shared with each other what little we had. Yet if the lunch break lasted more than ten minutes, the girls were almost indignant. In their keenness for biblical teaching on priestly service, they couldn't bear to miss a single minute. Prayer, worship and praise filled the day.

We were overjoyed to see our young people blessed with the spirit of worship. For this we had prayed ever since meeting Pastor Riedinger and the Egloffstein group. Since summer 1944, the last summer before the war ended, we had considered asking one of their number to come and introduce the Girls' Bible Classes to worship. The ravages of war prevented that ever coming to pass. But God's hand was in this. First He intended to lay the proper foundation with repentance – a lesson He would often repeat in our sisterhood. Judgment on our city taught us to walk in daily repentance, the source of first love for Jesus, from which worship naturally flows.

The Lord blessed us abundantly, so that we were "not lacking in any spiritual gift", as Paul expresses it (1 Corinthians 1:7 RSV). Along with the gift of worship, we received the other gifts of the Spirit mentioned in 1 Corinthians 12 and 14, such as healing, prophecy and speaking in tongues. We were thankful for these gifts, because they were for the benefit of all (1 Corinthians 12:7). They never played a predominant role in our spirituality, though. The source of our spiritual life is love for Jesus, flowing from repentance – a discovery resulting from our long struggles.

Our links with revival groups operating in the gifts of the Spirit were part of the Lord's plan. From the outset He taught us to take a biblically sound approach to the charismatic gifts. Amid the joy and, initially, a slight over-emphasis on the part of our youth, we stressed the importance of the proper use of the gifts as defined in the Bible. Right from the beginning of this new move of the Spirit He laid a solid foundation – not the baptism of the Spirit (a term we didn't use) but love for Jesus, born of repentance and leading to uncompromising discipleship.

Next to the proclamation of the Word, prayer took centre stage in our meetings now. The hours flew by as we interceded for individuals and our nation as a whole, spurred on by love for Jesus. What a difference from the prayer meetings for the nation we used to hold in the Girls' Bible Classes! Intercession was no longer a burdensome duty. Gripped by the burning issues of the day, we now wrestled in prayer for the persecuted Jews and all those affected by the ravages of war and the political collapse: the refugees; the displaced and exiled; the starving; the prisoners-of-war; the women abused by occupying forces, paying so dearly for the crimes of our nation. And lastly for the guilt-laden Nazi war criminals in Nuremberg, soon to meet their Maker.

The backlash was swift. A massive counter-attack was launched by the evil one in his fury at this prayer-led invasion of his territory. He stirred up opposition designed to crush this new life, using human agents to spread false rumours. Indeed, "Herod and Pilate became friends" (Luke 23:12). God in His wisdom was answering the prayer I had written in my journal as a twenty-year-old:

Lord Jesus Christ, if only I could demonstrate my overflowing gratitude to You! Oh, let me suffer, let me be held in contempt, if it seems good to You; if it serves to purify me and enable me to honour You all the more ... I don't know whether I can bear it yet, but I long to suffer for Your sake. May Your love be so deeply rooted in my heart that it stands the test of suffering. If I only have You, surely I can bear everything gladly.

May 1, 1925

Recent developments had caused an uproar among many of the girls' families. Parents with other hopes for their daughters were dismayed at the direction their lives had taken: the girls had become far too "religious". Accusations were heaped on us from all sides, whether verbally or in writing: stern warnings, indignant outbursts and even threats. Once respected in Christian circles, now we were suspect, our reputations ruined. People distanced themselves from us. We were labelled everything from fanatics to sectarians, Catholics to Pentecostals, or extremists forever talking about repentance.

Waves of contempt and even hatred rolled over us, finally coming from all over Germany, including Bible-believing churches and fellowships where I had held meetings during my travelling lectureship. Even before the postal service was restored, news of our revival spread like wildfire, with the enemy fanning the flames. Much to my sorrow, even my old Bible college withdrew from me. For a while the sisters were forbidden to correspond with me.

Now the price had to be paid for all the revival blessings of new life and love for Jesus our young people had received. Erika was abruptly dismissed from her position as youth leader of the Girls' Bible Classes, which were affiliated with St. Paul's Church. She had a distressing talk with the senior pastor, who made demands she could not fulfil in good conscience. I'll never forget the night she came back home grieving over the breach with St. Paul's. For years she had enjoyed a good working relationship with the pastor, and I for my part too. That night as we talked and prayed about all the criticism directed at us, the Lord gave us the following verse: "For you have upheld my right and my cause, sitting enthroned as the righteous judge" (Psalm 9:4).

Only months later I found myself in a similar situation. The missionary society asked me to avoid certain topics in my talks. Like Erika, I was unable to comply: I had to follow my conscience. So I resigned. God's hand was evidently in this too, for now I was where He wanted me. I was to become fully involved in shaping the fledgling sisterhood. Though currently without any income, we were not unduly concerned. We had faced uncertainty in the past and God had always sent help in time.

Nor were the girls spared their share of troubles. Many faced opposition at home, as the Lord tested their commitment right from the start. Yet hadn't we pledged ourselves to follow Jesus? Wasn't He the Man of Sorrows, who endured the shame of the cross? Personal humiliations were nothing new, but we had never encountered disgrace and persecution for His sake. This mark of discipleship had been missing in our lives, and we had always felt a sense of unease about it. Now our one desire was to go wherever the Lord led.

"Rejoice in so far as you share Christ's sufferings." (1 Peter 4:13 RSV) This verse, which the Lord had given me a number of times in prayer, came true especially during my last speaking tour for the missionary society. Before the revival I had enjoyed considerable respect and recognition: invitations poured in from churches and fellowships, and meetings were well attended. Now my travelling ministry bore the stamp of disapproval.

Rumours about the revival preceded me wherever I went. The general consensus was that I had fallen into error and was promoting false teaching. Meetings were suddenly cancelled – and the reasons given were humiliating. On July 4, 1946, I wrote to Erika:

> *Here in M. I had to go through a refining fire. The word the Lord gave me for this time came true: "Rejoice in so far as you share Christ's sufferings, that you may also rejoice and be glad when his glory is revealed"* (1 Peter 4:13 RSV). *In all the pain I was comforted at the thought of my Lord. So I can only give thanks. The team of intercessors, ranging from students to the staff at the Inland Mission, were up in arms against me, warning everyone about my teaching. They didn't come to the prayer times and mostly not to the meetings either. When they did come, the antagonism was so intense that I could barely speak. You could*

have cut the air with a knife. Dwindling numbers at the meetings – I've never known that happen before. I feel like an outcast.

One loyal supporter stood up for me and my message, but at a cost to herself. She really struggled. After all, the others are believers and they reject my message. So I had a difficult time with her too. For instance, she didn't think my words about judgment and repentance were theologically sound. The Bible college in X has a lot to answer for. Just two years ago people were so keen to hear my talks, saying how helpful they found them. They valued copies of the transcripts and passed them on to others. And now they are so antagonistic.

My travelling days are virtually over. My reputation is ruined. Local pastors have spread the word that I belong to the Pentecostal movement or some sort of high church.

What the Lord impressed upon my heart has come true: You will stand alone and forsaken, outside the camp, despised and held in contempt by all, unwelcome wherever you go, and with no ministry to fulfil. – But for me, to be one with Jesus in His anguish and the shame of the cross is my deepest joy.

The fewer people at the meetings, the more joyfully I delivered the message. I looked to Jesus alone and simply proclaimed His glory. In private talks afterwards I noticed that some had been challenged and made commitments to the Lord.

Tomorrow morning two or three women students from the Bible college want to come and tell me what their reservations are. I need a lot of love and humility ... The main thing is not to grow weary in the face of so much opposition, first at home and now everywhere else – and this is only the beginning. Yet didn't we choose the thorns of Jesus?

In view of mounting antagonism in Darmstadt it seemed doubtful whether our home could still serve as a meeting place for the young people. Very wonderfully, God came to our aid in that moment of acute need. He sent us supportive friends who encouraged us and spoke up for us – above all, Pastor Riedinger.

Loving, caring and understanding, he backed us wholeheartedly as we followed the Lord's leading. Although we had known him since 1943 when we met in Egloffstein, this was his first visit. The timing was significant.

A remarkable sequence of events led up to this visit. In August 1945, Erika and I were on our way to Nuremberg in a coal truck, as there was still no long-distance public transport. I had kept in touch with a pastor we knew from Hof and Egloffstein, and we wanted to visit him. We hoped to talk over various matters that were on our hearts in connection with the revival, and get his advice. Before we reached our destination, we were stopped and ordered down from the truck by American soldiers. Along with several other people we were taken into custody at Erlangen Prison, as they claimed our papers were not in order.

With the benefit of hindsight, we realized that God must have placed these "angels with fiery swords" in our path. On this journey He intended us to meet the man who would become our spiritual father – Pastor Paul Riedinger, a district superintendent of the Methodist Church. The following day we were released from prison and ordered to take a direct route back to Darmstadt. At that point God gave us the idea of visiting Pastor Riedinger in Ansbach, which was pretty much on our way. The plan worked and we stayed with the family for a week. Strong bonds of fellowship were forged. We were able to talk over the various issues and questions in our hearts about the way the Lord was leading us, and we left feeling richly blessed.

It was early November 1945 when Pastor Riedinger came to visit us in Darmstadt. He had an instant rapport with our young people; it was as if they had always belonged together. Keen and spiritually hungry, they opened their hearts wide to him, receptive to what he had to share from the wealth of his spiritual teaching and knowledge. He talked about the calling to priestly service, bridal love for Jesus, love for Christians of all traditions, and about heaven. No one could speak as he did about the City of God and the priestly ministry of worship in God's sanctuary with its sacred laws. From then on he was a regular visitor and we were soon calling him our Father Riedinger. His visits were happy and special occasions for us. As he spoke, the presence of God seemed to descend upon the room.

On his first visit he mentioned in passing during a Bible study that Christianity has a long tradition of believers living in community. It was like hearing something we had always known. All those months we had been aware of a deep desire for a shared life of poverty and prayer, loving Jesus with the love of a bride. An inner constraint had so far kept the girls from applying to deaconess houses or Bible colleges, though some of them, knowing they were called to the Lord's service, had sent for brochures. Once again we were aware of an inner conviction guiding us. Without knowing it, the girls were waiting for the Sisterhood of Mary, which God had already planned for them in His heart.

The first time Father Riedinger, Erika and I shared with each other our thoughts and plans about beginning such a communal life, the Lord spoke to us through a Bible verse: "All this also comes from the LORD Almighty, whose plan is wonderful, whose wisdom is magnificent" (Isaiah 28:29). We spent much time in prayer, seeking the Lord's will in detail, and as we did so, the inner structure and mission He desired was revealed.

The Girls' Bible Classes were to give rise to the Sisterhood of Mary, which was already in embryo before my travelling lectureship. It naturally followed that this new work of God would be based on the same spiritual principles He had been teaching Erika and me during the long years prior to the founding.

My vision for the emerging sisterhood became clearer. It was to be a community grounded in daily repentance and walking in the light; a fellowship rooted in bridal love for Jesus. God was calling us to a life of faith and dependence upon Him for provision; a life of prayer, worship and sacrificial love.

This was the path the Lord had shown me for my own life. It was the path He had taught me to follow during the long years of struggle and hardship. During the winter of 1946–1947 we earnestly sought the Lord concerning the right structure for the sisterhood's spiritual life and mission. We knew we had to be faithful to the principles He had shown us.

But now the practical issues had to be dealt with, paving the way for the founding of the sisterhood. Insurmountable obstacles faced us. In those days a license was required to found a sisterhood, and when I went to the local government offices in Wiesbaden in late January 1947 I received a flat refusal. That evening Erika and I sat together at home, our hopes dashed. It was a repeat of the disappointments of the last eleven years, by now an all-too-familiar experience. Again we had to lay our "Isaac" on the altar: the God-given promise of a ministry in Darmstadt. Night fell on our souls. As we prayed that evening we received the verse, "Fight the good fight of faith" (1 Timothy 6:12 KJV). That revitalized us, spurring us on to continue battling in faith, even when there was nothing more to hope for.

Next morning God suddenly put a thought into my mind. *Go to the American information centre in Darmstadt. Find out if there is another way of obtaining a licence.* Humanly speaking, there was no point, since I had already been turned down by the one agency authorized to issue licences. But trusting in the God who works miracles, I went to the American information centre.

The woman I spoke with referred me to the Municipal Youth Council of Darmstadt, and that very day I was granted an interview with the official in charge. It turned out that he knew my father and was grateful for the help his son had received while studying under him. His heart was moved to help us and he made an unexpected recommendation: to have the sisterhood licensed as a youth club. I learnt that the relevant committee met only four times a year but was due to assemble the following week! I could scarcely believe this wonderful guidance and hurried home to share the good news with Erika. Without delay we handed in the necessary documents.

And so it happened that on February 4, 1947, one of the Bible class members called on us, joyfully waving a newspaper. What did it say? The Municipal Youth Council, the body responsible for issuing or denying permits to start an organization, had met last Friday in the town hall. Licenses were granted to the following: the Solar Corona Youth Group, the Schlaraffia Tarimundus Club, ... the Arheilgen Social and Paddle Club, ... the ecumenical organization "The Sisterhood of Mary"...

God often chooses strange ways to accomplish His purposes. Years later we discovered by chance that this permit was not valid, but by then the sisterhood was well established and thriving, so the authorities had no other option but to license it retrospectively. In view of the insurmountable difficulties standing in the way of our founding, the Lord had given me the Bible verse, "The mountains melt like wax before the LORD, before the Lord of all the earth" (Psalm 97:5). True to His word, He caused this huge mountain to melt, along with other obstacles. Parents who had tried to prevent their daughters from entering this new sisterhood, which seemed to offer no security, now gave their permission.

The next major problem was the obligatory residence permit for each member. In post-war Germany the housing shortage was acute and strict regulations were in place for relocation. There was no chance the Housing Authorities would issue permits for special cases like ours. Seven prospective sisters wanted to join, but where were they to sleep? Erika had already given up her study-bedroom, turning it into a multi-purpose room – dining room, living room and classroom in one. I had moved into a small storeroom so that three sisters could use my room.

But where were the other four to sleep? The girls were due to arrive within a week, and we prayed and trusted God to intervene. Then a neighbour came round to ask if the student who lodged with my parents could move into her house for the next term. He wanted to study with her lodger in preparation for the exams. Since he would not be paying rent, my parents were free to use the room as they pleased during this period. Our hearts rejoiced over God's unexpected provision, enabling us to start our community life.

On March 30, 1947, the founding ceremony was held, and Pastor Riedinger joined us for the occasion as our spiritual father. God had shown him the name for our sisterhood. We were to be called the Sisterhood of Mary after the mother of Jesus. She was His first disciple, and from her life we see what it means to tread pathways of faith in loving surrender to the will of God.

The oneness in the Lord demonstrated at the founding ceremony was significant. The address was given by the pastor of our parish, whose predecessor had dismissed Erika. The youth pastor of Darmstadt, the Methodist minister of Darmstadt and the Catholic priest from a neighbouring parish each gave a word of greeting. My parents, who had welcomed the newly founded sisterhood into their home, were also present at the ceremony – full of joy.

And where did it take place? In the very rooms that had stood empty for years, waiting for the students of the Steinberg Bible Courses. For so long, the vacant beds had stared us in the face, underscoring the futility of all our ways. Now the room was full, not only with the seven sisters dressed in white as candidates (it was a year later that we received our proper robes). We were joined by many other young girls from the revival, a number of whom also sensed a call to the sisterhood.

In 1935 we had imagined that the Steinberg Bible Courses were the purpose of God's leadings. But that was too small for God. He had something far greater in mind! He wanted to form a company of people who would surrender their whole lives to Him and follow paths of faith – just as He had taught us – so that His name would be glorified. He wanted to give us spiritual daughters who would share His path of sacrificial love, His way of the cross, which bore the stamp of poverty, disgrace, lowliness and obedience – all for love of Jesus. On the founding day we could only worship God for what He had done.

Now, after twelve years, believing was rewarded by seeing. The long, dark pathways had led to a wonderful goal: we were privileged to found and lead the Sisterhood of Mary as a work of God for His glory. We couldn't help feeling awed and humbled and could only say, "The LORD has done this, and it is marvellous in our eyes" (Psalm 118:23). We are not worthy of all His faithfulness and mercy.

PART 2:
WONDERFUL IN COUNSEL

IN JESUS' FOOTSTEPS: INNER CONFLICT AND THE SHAME OF THE CROSS, WEAKNESS AND POVERTY 1947 – 1951

MOTHER OF THE SISTERHOOD – BUT WHO?

It was 1947, the first year of the Sisterhood of Mary. One evening as we were sitting together, sharing about our communal life, one of the young sisters suddenly asked, "Couldn't we call you 'Mother'? After all, you're our spiritual mother." Everyone agreed. Mother of the Sisterhood of Mary? For twelve years the Lord had led me through trials and disappointments in preparation for this task. Now as I embarked on the second half of my life, He was entrusting me with this commission – with its joys as well as responsibilities and burdens. Yet it seemed as though it was not to be.

In this very room we had sat together with a pastor just months ago, prior to the founding of the sisterhood. This brother in the Lord had been in close fellowship with us for several years. He had shared what he believed God was showing him about the new sisterhood. A mother was to be in charge, but that would be someone else. I would have a pastoral ministry which would include speaking engagements in various churches. In addition to the sisterhood, an ecumenical Bible college open to all Christians was to be established in my parents' home, Steinberg House – and I would be teaching there. The sisterhood was to be affiliated with another Christian organization.

The announcement came as a stab to my heart, for it would have serious and painful consequences for me. I was not to be mother, not to have an active role in leading and shaping the sisterhood. Yet hadn't the sisterhood grown out of the 1944/45 revival in the Girls' Bible Classes Erika and I had led? Hadn't the Lord clearly shown me the direction it was to take? Months earlier I had already put my case to this pastor and his friends. After much heart-searching, I felt sure of God's leading. Contrary to what they believed the Lord was saying, I had become increasingly convinced that His plan for us was not an ecumenical Bible college, nor an affiliation with another organization. He wanted to create a new offshoot on the tree of the Church, with its own God-given commission: the Sisterhood of Mary.

Although the details were still hazy, an outline was taking shape. At the heart would be a shared life, walking in the light and in daily repentance. My vision was a life lived in love for Jesus, leading us to forgive and love one another, and to share His path of poverty and lowliness as disciples of the cross. From this would flow the anointing and authority for each new ministry the Lord would entrust to us. Such is the power of living out the call to love. In embryo, this vision already contained the calling of our future "Land of Canaan" to reflect something of the kingdom of heaven, God's rule of love. I sensed that the Sisterhood of Mary was a creative thought of God, originating in His heart, rather than a response to human need or force of circumstances.

Our friends, however, did not understand the burden of my heart. This too was part of God's plan. The foundations of our sisterhood were to be laid deep with trials and temptations. God wanted the full measure of my trust and the surrender of my will. As long as I was firmly convinced that a commission was from God, nothing could shake me. In each new venture of faith the real suffering lay not in the insurmountable difficulties but in the inner conflict, which now broke over me in full force.

Letter upon letter arrived from friends telling us what God had shown them about our emerging ministry. The advice came thick and fast: *the sisters were not to be trained within the safe confines of their own motherhouse ... they were to be sent out to existing sisterhoods … they were to die to self, devoting themselves to social welfare work … our sisterhood was not to be something new and different …* All this clashed fundamentally with the vision God had given me.

The letters went back and forth. There were talks in private and in groups. I was caught in a thicket that grew denser by the day. For Jesus' sake I was sincerely willing to die to my own opinions and everything that mattered to me. On the other hand, I had to be true to what God had called me to. As a disciple of Jesus I was committed to following the way of the Lamb and not fighting for my rights. But did this mean abandoning the directives I was sure God had given me? Wouldn't that destroy the new life that was finally budding after many long years of waiting and believing? Was I supposed to cling to my convictions or let go? Was I supposed to resist the guidance of others or submit?

It nearly broke my heart to think of the sisterhood developing so differently from what God had clearly shown. If I was to take on a travelling ministry and the sisterhood was to be led along other lines, surely it would lose its God-given mandate. Was this to be the outcome of the twelve dark years of waiting for the fulfilment of His promises? Hadn't He given me the vision for a new ministry at Steinberg House? Hadn't He called me to be the spiritual mother?

In my heart a battle raged. Shouldn't I insist that this was *our* ministry, which God had entrusted to Erika Madauss and me back in 1935? It had all grown out of our Bible classes. And God had given me the vision in the first place. In fact, revival had not come through the preaching of these brothers in the Lord, as we had expected. Instead, it came through the bombing of our city shortly before the planned mission. New life broke out in our youth groups at the very time when communication with the brothers was interrupted, and during that first year we had tended this young shoot all on our own.

Certainly I could have expressed myself in this way, but I felt the Lord restraining me. I knew I could only fulfil the role of mother with the confirmation of these brothers who were spiritually close to us. Only if they agreed that God had appointed me to this position would I have the freedom to take it up. I battled through to a place of faith: if God had given me the inspiration for the sisterhood, He would contend for me. All that He had given me, I now laid back in His hands, letting go completely.

> I follow now close in His footsteps
> The path that He trod here below.
> I only desire what He gives me,
> And only His way I will go.
>
> O NONE CAN BE LOVED AS IS JESUS, no. 32

At the time all this came at great cost. With hindsight I see that the flames of revival are not enough to sustain a work of far-reaching significance in God's kingdom. He lays the foundations according to the type of building He has planned. He digs deep with inner turmoil and pain as we learn to die to self. The greater the trials and sacrifices, the more solid the foundations. Each painful act of surrender God requires in a founder's life will have bearing on later generations and the future development of the ministry. This is why founding periods are often so very painful. God presented us with many hardships to be laid, brick by brick, into the foundations.

More bitter than all the disappointments of the twelve years of waiting was the realization that God wanted me to go along with the brothers' plan and be consecrated for the office they had assigned me. The sisterhood had risen like a bright star on the horizon: surely now the time had come for God to fulfil His promise. This hope now lay dashed and broken. But by the grace of God my heart, softened after the twelve years of waiting, now yielded more readily to the will of God without breaking under the strain or rebelling against His leadings.

In 1947, at the founding of the Sisterhood of Mary, the Lord did entrust me with the leadership, but only temporarily. The person who was to become mother was not yet free to assume her post. Together with Erika Madauss, who was consecrated as "novice mistress", I was to lead the sisters during that first year as Dr. Klara Schlink.

For six or eight months I remained in this uncertainty. As the leader, I was the spiritual mother of the first sisters who came to live with us at Steinberg House – and yet I wasn't. Day by day I handed back the leadership to God, surrendering unreservedly to His will and sacrificing the desires of my heart. Little did I realize that the Lord was deliberately leading me this way. He was teaching me to let go of what I held dear, to make room in my heart for Him. He wanted to become the love of my life as never before. The love of God is a mystery. He takes away something we have looked forward to all our lives in order to give us something infinitely greater and more satisfying: Himself. Only His love can make us truly happy, as I was later to discover.

Finally God intervened. What these brothers in the Lord had planned, failed to materialize, and there was no more talk of the other leader they had envisaged for the role. God gave back my sacrifice. He Himself confirmed my calling, in that these same brothers gradually came to regard me as mother of the Sisterhood of Mary. The sisters had no idea what had transpired, and after the first year under my leadership they naturally looked upon me as their spiritual mother. And so it happened that a year later, in March 1948, Erika and I had our investiture along with the first seven sisters. Father Riedinger, who conducted the ceremony, blessed me with the name Mother Basilea, and Erika with the name Mother Martyria.

With childlike joy I accepted this name as a gift of God, rejoicing in the assurance, "I'm a child of the King, with Jesus my Saviour I'm a child of the King," as the chorus goes. My name pointed to the Lord's promise that we are redeemed by His blood to be kings and priests (Revelation 1:5-6; 1 Peter 2:9). The names we receive as sisters are of spiritual significance: something to aspire to in faith. A biblical calling was sacred to me, and the calling to the royal priesthood was especially close to my heart. I was always conscious that we can only live up to this by following the example of Jesus who in self-giving love humbled Himself, relinquishing all that was His by rights and making Himself nothing. At that time I could never imagine how much grief, shame and hostility this name would bring me. I would be accused of wanting to make myself a queen in my pride, and of trying to steal God's glory.

In 1947, that same year when God kept asking me for the total surrender of my will – my "Yes, Father", come what may – I spent a week at a Christian retreat centre. While I was there, Jesus drew very close, overwhelming me with His love. For the first time I understood how people in acute suffering could say that the love of Jesus completely absorbed and refreshed them. The psalmist writes: "You give them drink from your river of delights" (Psalm 36:8). And so it was for me. In the midst of my distressing situation I could hardly take in the bliss of His love. In freely giving up our life and what makes life worth living for us – as I had done by giving up my heart's desire and my rights – we will find Jesus, the very source of life. We will taste the inexpressible joy of His love.

Jesus was calling me to a closer walk with Himself. He wanted me to catch a deeper glimpse of His heart. We are meant to grow in the knowledge of God, so that our love for Him will increase and abound. Coming to know Jesus as our Saviour and the Bridegroom of our soul is like entering a glorious new land. At every step we encounter more beauty, more treasures waiting to be discovered. Words can never describe what Jesus is like. In Him is the fullness of the Godhead. All the beauty of heaven and earth is to be found in Him. He is King of kings, awesome in power and majesty. He is both Ruler of the universe and Lamb of God, bearing the sins of the world. Over the years God would open His heart to me more and more, as my relationship deepened with the Father and with the Son. Discovering the heart of God became a source of profound joy, an inexhaustible mine of treasures.

But where does God reveal His heart? Jesus shows us the way. Nowhere else is He to be found but on the path He trod. The

Lord reveals Himself to those who keep His commands (John 14:21). And what is His command? To walk where He walked – in poverty and anguish of soul, in self-surrender and humility – and to embrace the shame of the cross. This was where the Lord was calling me, and there I found Him as He truly is.

THE SHAME OF THE CROSS

In later years we often sang, "As we follow the way of the cross, You reveal Your heart to us." But the way of the cross is marked by suffering of all kinds. And shame for His sake increasingly marked the path I was to follow. It was a rough path that left my feet bruised and bleeding. Almost twenty years of Christian service lay behind me. From 1926 to 1945 I had been a city mission youth leader, Bible college teacher, national student leader, and travelling lecturer for a missionary society. I had held Bible courses in churches and fellowships throughout the country. I was respected – even looked up to – in Christian circles. This recognition was a part of my life and I took it for granted.

The hostility that flared up as revival broke out among our youth in 1944 and 1945 continued unabated after the founding of the sisterhood. I discovered what it means to be controversial, a target of criticism and defamation. Opposition was my constant companion, as the Lord stripped me of my good reputation so that I wouldn't stand in the way of His glory. He allowed me to suffer contempt so that I would learn to be independent of others. He wanted to be my first love. And He accepted my pledge to follow Him on the path of shame and disgrace for His name's sake.

Humiliation became an integral part of my life. In the attic apartment of Steinberg House I would often sit and read the incoming mail in my little room, previously a small storeroom. Some letters pierced my heart. One well-known evangelical leader was adamant that our ministry was demonic because we had the gifts of the Spirit. Sinking to my knees, I laid the letter before the Lord in prayer, tears flowing. Another time a prominent theologian vehemently accused me of disgracing the Protestant church. He was convinced we wanted to become Roman Catholic and would cause a schism in the church. Nothing could have been further from our intentions – our aim had always been reconciliation, the fellowship of love across denominational divides.

The rumours spread; friends distanced themselves from us and sided with our opponents. Speaking engagements were cancelled because people had been warned against us. Yet no one ever came to check the facts before passing on untrue reports. From a student at my former Bible college I learnt that I was a topic of discussion at a conference there. I was declared a stain on the reputation of the entire organization because we had received the charismatic gifts. Everyone was advised to dissociate themselves from me.

At a big evangelical conference the speaker warned against us, claiming that at Steinberg House people rolled around on the floor, screaming. My father, who happened to be present, asked him afterwards how he came up with such statements. It turned out that these incidents had occurred in a fellowship somewhere completely different, and had nothing to do with us. In private, the speaker took back his words – but not in public. So for the many participants this false rumour was the truth. Returning home, they spread it in their churches and fellowships, warning against us everywhere. Later, so we heard, believers were instructed to burn my books. Allegedly I was possessed by the devil, and everything I wrote was demonic. People were advised not to set foot on our grounds.

A former preacher had been circulating a forty-point list of accusations against us. In a talk initiated by a third party he subjected me to a veritable cross-examination. Though obviously embarrassed when I pointed out the fallacy of his claims, he continued to disseminate his publication. Then there was the clergy wives' conference in our state of Hesse. A member of our women's Bible class returned greatly upset: she had been cold-shouldered because of her association with us. Rumour had it that we had left the church. In fact, our young sisters helped out with church activities such as Sunday school classes and youth groups.

My little room became a place of tears. The word the Lord had given me when I moved in now came true: "I, even I, am he who comforts you" (Isaiah 51:12). What a kind and gracious assurance from the Lord at a time like this! On all sides we faced distrust, even outright opposition, not just because of the gifts of the Spirit, but because of misgivings concerning the practical outworking of the revival. Our young people were full of new spiritual life, and their enthusiasm was unsettling. Complaints and even intimidating letters came from parents resisting their daughters' desire to be all out for Jesus. The idea that they might forego marriage in order to follow Jesus' call into a new and financially insecure sisterhood filled parents with dismay. And other Christian organizations, disappointed not to find recruits among our young people, distanced themselves from us.

Why this rejection and even hostility? As far as the charismatic gifts were concerned, it was especially hard to understand. In our sisterhood the gifts never took centre stage, as perhaps elsewhere, and 1 Corinthians 14 was our guide. The revival in the Girls' Bible Classes, fundamental to the Sisterhood of Mary, had a different focus. The Holy Spirit's gift to us was a new intimacy with Jesus through an ever deeper experience of repentance, the source of spiritual life. The need for daily repentance, as stressed by Martin Luther, was the defining force in our youth work and later our sisterhood.

Another reason for the widespread rejection was our ecumenical outlook. We were ecumenical only in the sense that we sought fellowship with our brothers and sisters across denominational divides. For love of Jesus we wanted to honour His last request "that all of them may be one" (John 17:21). Some evangelical groups with an anti-Catholic attitude criticized us for what they considered a serious error. Yet it was never our intention to align with Catholicism. Love for Jesus was our motive for seeking fellowship. It was my growing conviction that the closer we are to the loving heart of God, the closer we are to each other. For us, the love of God was the only basis for true unity, and the cross of Jesus the only place where we could meet as brothers and sisters in Christ. But how to clear the misconceptions when, in spite of our requests to meet together, all doors for communication remained closed?

God evidently wanted me to take my share of injustice and humiliation, bearing it patiently as a follower of Jesus. People were merely His instruments. Yet it was all grace that God led me this way, for the servant is not above the master. The way of the cross became a reality for me. Sometimes I was reminded of an incident in my college years when I was asked to give a talk on 2 Timothy 3:12, "Everyone who wants to live a godly life in Christ Jesus will be persecuted." I was at a loss what to say. What did I know about persecution, disgrace and rejection? Did this verse even apply to me? Could I count myself among those who led a godly life in Christ Jesus? Now, however, the Lord let me taste this suffering almost to saturation point. What hurt most was when it came from those who had been closest to me.

It is humiliating to be shamed in public, but humiliation is the way to humility as we follow Jesus, the Lamb, who did not return insult for insult but showed love and forgiveness. I, too, was to learn long-suffering, forgiving love. I was to learn to bless my enemies. In order to draw me closer to His heart, He humbled me and gave me a greater love. God had a new commission in store for me, but before I could be entrusted with it, my sinful ego had to be dealt a death-blow. Ultimately, God was answering my life-long prayer:

May Your name shine forth gloriously. I want to live and spend myself for Your glory. Obliterate all that is of self, so that Your glory can shine forth mightily.

Embracing the shame of the cross brought me another gift. By losing the respect and recognition of others, I gained something far more precious in return. I came to know Him more intimately and share in the fellowship of His sufferings (Philippians 3:10). The testimony of various fathers in Christ became true for me: only if we suffer personally can we understand the Passion of Jesus.

In that year of 1948, as I walked the path of suffering, my eyes were opened to something of unimaginable value. For the first time I discovered the treasures that lie hidden in the sufferings of Jesus. I came to know and love the Man of Sorrows more deeply than ever. During that time I wrote in my journal:

O Jesus, meditating on Your Passion is sheer bliss: to do so is to behold the greatest miracle of God. Greater than His omnipotence that brought all worlds into being, greater than His wisdom spanning eternity, greater than His unsearchable understanding is the miracle of His saving love. God takes on human flesh. God suffers at the hands of sinners, the hands of those He made. In Jesus, God went to His death, allowing Himself to be gashed and wounded like a sacrificial victim.

Every thought and word of God, every work of His hand, is holy. But holiest of all is the Passion of Jesus. Here God reveals His nature completely, granting us a glimpse into His heart of perfect love. "O love of God, how great, how strong! Low in the grave You laid Your Son, whose presence rends the mountains." [Paul Gerhardt]

I continued:

You have given me a completely new love for You as the Man of Sorrows and Bridegroom of my soul. Your anguish for the world and for human souls has finally begun to touch my heart of stone. You have set my cold heart aflame with the desire to share in Your sufferings. January 10, 1948

And so amid the pain I knew the reality of Jesus' promise: "Blessed are you when people insult you ... because of me ... Great is your reward in heaven" (Matthew 5:11–12). And the reward begins this side of eternity. Jesus loves us too much to wait till we get to heaven. Here and now He blesses us abundantly as we walk the way of the cross, suffering for His name's sake. For everything we have given up, Jesus gives us a hundredfold in return, as I came to discover myself. For all the brothers and sisters I lost, I received a hundredfold in return – believers the world over, too many to be counted, with whom we are one in the Lord. The joy of the Lord and His love welled up in my heart. He gave me life in all its fullness, a growing knowledge of Himself and the fellowship of His suffering.

But His love didn't stop there. He sovereignly watched over us so that ultimately libel and slander couldn't destroy our organization. Strange things happened. Men who had met together with this intention were suddenly at variance with each other. Or they inexplicably changed their minds in the course of the meeting. As our Protector, Jesus was lovingly watching over His work, preventing unfavourable resolutions from being passed. Here too I discovered the truth of His words, "Whoever loses their life for my sake will find it" (Matthew 10:39). Life for me in this case meant enjoying a good reputation and not being constantly vilified.

Even in my youth I was quick to take issue if someone was unfairly treated. Perceiving untrue allegations, I would not rest till I got to the bottom of the matter, even at the cost of my own popularity. Later Mother Martyria would jokingly say, "You should have been a lawyer!" So for me injustice was especially hard to take. In a sense it meant "losing my life". Now I had countless opportunities to give up my rights and good reputation. The Lord had a reason for leading me into such situations. He was teaching me to follow His example. "When they hurled their insults at him, he did not retaliate; when he suffered, he made no threats. Instead, he entrusted himself to him who judges justly." (1 Peter 2:23)

For years I had searched for a more intimate relationship with Jesus, and for true life in all its fullness. And yet I had missed the way that would have led to it. Now I found the deep joy I had been looking for. I discovered it as I followed Jesus step by step on the path of the cross, which for me at that time was paved with humiliation and unjust accusations.

TREASURE IN THE CROSS OF ILLNESS

During the winter of 1947–1948, with serious food shortages widespread in post-war Germany, I developed a stomach disorder. Physically I was so weak I could hardly stand and would force myself to get through the day. This marked a new phase in following Jesus, with the path of discipleship growing rougher. I struggled when comments were made about how ill I looked – not only from members of the sisterhood family. Barely able to collect my thoughts, let alone hold teaching sessions for the sisters, I found it hard to fulfil my obligations. It was humiliating not being able to carry out my ministry as fully as I wished. Hardest of all, I could scarcely pray in this debilitating condition. The illness was persistent, and I was distressed that this new cross was getting me down.

Then the Lord reminded me of the treasure hidden in every cross. Praying "Yes, Father" is the key to unlocking this treasure trove. But to pray this from the heart we have to believe that God does have something precious in store for us. This is not about repeating "God is love" like an empty formula of faith. It's about firmly expecting that when God takes something away, for instance health or strength, He will give us something far greater and more satisfying in His fatherly goodness. That is love's way. It was all about reckoning with the blessing hidden in this small but painful cross. Love is always giving gifts and making others happy. And God is love!

Now I wanted to learn what it means to hold on in faith to His loving promise. In this difficult situation I began to put my faith into action by saying "Yes, Father" with complete trust in His creative power. The transformation was wonderful. Two great treasures were now mine.

First, God gave me a degree of independence from my physical condition. This would be of great significance in the future. I found that the Holy Spirit triumphed over the flesh, over tiredness and physical ailments. To my surprise I discovered that I could accomplish more in this condition than when in good health. God's power is made perfect in weakness. After I said "Yes, Father", trusting in His loving care, I was able to stay up late praying and, in spite of my weakness, still go about my work during the day. Weakness seemed to be part of God's loving plan for me, with sickness and frailty accompanying me more or less for the rest of my life. The greater part of my writings were produced in a state of weariness. Writing in obedience to God, often at night, I found it difficult to collect my thoughts and was doubtful of the results. Later I was amazed to see that the Spirit of God must have been at work as I wrote. My heart was filled with praise.

I saw this principle at work in my travels and speaking engagements, and also in meetings with our spiritual daughters and other day-to-day commitments. God heard my prayer that no one would notice my physical weakness. People even commented how bright and lively I looked. Often I sensed new strength flowing into me at the very last moment, even after I had begun to speak – though it didn't always happen. When people thanked me afterwards, I could only quietly praise God for working in their hearts even though I had felt nothing.

Ever since then I have been able to rise early for prayer, even if I had been up late. Time and again I have marvelled at what the Lord can do. Thanks to His heavenly power, He enables us to accomplish more in our weakness than when we are in good health and full of energy. Of course, I respect doctors as a gift of God and am especially grateful to our family doctor for all his assistance. Yet I have also experienced the Lord's healing touch when neither treatment nor medication could help. God intervened and the symptoms of illness vanished. Other ailments He chose not to remove but left as lifelong conditions in order to demonstrate His power in my weakness.

There was a second treasure I discovered in the cross of illness. Often waking at four in the morning, I would rise, driven by the desire to pray. In those quiet early morning hours I inwardly beheld the face of Jesus, so holy and awesome, and drank in His loveliness with an unquenchable thirst. Song after song flowed from my pen as I celebrated the beauty of the Lord. It was a recurrent theme in my songs and writings, prompting my spiritual daughters to ask if I had ever seen Jesus. In reply, I could only describe it as seeing with the heart rather than the eye.

The first morning it happened I found a note slipped under my door from a sister sharing an impression she had received in prayer. An angel was giving me a paintbrush to depict something of the beauty of Jesus' face, lovely beyond words. That same morning another sister wrote me a Bible verse in calligraphic lettering: "When I awake, I shall be satisfied with seeing your likeness" (Psalm 17:15). Neither sister knew what I had experienced early that morning.

Following Jesus the Cross-Bearer, I learnt not to trust in my own strength and abilities, and so a space was created for the strength and beauty of the Lord to shine forth. Through the cross of illness He humbled me and made me weak in order to reveal Himself in His love, glory and beauty. The sheer bliss of Jesus' nearness was almost more than I could bear. It was a foretaste of heaven. Such joy amid suffering! Didn't I have every reason to give Him thanks and praise for my cross?

A CHAPEL BUILT BY FAITH

Never will I forget May 4, 1949. I was praying in my room when I experienced one of those rare moments when heaven invades earth. *Build Me a chapel, where worship will rise up to Me,* the Lord was saying. The very thought set me ablaze with love: I would do everything possible to create a house of God, a place where hearts would overflow with love and adoration. There, anthems would rise to heaven, word and song inspired by the Holy Spirit, proclaiming before the visible and invisible world who our Lord and God is. He is the Lamb enthroned on high – the King of all glory, power and majesty – the Father, the Almighty, the most holy God. There, countless numbers would be drawn into His presence. Coming face to face with His holiness, they would offer heartfelt worship.

For all my joy, anxious thoughts arose. *How could I possibly build a chapel for the Lord? How would this plan materialize?* We lacked funds, and land to build on. Months later, as I prayed the matter through during some days of quiet, the Lord in His abundant goodness strengthened me. He encouraged me with scriptures that were like a personal greeting from Him. After much prayer, I drew the following Bible verses from a selection of a thousand references:

> Consider now, for the LORD has chosen you to build a house as the sanctuary. Be strong and do the work. 1 Chronicles 28:10

> Then let them make a sanctuary for me, and I will dwell among them. Exodus 25:8

I was in real need of such encouragement. Though Mother Martyria wholeheartedly supported me, I was soon to discover that many friends and even some of my spiritual daughters did not understand the commission. Build a chapel for God? Minister to the Lord through worship? Even those closest to us expected us to devote ourselves exclusively to nursing and charitable works. Building a chapel was a new idea to me as well, but what was so painful was the lack of understanding. Sadly, I was to encounter this again in various other commissions the Lord would entrust to me. Believers are all in favour of building hospitals and care homes, and of sending sisters to work there. Undeniably this is an important ministry, and later we would engage in it on a smaller scale at our property, which we call Canaan after the Promised Land. But we found there was less understanding when it came to the ministry of prayer and worship, or even proclamation of the Word and pastoral care, areas into which the Lord increasingly led us.

This meant that few friends supported our ministries with their donations. Inwardly I felt restrained from asking for gifts and contributions. Even so, everything came together, for when God gives a ministry He also provides. Admittedly He often tested our faith first. With no human resources to draw upon, we were thrown completely on Him, and help was often a long time in coming. Yet this too was part of God's plan. In the end it would be clear for all to see that it was His work, His doing alone. We were humbled in the process – and He received the credit.

Our building project, launched with a mere thirty German Marks, was a venture of faith. I felt especially challenged, as God had entrusted me with the main responsibility for the sisterhood. Naturally I was aware that every commission from God, every vision, needs to be confirmed by someone else. For me, this was Mother Martyria, who stood faithfully at my side. I never took a single step unless she was in agreement, so that we could forge ahead together. Yet the ultimate responsibility rested on my shoulders, as God had given me the inspiration and District Superintendent Paul Riedinger was no longer with us. Shortly before his passing earlier in that year of 1949, he was shown that no one would succeed him as our spiritual father.

In the next two years of building I was to discover just how hard it was to carry out this commission without male support. To build a chapel for the Lord and a motherhouse was a daunting enterprise. We had no funding, no expectation of help from other quarters, nor the freedom to make an appeal. Such a project seemed to go against all common sense.

Living by faith is a balancing act, like walking along a ridge with unforeseen dangers at every step. Later, even friends advised us to abandon the project. In their opinion, to continue would be tempting God.

In my turmoil I would often cry out to Him, *You are a Father to the fatherless and an advocate of widows, so I know You'll care for me.* And God stood up for us and His commission, showing me each step when the way became precarious. He encouraged me with many miracles and answers to prayer as we were working on the basic structure of the building in 1950.

Work on the interior began in the summer of 1951. Suddenly, the windows of heaven closed: answers to prayer were few and far between. At the time I was away from home, recovering from severe concussion following an accident. Confined to bed, I often prayed in the words of the psalms:

> All Your waves and breakers have swept over me. My tears have been my food day and night, and my soul cries out, "Where is my God?" (see Psalm 42)

Bills were piling up and I cried to the Lord to be gracious for His name's sake. I pleaded like the persistent widow in the parable (Luke 18:1–8). Still there was no answer. God was silent.

This sudden silence must have a reason. Up till then the Lord had wonderfully fulfilled His promises for our building project. Of one thing I was sure: if no help was forthcoming and our prayers remained unanswered, the fault did not lie with Him. Before He could bless us again with His good gifts, hindrances needed to be removed. In this situation I was aware of the love of God. In holy zeal He was purifying me and the Sisterhood of

Mary of all that was unworthy of Him, all that obscured His true image. That is why He had put me into the crucible of suffering and of financial pressure.

In the light of His presence the Holy Spirit convicted me of sins I had not taken seriously enough. The past four years since the founding of the sisterhood flashed before me like a film. Various sisters came to mind and I recalled incidents when I had been unloving. Deeply sorry, I felt a compelling urge to ask forgiveness of each one individually. And God continued to speak, showing me where my work was unfruitful because I hadn't done it in unity with Him but had yielded to sheer busyness.

Deeper and deeper the Lord led me into spiritual darkness and inner conflict. Our financial problems grew from week to week, with no help in sight.

Socially isolated due to concussion, I had nothing to divert my attention. So I was compelled to face the gravity of our situation – God's *no* to me and our sisterhood. I drank that cup to the bitter dregs. In the stillness the Lord judged me to the core of my being, so that I lay before Him with a contrite and broken heart. In my journal I wrote:

> *Another week with almost no money coming in. Costs for the building materials are mounting up – thousands are due. How are we to pay it all? It is darkest night in my soul. Day after day book parcels are sent out, but no money comes in, only bills, bills and more bills. And the Lord is silent.* May 5, 1951

This time God was probing deeper. Months passed by with no prospect of help. For Mother Martyria and me, the sole comfort was a Bible verse received twice in prayer: "No one who hopes in you will ever be put to shame" (Psalm 25:3). But the financial difficulties persisted and I could only respond by confessing that the fault lay solely with me. God's Word says, "Surely the arm of the Lord is not too short to save, nor his ear too dull to hear. But your iniquities have separated you from your God; your sins have hidden his face from you, so that he will not hear" (Isaiah 59:1–2).

If God was disciplining us by not answering our prayers, I knew He was holding me personally accountable as a shepherd of the flock. God spoke so clearly that I could not evade the truth. It was deeply painful to realize I was to blame for the plight of our sisterhood. In a letter to my daughters I apologized, asking forgiveness for the times I had been too hard on them, or spoken harshly, failing to serve them in true love and humility.

During those weeks I shed bitter tears. My one fear was that we could fall into debt, bringing dishonour to God's name. That I dreaded more than anything else. We had always proclaimed that God is alive and answers prayer today. What about all the people who had been encouraged by the miracles and answered prayers we had been experiencing? They would be disappointed, disillusioned, their trust in God shaken – and all because of me.

God's silence broke my heart of stone. Month by month the bills piled up, and with them the danger of debt. Yet amid tears I was overflowing with thanksgiving for the grace of His light: *You cast me down, Lord. And where? – into the depths, only to enfold me in Your loving arms.* The holiness of God broke into my life as seldom before. From my innermost being rose a cry that after all those months He would send me back to my spiritual daughters a different person – humble and contrite of heart.

God is love, and He never lets us be tested beyond our endurance. In those weeks of tears there was a blissful interlude as the triune God drew near. It was a foretaste of the blessings yet to come. Grief was swallowed up in joy as God made His dwelling in me (John 14:23) and I tasted the rapture of His love. This is why He first had to empty and cleanse the inner sanctuary of my heart.

At the peak of our financial crisis the hour of deliverance finally dawned. God turned His face towards us in favour. A friend of ours, a Christian wholesale dealer, showed us the way out of our predicament: instalment plans. The concept was new to us, but our friend explained this was standard practice in building projects. He was even willing to accompany a sister to the various firms, who immediately agreed to do business with us in this way. It was a huge relief to have the greatest burden lifted from our shoulders. By the grace of God we didn't miss a single payment.

Yet despite this turn of events, God still opposed us until, by the end of that summer, we lay humbled before Him and others. The dedication of the chapel had already been planned for the September, and friends invited. But although the interior was almost completed, the ceremony had to be postponed. In a newsletter, which Mother Martyria sent out on my behalf, I felt a compelling urge to take responsibility, explaining that this was God's judgment on us. We headed the newsletter with a Bible verse: "I thank you for humbling and helping me" (Psalm 118:21, according to Luther).

Soon afterwards, I moved into our newly built motherhouse, still feeling physically frail. In deep repentance I went to each of my daughters and asked for forgiveness. On September 23, 1951, the day the chapel should have been consecrated, a group of sisters gathered round my bed. How often we had spoken of the moment when the chapel bell would ring for the first time, summoning the guests to the dedication ceremony. What songs of praise would be raised to God for enabling us to build the chapel without incurring debts – all thanks to His power to work miracles.

Now the big moment had come. The chapel was built, the bell was ringing – but there were no guests that day, there was no consecration, for we still stood under God's judgment.

Never had the ringing of a church bell filled me with such sorrow. It sounded more like the tolling for a funeral. Silent were the voices that were to celebrate Him in song. Heart-rending sobbing broke out among us. It was because of our sins that God allowed all this to happen. In that hour, as God spoke to us through the ringing of the bell, a wave of repentance swept across the sisters as well.

Ultimately, this holy hour of God's judgment was an hour of grace. A fresh wind of life blew through our sisterhood under the forgiveness of Jesus. And just months later I was to see a sun of grace rise over my life too. It had been a summer of distress, and God's *no* to me had driven me to a deep repentance. Now He was about to do something new.

GOD BREAKS INTO MY LIFE: THE CALL TO SECLUSION, 1952

HIS EXCLUSIVE CLAIM

The sparrow has found a home, and the swallow a nest for herself." (Psalm 84:3) In September 1951 we all moved into the new motherhouse, where the sisters working on the building site had been living in makeshift quarters. The upper storey was not quite finished, and there was still some interior work to be done, but at last we were reunited as a family. From then onwards we focussed on our primary mandate as a community: prayer and proclamation. Never could I have envisioned the foundation God would lay for this far-reaching ministry. It was tied up with a specific call.

God was calling me, as mother of the sisterhood, out of our normal sphere of work and duties and away from active service. He was leading me in a different direction. I was to come apart with Him in quietness and solitude.

God's call and claim upon our love are so powerful that people in every generation have responded by treading paths they would never have chosen, had they followed their natural inclinations. So it was with me when God called me into seclusion – me, the outgoing, proactive and creative type. During my student days in Berlin I found it hard to stay alone in my room for more than an hour or two. I was in my element when I was with others. Nothing and no one could have induced me to lead a life of seclusion: only Jesus Himself.

The call to solitude, so foreign to my nature, was to be the foundation for our future commissions. I had often heard that all great things for the kingdom of God are conceived in the quietness of prayer. Examples from the Bible demonstrate that solitude is often the birthplace of new spiritual life and fruitful ministry for God.

In theory I knew that if God calls us apart for an extensive period, our ministry will have a special anointing, as we make ourselves available to Him, listening to Him and speaking with Him. Though from time to time I had withdrawn for hours of prayer, this had been on the periphery of my life. My common sense had too many arguments against a prolonged absence. *You're indispensable ... Think of your commitments ... It would be irresponsible towards the sisterhood ... etc., etc.*

The Lord Himself had to break into my life powerfully for this to happen. With loving overtures He had prepared the way in previous years. There were special moments when He drew close in infinite grace. Now He came in the full force of His love, which surpasses all understanding. I sensed Him beckoning me to come apart and be His alone. In early January 1952 I responded by committing myself to several weeks of solitude and prayer.

The pain of summer 1951 lingered on as my heart mourned for having grieved God and others. Then one evening while I was in prayer, the holiness of God descended upon me – this time not in judgment but in His overwhelming love, to make good His total claim on me. He came in the power of His holy fire and I felt as if I were being consumed with an unquenchable ardour and divine zeal. What could this experience be? The infilling of the Holy Spirit? No, my experience of the coming of the Holy Spirit and His gifts had been quite different. This time Jesus drew near as the Man of Sorrows. He had come, in keeping with Scripture, to baptize us with the Holy Spirit and with fire (Matthew 3:11). Something of the overwhelming power of His love and suffering broke into my life.

Out of this arose a burning desire to suffer and sacrifice for Jesus' sake. For years I had prayed for such love. I knew it was missing in my life. In that holy hour something stirred in my heart as He awakened this love in me. I was gripped with a passion to see souls saved.

A holy fire marked my life from that time onwards. To prepare me as a true bride of the Lamb, the Lord set my heart ablaze with love for Him. As His Word says, "Love is as strong as death, its ardour unyielding as the grave. It burns like blazing fire, like the very flame of the LORD. Many waters cannot quench love; rivers cannot sweep it away" (Song of Songs 8:6–7, alternative rendering). During my first years in seclusion this resulted in many hours of worship and prayerful pleading, even at night. And the flame of prayer in my heart burned on even when my work required intense concentration.

As the Bible demonstrates, direct encounters with God are a reality. Often linked to a new commissioning, such a dramatic intervention, such a touch of God, marks a radical turning point in our spiritual life. He Himself breaks through with power. Shortly afterwards I, too, was to receive a mandate from God which was to be of great significance for the ministry of the Sisterhood of Mary.

First of all it meant following the call to quietness and solitude. It was as if Jesus were entreating me: *Give yourself wholly to Me.* This request would impact my life profoundly. Until then, being active for the Lord had been my main focus. Service, rather than Jesus Himself, absorbed my attention. But now it was to be all about Jesus. The ministry *for* Him was no longer my primary concern, although it continued as the fruit of my times in seclusion. First and foremost I was to minister *unto* Him. That meant spending far more time with Jesus. Because of His inexpressible love for us, He longs for our love in return. Yet, as I came to realize, I had been neglecting His claim on our love. It was as if He gave me a glimpse into His heart, full of sorrow because He is loved so little.

Jesus showed me His pain that we are there for others but seldom for Him. I could almost hear Him lamenting, *Who is there for Me?* (Luke 10:41–42). So often people, things or our service for Him mean more to us than Himself. Yet where can we find a heart like His, so full of love for us? That is why He longs for our response of love. Later I wrote to my daughters:

> *Hear the plea of the Bridegroom of your soul: "I am waiting for you, will you come?" What does He expect of you? Very few are called to lead a life of seclusion, but there is one thing He is clearly asking of each one of you – that your love would be His alone ...*
>
> *The best, the most blessed gift in heaven and on earth – Jesus and His love – is for those who surrender all they hold dear. Such love doesn't become ours automatically, but only as we give Jesus our all ... So do not cling to human, soulish love. Do not nourish it. It will blight your bridal love, or prevent it from blossoming. Jesus will not accept a divided heart. Be willing to pay the price for the overwhelming joy of His love. It's worth everything.*

In the course of 1952 His loving overtures grew stronger still, as later expressed in the following lines that I wrote:

> Where is the soul for whom I can be all,
> The soul who seeks My heart, seeks Me alone?
> I ask you now, "Am I enough for you?
> Will you in truth leave everything for Me, for Me alone?"

Jesus' request stirred me to the depths of my heart. Overwhelmed by the revelations of His love in the following months, I could only give Him my *yes*.

> My dearest Jesus, how can I refuse?
> Lord, I am Yours, to go where You should choose.
> For You alone I'll leave all else behind ...

In my case, it meant adopting a new life-style in response to His love. In the winter I spent most weeks in seclusion, away from the sisters, while in the summer there were interruptions owing to journeys the Lord called me to undertake. My life had taken a new direction – I would spend most of the time in solitude, alone with Him.

With a bleeding heart I made the break in 1952. Letting go of the sisterhood was painful, especially so soon after the Lord had entrusted it to me. Since 1935 Mother Martyria and I had been waiting for this ministry to materialize as God's gift in fulfilment of His promise. Now for many months I would be separated from my beloved spiritual daughters, just when we had been looking forward to being reunited after my long absence.

For their part, too, the sisters had sacrifices to make. Later they said that during the two years of building they used to comfort themselves with the thought, *When at last the motherhouse and chapel are finished, then—!* Then they would catch up on everything they had missed. It would be a spiritual feast with celebrations – mealtime fellowship around a table rather than amid piles of old bricks and sand heaps on the building site. There would be evening get-togethers when we would go deeper into the Lord's purposes for our ministry as I shared more of His heart. Now they had to give up everything they had been looking forward to.

Because Jesus loves us, He seeks tokens of our love – and these are sacrifices. That's why He challenges us, *Anyone who sacrifices ... for My sake* (Matthew 19:29). Sacrifices inspired by love are proof of our devotion. Jesus values them highly, thanking His followers with the promise of a reward. They are to receive a hundred times as much here and now, and inherit eternal life. How few proofs of my love, how few sacrifices had I brought my Lord up to that point! What unbelievable grace that He should now ask me to forsake all I held dear, all that made life worthwhile – giving my very self for love of Him!

Then came October 21, 1952, the day I would make good my promise and part with Mother Martyria and my daughters. Some weeks earlier I had already sealed my dedication for this new way of life during a time of prayer in a Bavarian village. There I wrote a farewell letter to my daughters in order to prepare them. Now, on October 21, they came to me in small groups. Together we sang songs of love and surrender to Jesus, and I blessed them. Then the door closed. Tears flowed freely. The pain was very real. It had to be that way. A sacrifice for Jesus is worth only what it costs us.

With this act I had laid aside the hands-on leadership of the sisterhood, while still exercising the spiritual leadership through correspondence with Mother Martyria or discussions with her in special cases. Occasionally I would join the sisters for an evening meeting if the Lord gave me a message to share. For many weeks, however, solitude was my lot, and I was alone in my room with Jesus.

Loneliness has tormented people in every age. Just how hard it is I was now to discover for myself. I found myself in a dying process where the lights of joy were extinguished. Instead of happy mealtimes with my daughters where we shared our news and concerns for the Lord's service, I took my meals alone in my small room. In the evenings I could hear my daughters singing joyfully in our Hall of Zion, and my heart ached to be with them. Sometimes I could hear the hum of voices in the next room as Mother Martyria discussed work and practical matters. Of course I was consulted in writing when important decisions had to be made, but being naturally interested in everything that happened, I sometimes wished I had more details. Now I was like an outsider. The Lord had effectively cut me off from the day-to-day running of the sisterhood.

For weeks at a time I rarely saw anyone, and there were days when my room seemed like a prison cell. I was a captive of His love. We are all familiar with quiet times when we can't feel Jesus' presence and prayer does not flow naturally. A sense of desolation engulfs us. On such days we feel so trapped, empty and spiritually dry that we are tempted to break free. But that would be to forfeit the spiritual treasures Jesus has for us in times of loneliness. Only after a long stretch in the desert did Moses encounter God at Sinai.

One occasion during those first months in seclusion stands out in my memory. Mother Martyria had been in another town for a speaking engagement. My impulse on hearing her return to her room was to join her and learn how it had gone. One step through the door and I would have been with her. At that moment I literally experienced what it means for Jesus to have first claim on us. He was like the master of the house, holding the key to my room. Gradually I began to understand His pain that we are so rarely there for Him. When visitors arrive, it's only natural to lay everything else aside, even if we are in the middle of important work or a lively family discussion. We make ourselves available to our guests. But do we make ourselves available to Jesus when He wants to come? How often we turn Him away, feeling more drawn to work and people. Jesus is little more than a beggar, knocking at the door of our hearts, waiting to see who will receive Him.

Jesus with love still is seeking
For hearts aflame with love,
Their lives and longings yielding
To Him who reigns above.

Once more the Saviour is knocking
At every heart and door.
Oh, listen, hear Him pleading,
"Accept Me as your Lord."

As the implications of responding to His call dawned on me, the enemy attacked. *This is senseless – irresponsible. What about Mother Martyria?* Doubts nagged me, even though she actually made things easy for me, saying with exemplary selflessness, "When Jesus calls, you must follow. For His sake, I am glad. We can never love Him enough." Still, it was hard to think of her having to shoulder so much additional responsibility. Was it fair on her and our spiritual daughters? Wouldn't I be failing them if I couldn't serve them as I had so far? Were God's purposes for the sisterhood really to be fulfilled through my drawing apart? Wasn't this unusual lifestyle likely to give rise to misunderstanding? Wouldn't it cause more harm than good?

In my limited understanding I had perceived my role as mother of the sisterhood quite differently. Unforgettable was the day in

December 1949 when Father Riedinger asked Mother Martyria and me to visit him as he lay dying. A man of God, full of love and humility, he gave a prophetic blessing. God, he said, was now entrusting me with the responsibility he had borne as spiritual father of the sisterhood.

At the time I had naturally assumed that this would take the form of active ministry, which I would have welcomed despite the struggles and challenges. Now I found myself on a very different path, where I was required to give up all active ministry.

At times my four walls stared at me cheerlessly, so great was my inner turmoil. All too easily I started comparing myself with university peers. Like me, they were in the prime of life. Unlike me, they were where the action was. They held key positions. They were needed and listened to. Now when I was asked to give a talk, or when visitors came, Mother Martyria would have to excuse me or stand in for me. My rheumatism caused me constant pain. But worse still was the spiritual night as loneliness threatened to engulf me. If we follow the Lord's call in concrete ways, even when it goes against all common sense, the tempter will be at hand to divert us. He fears the consequences. Dying to self leads to fruitfulness. The result is an invasion of his territory.

Again and again I reminded myself of this truth. But I still went through moments of anxiety. What if the Lord called me to long weeks in seclusion not just for a few years but for the rest of my life? I was not cut out for this. Would I be able to survive a prolonged period in the wilderness, or would something in me break?

No, that could only happen if I was walking in self-chosen asceticism – not by following a call of Jesus for love of Him. Connected with the source of life, Jesus Himself, I would not suffer emotional damage. Such a path could only lead to more life-giving fullness in Jesus, more tokens of His love and grace.

Though Mother Martyria and the sisters missed my presence and help, they too were blessed in the sacrifices they made. As they would often say later, ever since I followed the call to seclusion Jesus was closer to them than ever. "Whoever forsakes will receive" applied equally to them. Their bridal calling was revitalized as the love and sufferings of Jesus became more real to them. They gained a new vision of God the Father in His holiness, power and goodness, as well as His grief for us, His children. The creative power of the Holy Spirit impacted them afresh. During the brief times I did spend with them, they received spiritual insights beyond anything that I had previously been able to convey. God had called our sisterhood into being for a specific purpose in these end times. And by calling me into seclusion, He was preparing us all for a far-reaching ministry.

At the time I saw no evidence of this. But in hours of inner conflict, when my path seemed senseless to me, a star of promise shone in the darkness: a prophetic word received by a friend of the sisterhood. "The more you withdraw from public life, the further the call will resound one day. The commission of the Sisterhood of Mary will be worldwide." Back then I found it hard to believe what the Lord was saying. All I could do was hold out in obedience day by day. The holy fire of prayer that God gave me would later find its own channels in the specific ministries He entrusted to us.

ALONE WITH JESUS

For all the turmoil, the isolation and the inner pain for Jesus' sake, there was another side to seclusion. Increasingly I became aware of the privilege of such a life – away from others, hour after hour in deepest communion with Him, fully surrendered to His will: being there for Him alone. John's Gospel shows us what it means to share in His innermost joys and griefs as we rest, like the beloved disciple, on the heart of Jesus. Could there be a greater blessing than drawing near to that great fount of love that never runs dry? His heart is so vulnerable, so easily grieved by our sins, and yet so merciful. From the wounds we inflict flow salvation, forgiveness and love. Who can fathom the heart of Jesus? His love is infinitely gentle and tender towards those who love Him. As God's Word assures us, "I love those who love me" (Proverbs 8:17).

The stillness of eternity would rest upon my room while I was in prayer. At times the holy presence of God and His love were almost tangible. And as He drew near, reaching down to the heart of a sinful human being, one felt the very breath of God. His peace was like a river. Now His tender love was like a veil enfolding me; now it was like a blazing fire, setting me aflame with love for Him.

How can the One who loves us so dearly stay away? Will He not draw near, visiting us with His love? This is His pledge: "We will come to them and make our home with them" (John 14:23). The King of Love longs to make His dwelling with those who love Him with the single-heartedness of a bride. He knocks at the door of their hearts. "Arise, my darling, my beautiful one, come with me." (Song of Songs 2:10) Yet why does Jesus choose to come when the shades of night have fallen and the beloved is walking in the darkness of a deep valley? Drawn by the love of the beloved, He comes to console, refresh and overwhelm with love. This is true even of an earthly bridegroom; but the Bridegroom of our souls is infinitely more caring. His is an undying love.

Yes, Jesus comes. He is the coming Lord – today, tomorrow and one day when He will come again in glory for His bride, who eagerly awaits her King and Bridegroom. He comes, filling us with the rapture of His love, far surpassing all human love, for no one can ever love us as He does. What love is so pure and gentle? What love so ardent as His, a blazing fire from the heart of God? What love so strong, charged with the infinite power of God? Who can describe the sheer force of such love, drawing near to make a fragile, sinful human soul all His own? What love is so expressive of warmth, compassion and mercy? Human love is limited in scope and capacity. But the love of Jesus, which is from above, knows no barriers. From His heart it flows, limitless and undying, a stream without beginning or end.

If His love can fill the human heart with rapture in this life, as described in the Song of Songs, how much more in the next world? Even here and now we taste heavenly peace when Jesus draws near to make us one with Him in the Father (John 17:23). All pain is soothed, all restlessness stilled, for Jesus is there. Time merges with eternity as we rest in His embrace, and from the core of our being a cry rises: *When, oh, when, will we be united for ever with the Lover of our soul?*

The times spent in quietness and prayer brought many blessings and new commissions. But of all the gifts of grace none could compare with the privilege of drawing close to the heart of Jesus and sharing His innermost concerns. In His heart is a wealth of love, but also the fullness of pain. What could be greater than loving Him and being loved by Him? Could anything be more wonderful than Jesus coming to us in keeping with His promise? Out of this oneness with Him flowed each new inspiration for our mission and our spiritual life as a sisterhood. Abiding in Him, as Jesus teaches in John 15, is the source of all activity and growth in the kingdom of God. It has eternal value because it unites us with God, who is life everlasting and the fount of all blessing.

THE MIRACLE AND MYSTERY OF CHRISTMAS

The long weeks of seclusion prior to Christmas 1952 were especially dark. Occasionally, though, a bright light pierced the night. All of a sudden the wonder of Christmas shone forth, the mystery of the Incarnation: *God became man!* The Child of Bethlehem became very real to me. Suddenly I was able to relate to Him more deeply than ever before. Night after night I would be awakened as the Spirit moved me, in spite of my tiredness, to write songs about the Child in the Manger. Why? – Because for most of us the mystery of Christmas was little more than a concept, a historical fact, a familiar tradition. It hadn't yet come alive for us here and now. I sensed that this Christmas God wanted to do something new among us that would impact our hearts and lives. The songs the Lord had given were part of His plan to inspire greater love for Jesus, the Child in the Manger, revitalizing our worship.

Despite this time of spiritual preparation for Christmas, anxiety rose in my heart. Would it be a repetition of the disappointing Christmas we had celebrated two years earlier? Back then in 1950, we had just started building the Motherhouse Chapel. My heart was on fire with love, consumed with the one desire: *All glory be to God! He is worthy of our worship!* The Holy Spirit had given me some new worship texts, and in glowing colours I tried to depict for the sisters what it would be like when the Child Jesus drew near to win our hearts. Overwhelming love and joy would be ours as we celebrated His coming.

But where was the flame of love in the sisters' hearts that Christmas? I could hardly believe it. The songs hadn't been practised, the singing was lifeless, an atmosphere of boredom prevailed. It was a deep grief for me. How could we build a chapel if our hearts were not ablaze with the love of Jesus, if the spirit of worship was missing? Hadn't the Lord shown me we would have a choir of sisters singing songs of worship in the power of the Holy Spirit? Heaven would come down, inspiring many others with the spirit of adoration. Yet Christmas 1950 showed no sign of this.

During the Christmas season the following year I even had to disband the sisterhood choir temporarily. The singing, so uninspired and lacking the Spirit's anointing, seemed more like an affront to God. For several months we were without a choir. During that time we pleaded that the Lord would remove all hindrances and infuse new life into our singing and worship. Would Christmas 1952 be any different?

With a sense of expectation I came out of seclusion to celebrate Christmas, my heart overflowing with love for the Child Jesus. Yet once again a crippling weariness and heaviness hung over Christmas Eve and Christmas Day. Still, the longing burned in my heart: *This time the Child Jesus must receive the worship that is His due! This time heaven must come down!* On the Second Day of Christmas the miracle happened. It was a creative act of the Holy Spirit. Suddenly our Hall of Zion was much more than a meeting room: it was transformed into the very threshold of heaven. Instead of the sisters quietly listening to a talk about the miracle of Christmas and then singing a few carols, they were caught up in the momentum of what God was doing. Like the shepherds making haste to adore the new-born King, small groups of sisters knelt around the manger scene to express their love in song. Late into the night we sang the traditional carols as well as new songs the Holy Spirit had given me during my weeks of prayer.

O Child of heavenly beauty,
Whom angels magnify,
You radiate the glory
That comes from God Most High!
O Child, O clearest image
Of God's most tender love,
Now sinners dare to praise You,
Whom angels laud above!

Since You to us descended
No more seems heaven far;
You bring it close to all men,
O radiant Morning Star!
With You love came from heaven,
Among us to abide;
O rapture for all sinners;
Their thirst is satisfied!

We made up verses on the spur of the moment to celebrate the newborn King for who He is and for what He brings: forgiveness of sin and salvation, love for one another – a foretaste of heaven. In a burst of joy we would leap to our feet and, joining hands, dance before the Lord, awed that God became a human being, a little child. Our worship was constantly fanned into new life.

The Child Jesus had come alive for us. What happened in Bethlehem was happening now among us. That year we celebrated Christmas, the festival of joyous song, as never before. Heaven's glow was all around. Since Christmas was far too short, we went on celebrating till Epiphany. Evening after evening we came together, often worshipping until far into the night.

Those two weeks that I spent with the sisters were truly a foretaste of heaven. Our happiness together more than compensated for the times apart. By coming to us as a child, Jesus had made us children again, who love freely and joyfully, oblivious to what others might think. He had begun to free us from our intellectual mindset and sophisticated ways. The seed of adoration was planted in our hearts as we reclaimed a child's sense of wonder at Christmas. True worship can only be offered from the place of childlike humility.

The Child of Bethlehem, love eternal in human form, had called us to live together in oneness of spirit and in reconciliation, the distinctive mark of Christian love. What God did at Christmas 1952 didn't stop there. Love sparks new life. A far-reaching ministry grew out of God's gift to us. The following Christmas we invited friends and neighbours to celebrate with us. In the Motherhouse Chapel the sisters performed a nativity play the Lord had given me during my months of prayer. For all its simplicity and our lack of experience, the play spoke to people. It was inspired by love for Jesus, who came to this earth as a newborn child. And it was written in the fervent prayer that love and wonder would be awakened in those who came, in turn prompting them to love and make their peace with others.

And so it happened. Toward the end of the nativity play sisters gathered at the front, standing or kneeling. Then one of the guests came forward to light a candle, and others followed. Song after song was raised until everyone was caught up in the atmosphere of worship. At that moment two families not on speaking terms were reconciled at the manger. What a victory for Jesus! As love eternal He came into this world so that love would triumph. And Jesus lives today, transforming people and enabling them to love. Where Jesus is loved and worshipped, miracles happen!

Rediscovering the mystery of Christmas had a ripple effect. Indeed, the Child of Bethlehem had begun His victory parade, just as I had been shown in prayer before Christmas 1952.

Later the ripples could even be felt in Bethlehem. When sisters began their ministry in Jerusalem, on the Mount of Olives, I shared with them my grief about the feuding between rival Christian denominations year after year in Bethlehem's nativity grotto. Sadly, tensions often reached fever pitch on Christmas Eve, the very night when love and reconciliation ought to triumph. I was also grieved for Jesus' sake that tourists were often rushed through the church marking His birthplace.

Making this a matter of prayer, the sisters were determined that each new Christmas would see an outpouring of thanks, praise and honour in the nativity grotto. They prayed that the flame of love would be rekindled in many hearts.

What was humanly impossible, then happened. Instead of stopping only for a quick look round and a photo, crowds of tourists found themselves drawn into worship as the sisters sang. The Child of Bethlehem had made His presence real to them. Soon the grotto was transformed, now truly a place of prayer. For hours on end people of all nations, young and old, whether churchgoers or not, reverently joined in the singing. Even the Muslim guard forgot his duty. After listening for two full hours, he whispered to our sisters, "Did you know that nothing like this has ever happened before? It isn't really permitted."

Year after year on Christmas Eve the same scene was repeated. Our sisters not only sang in the grotto but shared something of the joy of Christmas in the streets of Bethlehem, which were teeming with pilgrims, tourists, spiritually starved hippies – and also Jews drawn by the mystery of Christmas. Handing out

Christmas greetings, our sisters were struck by the responsiveness of the young, whose sad faces would momentarily light up.

Like rays of light filtering into dark nooks and crannies, the joyous message of Christmas – God became man, born among us as a baby – was spreading. There was singing and worship, not just in Bethlehem, but in more and more places here in Germany too. In our own city centre, outside a large department store, our sisters set up a Christmas manger and began to sing. Amid the bustle of Christmas shopping, children happily gathered round. Lost-looking teenagers stood by wistfully, and grown-ups sang along. At a Christmas market in Berlin our Canaan Friends set up a manger among the stalls. Busy shoppers, their attention diverted from the eye-catching displays, paused to join in the singing and worship.

The Child Jesus was winning hearts the world over – through a manger scene at the heart of Coventry, in the poorest districts of our town, in Greek Orthodox circles in Thessalonica, in convents in Italy and Jerusalem, at Christmas services in Arizona, and via the American forces radio network. Leaflets placed in shops and doctors' waiting rooms, Christmas letters and song recordings – all helped to spread the message of His love.

He makes the sad happy and evokes in adults a child's sense of wonder. One and all are drawn into His orbit. A bishop, a research scientist and professional entertainers learnt the secret of simple, heartfelt worship at the manger, as did guests staying at our retreat house Jesus' Joy.

And that was not the end of the blessing. Our simple nativity play of 1953 was the seed of our Herald Plays. Over the years thousands would be reached through these biblical dramas with the call to first love for Jesus, discipleship, and trust in the heavenly Father.

I wonder if any of my daughters could have imagined in 1952 when I was separated from them, alone in my room, that the fellowship of love with Jesus would have such far-reaching effects.

THE FELLOWSHIP OF HIS SUFFERINGS

What was it that made Paul willing to give up everything he had counted as gain? His life as a Pharisee, his privileges as a Hebrew, his reputation among his people? All this he came to regard as loss, even refuse. All he once held dear he would gladly exchange for the privilege of gaining Jesus, becoming one with Him, sharing in His sufferings and being conformed to His likeness in His death (Philippians 3:7–10). For Paul, there could be no higher gift than the fellowship of Jesus' sufferings. This was his supreme desire. How often had I read this Bible passage without really taking it in.

Nor was Paul an exception, judging by accounts of early Christian martyrs. This same impulse has fired people of every generation and denomination, such as John Hyde, the missionary to India. "The closer we draw to His heart, the more we shall share in His sorrows".

Similarly, Francis of Assisi (who like Paul was no theorist) prayed that he might feel in his body and soul something of the pain Jesus endured in His Passion. It was the longing of a lover asking to share the pain of the beloved. And God led him into the fellowship of His sufferings. His grief-laden life, striking in its resemblance to the Man of Sorrows, is said to have reached its climax in bearing the marks of Jesus.

As my love for Jesus grew, so did this longing in my heart – first a gentle yearning, then an ever deepening desire. Starting with 1952, when Jesus overwhelmed me with the power of His love, the fellowship of His sufferings became real to me. I sensed that suffering – especially the fellowship of His sufferings – yields an abundance of fruit. Paul, for instance, writes, "We always carry around in our body the death of Jesus, so that the life of Jesus may also be revealed in our body" (2 Corinthians 4:10). Paul knew what it was like to share in the sufferings of Jesus, being conformed to His likeness. He prized this privilege, as is evident from his letters, especially 2 Corinthians 11, listing the many trials and tribulations he faced.

Leading a person into the fellowship of His sufferings, Jesus may grant them a Gethsemane experience, sharing something of His ongoing pain for a lost world. What grief can compare with the pain of God? Previously unknown depths of suffering, unlike any human sorrow, then break into a person's life. Unnoticed by others, a follower of Jesus can suffer inner torment rarely encountered by the average Christian and totally unrelated to any other challenges they face.

When the powers of death draw near, the soul tastes something of Jesus' agony and God-forsakenness in Gethsemane. A terrifying loneliness may threaten to devour the soul as in a yawning abyss. Even someone who has enjoyed deep intimacy with Jesus may suddenly be so overwhelmed by this sense of death and desolation that they cannot take the slightest comfort in the things of God. It is as if they had never known Jesus. Death seems to hold their heart in a vice-like grip. Numbed and incapable of thinking or feeling, they are aware only of torment. Yet deep down inside they are at peace, cheerful amid trials and able to fulfil their day-to-day responsibilities unhindered.

As Jesus leads us into the fellowship of His sufferings, He may also allow us to share in the dishonour He endured. Peter reminds us that suffering should not take us by surprise (1 Peter 4:12). This applies to the whole range of suffering Jesus underwent. If we long to share in His path of sorrows, He will grant our wish according to our capacity to suffer. There is no stretch of His path that He will withhold from us.

Jesus longs even to share His wounds, as some have been privileged to experience. Paul writes, "Let no one cause me trouble, for I bear on my body the marks of Jesus" (Galatians 6:17). Was he referring to a touch of God, painful but empowering? Did he in some form receive the marks of Jesus' wounds? We may assume so.

Painful encounters with God and their consequences are recorded in Old Testament days too. Jacob limped after wrestling with God and seeing Him face to face (Genesis 32:31–32). His limp was a sign that he was no longer the same man. Such a touch of God has far-reaching effects.

And such life-changing encounters are granted to members of the Body of Christ considered worthy to share in the life and suffering of Jesus, who is the Head of the Body. They are part of Him, for as Paul writes, "we are members of his body" (Ephesians 5:30).

A touch of God connects us with the Lord of life. And coming into contact with Him, we will not lapse into fruitless passivity and dejection on the one hand or spiritual pride on the other. If the Lord graciously chooses to lead us into the fellowship of His sufferings, the result will be humble dedication and a passion for His cause. Such a person lives wholeheartedly for the advance of His kingdom, whether in active service or in the sacrificial ministry of prayer. What Paul says can be said of them: "Christ's love compels us" (2 Corinthians 5:14). Love is their incentive. And the proof of authentic love is that it translates into action.

The mystery of the fellowship of His sufferings unfolded as Jesus shared with me something of the pain of His Passion. It was sheer grace. Now I began to understand with the heart, not just the mind. In the previous months there was one song I sang over and over again:

> Jesus, Jesus, my Beloved,
> Lamb of God, now glorified,
> once You chose the cross of suffering:
> willingly for us You died.
> Let me, Lord, with love now follow
> on Your path of pain and death,
> let me feel the grief and anguish
> You endured at every step.

All this began to come true for me, and often when I came apart for prayer with Jesus, He opened His heart to me and let me taste something of His sufferings. Even in those months before I entered seclusion, it was like being in Gethsemane. Darkness all around, I committed myself to a path that seemed meaningless. I sensed the grim reality of the onslaughts Jesus must Himself have endured in Gethsemane. His total surrender to the Father's will, His *Yes, Father,* became deeply meaningful to me. My one prayer was:

Let me bravely stand beside You
in my own Gethsemane
when Your presence seems so distant
in the night of agony.
Then, when tossed about by conflict
and assailed by hordes of hell,
let me lie before You prostrate,
yielded fully to Your will.

Surrender was what the Lord was asking of me. He was calling me to bind myself to His will and walk His path – a prisoner for His sake, with no opportunity for active ministry, no scope for creativity. Only because Jesus had entered my life so powerfully as a captive bound in chains for love of us, was I able to rise to the challenge. In spirit I watched in awe as the innocent Lamb of God was led to the slaughter, hauled before judge after judge. Faced with the holy presence of God, I too stood accused and condemned, as the Spirit convicted me of my sins more deeply than ever before.

Down this road the Lord led me, drawing from me the only response possible – tears, sorrow, love and adoration from a heart shaken to the core by the Passion of my Lord. What had begun in 1952 became even more real during Lent 1953. As the first fruit of this experience the Holy Spirit filled me with grief over my sin. The grace of repentance was to mark all future periods in seclusion. My heart ached to see that my sin was the cause of His suffering, and I wept for His pain. The Lord was answering the prayer I had brought Him the year before:

Let me weep with You, Lord Jesus,
in Your night of grief unknown.

All this spurred me on in my desire to refresh and console the heart of Jesus. I wanted to express my love with a readiness to endure suffering and a passion for souls to be freed from sin and Satan. I yearned for others to be inspired with love for God the Father, God the Son and God the Holy Spirit. This burning love for Jesus, which was to grow in intensity, was the incentive for my writings and songs.

In previous years I had held Lenten meditations for the sisters, but how different Lent 1953 was! Leaving the complete silence of my room, I would join the sisters for the occasional evening. Now there was a new depth as I shared from the heart about Jesus' pain, which had come alive to me. I was gripped with a passionate longing that we would find ever new ways of proving our love for Him. Who can fathom the agony He endured – all for love of us sinners – to save us from Satan and hell? God graciously heard my prayer. That Lent, the sisters opened their hearts to receive the Man of Sorrows.

As He drew near in His love, we were privileged to come closer to His heart. Suffering is sacred. Only to those nearest to us do we dare lift the veil covering the pain deep within. So it was a holy hour when Jesus revealed to us the holiest of all, His sufferings. Many of my spiritual daughters were moved to tears at the thought of what Jesus endured because of our sinning. His sufferings kindled their hearts with love. Our one longing was to show Him our thanks for what He did for us. With what love, with what tenderness, we now worshipped Jesus as the Man of Sorrows.

In me burned a single desire:

Love, to You our love we offer,
Such as we would give no other,
Love and comfort without end.

I WANT TO CONSOLE YOU, no. 14

Sharing with others about the Passion of Christ, inspiring them with love for Jesus – what a privilege! All the pain of my calling to seclusion paled in comparison.

THE WRITING MINISTRY

During my travelling lectureship from 1939 to 1946, I was often asked, "Can't we have your talk in writing?" In reply I would say, "None of my talks are on paper. I don't have the gift of writing." But God had a different plan. My lectures in those years had been taken down in shorthand, duplicated and distributed. Mother Martyria and I only noticed when orders came for copies of transcripts we had never seen. Once in possession of the texts, we started duplicating them ourselves.

Our primitive methods of duplicating soon proved to be insufficient to meet the demand. So we explored the possibilities of having the texts printed, as printing restrictions had been lifted after the war. It was a risky venture, and we prayed a long time whether we should take the plunge. The printing costs for self-publishing were prohibitive. The year was 1948 and financially we were at our lowest ebb. It was just after the monetary reform when everyone had a minimum start-up sum allocated by the government to tide them over when the old currency was taken out of circulation. Even so, we went ahead and had the first three booklets printed: The Royal Priesthood, Mirror of Conscience and a further booklet on the theme of overcoming.

The demand exceeded all expectations, and the first editions were soon out of print. New editions brought us more big bills, and we were not charging for the books. At this point Sister Martina came up with a suggestion. If we could acquire a small offset printing machine, we could save on costs by printing simple booklets ourselves. And God heard our prayer. Not long afterwards just such a machine was donated. Many copies were then printed upstairs in the motherhouse. Two more booklets followed. But I had no intention of writing anything more.

During my first winter in seclusion (1952–1953), however, the Lord called me to bear witness to Him through the printed word. No one could have been more surprised, for I was an unlikely candidate. I had never been interested in writing, considering it a man's job. Well aware that I lacked literary talent, I was only able to write at the prompting of the Holy Spirit. This often happened now after times of inner suffering with Jesus while I was in seclusion.

Sometimes the urge to write was so great that all previous objections were swept aside. My heart and spirit were aflame and I couldn't help writing for hours at a time. In obedience to the Spirit I would continue, sometimes for half the night, without growing tired. I recall an occasion in 1955 when I worked non-stop on a book from early in the morning till after midnight because the inner compulsion was so great.

Though I wrote as the Spirit led, this did not mean I was personally uninvolved, like a robot. Before writing about anything new, I first had to experience it for myself, so that my words would be backed by my life. What I expressed in writing was the fruit of my own experience. During times of solitude there was little to distract me. All the more I became aware of the radiance of Jesus' presence. Inwardly I beheld Him as the Lamb of God, our soon-coming King and heavenly Bridegroom. What I saw I wrote, painting pictures with words as I portrayed Him in my books and songs.

Certainly there were times when reason protested, "Now you've written enough." I was embarrassed at having produced so many books, and conscious of criticism from various quarters. What helped me was the knowledge that I was acting in obedience to God and His call. If writing was part of His plan for me, then it must be right. So I could only count it sheer grace to write at all. How wonderful to tell forth the glories of Father, Son and Spirit. What a privilege to proclaim the nature of God – holy and just, yet infinitely loving and merciful, overflowing with goodness. What a joy to sound the call to love Jesus above all else, acclaim Him as Saviour and prepare for His return.

Persevering faith and obedience were especially tested in this ministry. To reach readers beyond our existing circle of friends we needed connections with bookshops in our own country and also publishing houses abroad. For many years the doors remained firmly closed. Waves of slander ensured that hardly any bookshops, let alone publishers, were interested in having my books. Countless times the enemy of our souls tried to convince me that it was pointless to go on writing. It was only thanks to the Holy Spirit's fire and prompting that I didn't give up. I'll never forget the encouraging word of promise the Lord gave us in view of the closed doors in the English-speaking world: "I know the plans I have for you … plans to give you hope and a future" (Jeremiah 29:11).

And God was faithful to His word. When His moment came, the bookshops opened. Our readership grew to such an extent that the sisters in our publishing house at Canaan often had whole stacks of orders to fill. In our print shop, which began on a small scale in 1952, a total of four printing presses now struggled to keep up with the demand. An American publisher wrote that they counted it a real privilege to distribute our books. Other foreign publishing houses also opened up for our literature.

When the door to seclusion closed behind me in 1952, I little suspected what the Lord had in store. From my times apart with Him a wealth of writings would flow. He had in mind an international publishing ministry with over a hundred titles, and translations in many languages. We would be dealing with quantities none of us had ever reckoned with. Readers would be inspired with first love for Jesus through repentance, embracing the discipline of the cross and honouring God's eternally sacred commandments. But in 1952 all this was hidden from my eyes.

Back then who could have foreseen what the future held? Within a generation the Christian church would be in greater need than ever of the help, encouragement and spiritual direction that would emerge from the stillness of His presence, far away from all the controversy.

The writing ministry was one of the reasons why Jesus called me into seclusion. At times I was assailed with doubts: this way of life seemed utterly pointless to me. But God's thoughts are higher than ours. What seems pointless to our fallen intellect is often full of meaning and significance in God's sight, with consequences beyond all expectations.

CHRIST IN US

Long before the founding of the sisterhood the following Psalm verses had spoken deeply to me:

> For the LORD has chosen Zion; he has desired it for his habitation: "This is my resting place for ever; here I will dwell, for I have desired it." Psalm 132:13-14 RSV

What I experienced in fulfilment of this promise during those first months in seclusion encompassed far more than the awareness of Jesus' loving presence. This was a special gift from the Lord. But if He is actually to make His dwelling in us (John 14:23), this is not something that just happens. A process is involved.

The indwelling of Jesus! I had long yearned for Him to make this come true in my life. At the same time it seemed so remote. Jesus says He makes His dwelling in the hearts of those who love Him. And how do we show Him our love? By keeping His commands (1 John 5:3). Yet how seriously had I taken this? I now saw that I had bypassed the first condition – to obey His Word in the power of His redemption.

I was about thirty when God stopped me in my tracks and brought me to repentance about my failure to follow Jesus without compromise. It was a turning-point in my life. Now I took Jesus' commands as binding. That was the time when my first love for

Jesus was rekindled. This love drove me to take His Word seriously. Every word He said, every wish He expressed, was dear to me. What He asked of me I regarded as holy and binding. A longing was born in me. "If only the Lord would make His dwelling in me!" Yet how easily I was distracted by the many matters vying for my attention: people, events, work, worries, troubles and sorrows. The inner chamber of my heart was occupied. I believed in Jesus, but I did not allow Him enough space in my life. People and things were too important. Now the Holy Spirit moved me to renounce the hold they had on me.

One particular situation comes to mind. Some years before the founding of the sisterhood we had to move rooms in Steinberg House. Repair men were in, cupboards had to be emptied, belongings sorted. All day long there was a commotion. I still remember my concern that I would be so taken up with it all that I would lose the sense of Jesus' presence. So I entreated the Lord that by His Spirit He would enable me to stay close to Him. Throughout the day I made a conscious effort to do everything prayerfully, in the sight of Jesus, intent on not losing contact with Him in all the hustle and bustle. And I recall how grateful I was to Him for answering my prayer.

In my longing for Jesus to make His dwelling within me, I began to keep a strict check on anything that could totally absorb me. By nature a fast and keen worker, I was used to making a to-do list first thing in the morning. Usually I plunged energetically into my work, intent on accomplishing the goals I had set myself for the day. Now I took a totally new approach. Each morning I brought the various points to the Lord. I then laid my list completely aside, no longer referring to it.

Instead of focussing on everything I wanted to get done, I asked the Holy Spirit to guide me specifically. *Do You want me to do this or that? Stay here or go there? Continue with the task at hand or spend more time in prayer?* If there were deadlines or circumstances requiring immediate attention, I would naturally prioritize, seeing a project through. But my one prayer was that nothing would penetrate my innermost heart, preoccupying or unsettling me. And God heard me. He enabled me to respond with love and empathy to others, while abiding in Jesus and His peace.

At the same time God rekindled my love for Jesus. I couldn't stop praising and worshipping Him. My heart was full of my Lord and heavenly Bridegroom in His love and beauty. He is the wound-scarred Lamb of God, whose love extended even to those who mocked and scorned Him. He is the King, exalted and majestic, and He is coming again in glory.

Love alone compelled me to draw aside in solitude and prayer, in response to His call, breaking human ties and relinquishing personal wishes and desires, including the satisfaction of an active ministry. During this time, the Lord continued to prepare my heart to become a more worthy dwelling-place for Him.

Then came a day I will never forget. My room was filled with the presence of God. Jesus was so near I felt I could have reached out and touched Him. In that holy hour He granted me His indwelling in a special measure.

Now I understood why the Lord had led me through the valley of humiliation the previous year. The high and lofty One makes His dwelling only with those of a contrite and broken heart, as His Word says (Isaiah 57:15). Hadn't I prayed for years that He would make His dwelling in me? This is why He humbled me again and again. How else is He to fit us for His indwelling?

From that hour of grace flowed a stream of blessing into my life. Later, my daughters were to remark on my calmness amid the difficulties that come with the leadership of a ministry. That was thanks to the blessing of Jesus' indwelling. It was all grace. Though sometimes the waves rose high, inwardly I was like a tranquil lake. Jesus had made His dwelling in the depths of my heart. He is and was my Peace and Helper. In His wisdom He already had a solution worked out. He took my will and melded it with His own. When our will is united with His, we are yielded to Him even if His will goes against the grain. Disappointments, frustrations, opposition, trouble and suffering cannot destroy this unity.

The indwelling of Jesus brought me a further blessing, for which I am grateful to this day. I had often found it hard to discern God's will when faced with a decision, although as yet my burden of responsibility was not so great as in later years. In my turmoil I would often ask, *What does God want me to do? What is His will? How am I to decide? Which direction should I follow?* Often I had no real clarity. When I finally made up my mind, I agonized whether I had made the right decision. So how do you discern God's will? I still didn't have the answer.

At that time I didn't realize that it is impossible to discern God's will until we start taking it seriously. That means giving up our own will and the desire to have our own way. When we stop trying to run our own lives, then He can guide us. This is a process and takes time and practice. It starts with the resolution to let go. But losing is gaining. It's worth letting go of everything we value in this life in order to love Him above all else. It pays to surrender our will, personal wishes and opinions, until His will alone is binding for us. Then He Himself will come and dwell in us – He who alone can satisfy our deepest longings for love. He brings us everything we desire in the way of help, guidance and answers.

This has been my experience ever since that hour of grace. Whenever a new situation arose I would appeal to Him for guidance, well knowing I couldn't make the right decision on my own. Then it was as if Jesus took me by the hand. Later we saw that He had been clearly leading us in the many difficult decisions we faced.

Even in the small details of everyday life He was there to guide me. How I thanked Him when for instance He kept me from doing a task that later turned out to be superfluous. Sometimes I felt a check in my spirit not to have a consultation just now – and later it turned out to be unnecessary anyway. At other times I would be prompted to meet with one of my daughters, unaware that she had just prayed to the Lord for a talk with me.

When Jesus really abides in us, as He has promised, then it is He who is guiding and caring for us. He makes the decisions. But we must always be on our guard not to give way to self. Wanting to have our own way, clinging to our opinions and personal preferences, drives Jesus out of our hearts unless we are quick to repent. Only if we keep His word and do what He wants can He abide in us. As we walk in repentance with a humble heart, daily surrendering our will to Him, we will taste the blessings of His indwelling – peace, joy, utter bliss. It will be heaven on earth. This has been my privilege in a rich measure during the months spent in solitude and prayer.

Looking back, I can only praise the Lord for His wonderful plan for my life. Leading me into seclusion, He gave me the precious gift of His indwelling, His abiding presence.

JOURNEYS FOR RECONCILIATION AND UNITY: FRUITS OF TIMES APART WITH JESUS 1953 – 1955

HEALING THE BREACH

Acts of surrender we make to the Lord in private will one day have visible outworkings, impacting others as God takes us up on our promises. In all the suffering and inner conflict my times of solitude entailed, it was a great comfort to know that a genuine encounter with God will bear genuine fruit. For love of my Saviour, the Man of Sorrows, I now wanted to embrace my cross more wholeheartedly than ever and bring Him joy by my commitment to endure suffering. I yearned to walk in ways that would refresh His heart. Love is practical. It wasn't long before the Lord showed me the next step to prove my love.

During Lent 1953 I was gripped afresh by the reality of Jesus' present-day sufferings, the grief He still feels today, especially in view of the divisions within His Body, the church. All this was sparked by an experience during the previous year. In the run-up to a tent mission a group of believers was excluded from the prayer meetings held beforehand. A judging spirit had led to a painful disunity among the leaders. Despite extensive publicity, the meetings were poorly attended and the message failed to reach people's hearts. I was especially sad, having prayed a great deal for this evangelistic event. Disunity among believers had hindered the saving of souls. For me, it was a watershed moment. Now my prayer was to live for the healing of the wounds in His torn Body.

Following my first winter in seclusion, the Lord spoke to me about His grief that His last request "that they may be one" (John 17:11) had not been fulfilled. He reminded me of brothers and sisters in the Lord with whom relationships were strained or who were actively opposing our ministry. And so my commitment to Jesus, the Reconciler, resulted in various journeys of reconciliation in the summer of 1953. The Lord put it into my heart to do everything possible to heal the breach. This meant visiting those who had reservations towards us or had expressed disapproval of our ministry – in an effort to resolve our differences. False and even malicious rumours had caused damage since our earliest beginnings. Various Christian leaders and organizations with whom we should have been one in spirit still had their misgivings, or openly opposed us.

So how to bring about unity within the Body of Christ? Not primarily through theological discussions and doctrinal agreements, however necessary they may be. This is where the challenge of God's Word comes into play: "I looked for someone among them who would … stand before me in the gap" (Ezekiel 22:30).

What could I do personally? Give up my rights and stop demanding justice when unfairly treated. In practice this meant approaching the various organizations and Christian leaders and asking them for the handshake of friendship. Jesus showed me how much I lacked love and humility, otherwise I wouldn't have found these visits so hard. It was His love that compelled me to take the initiative, for the sake of His Passion and His last request.

So I set out, travelling north, south, east and west, to visit Christian fellowships and organizations. The journeys, all undertaken without a car, were strenuous, and the costs were a strain on our finances. We were completely dependent on God, trusting Him day by day for our basic needs and for our ministry. But money matters were the least of my problems. Far greater were the disappointments and humiliations these trips brought.

In one instance I went to visit a big Christian organization. The sister who met me at the railway station was polite but distinctly reserved. The leaders had come together to receive me, but I did not feel welcomed by brothers in the Lord. It was like walking into a courtroom. On the table lay a few booklets I had written, including one entitled THE WEAPON OF PRAYER. Various excerpts were read aloud, for example, "Prayer means being prepared to enter into the fellowship of His sufferings for the sake of those for whom we pray". The men maintained that such a saying diminished the value of Jesus' atoning death. They claimed that my "unbiblical" statements were spreading false teachings. My references to New Testament passages were not accepted, even though Paul speaks of the "fellowship of His sufferings" (Philippians 3:10 NKJV) and enduring everything "for the sake of the elect, that they too may obtain the salvation that is in Christ Jesus, with eternal glory" (2 Timothy 2:10).

This was typical of the criticism levelled at me. Individual phrases would be taken out of context with no consideration for the rest of my writings and my message as a whole. There was no opportunity to explain that I was concerned with the entire witness of the Bible, and I left bitterly disappointed. I had longed for fellowship in our Lord Jesus, but my visit had the opposite effect.

My visit to another organization coincided with a meeting of all members. There I hoped especially for oneness in the Lord. But these brothers set a condition: we must conform to their tradition and join their organization. I was unable to comply. Their guidance and the work they were called to were fundamentally different from our own. So instead of Christian fellowship, there was discord. At another Christian organization I wasn't even received. Yet here and there the Lord worked miracles of reconciliation and Christian unity. Fresh bonds of love were forged with individual brothers who had at times been reserved towards us. In the following years they would join us in our Motherhouse Chapel to praise and worship Jesus.

Summer 1953 drew to a close, but the journeys of reconciliation were still not over. That winter, while I was in seclusion, Jesus drew very close to me as the thorn-crowned Saviour. I was stirred to the depths of my being at the thought of the Lamb of God in His humiliation. Love and compassion would have shone out of His eyes as He looked upon His mockers spouting abuse and blasphemy. Maker of all worlds, King of kings, with myriads of angels at His service, He endured the constant jeering of the mob surrounding Him. Grief for His shameful humiliation dominated the beginning of the winter season of 1953–1954.

Further journeys of reconciliation followed in summer 1954. As before, my experiences during the period of strict seclusion had tangible results: again these journeys were marked by humiliation. How could a follower of Jesus walk any other path than His? If the Master was mocked and defamed, so will His disciples be.

Even before I set out on my travels, we discovered that a new defamatory publication about the sisterhood and myself was in circulation. Compiled by a regional evangelical leader, it found its way into committed Christian circles. As it so happened, that summer the libel reached the very areas where I was travelling. In His sovereignty God permitted it. I had been invited to speak at various places, but the main purpose of these travels was to seek reconciliation. That was my heart's desire. Hoping for healing of rifts, I visited various Christian organizations that were critical of us. But the libellous publication, carried by evangelical bookstores, had done its damage. As I wrote in my journal at the time:

> *It's like having the whole world against you. At each meeting it is the same. Most come with preconceived ideas. They are critical or even contemptuous. And all because of this book with its "statement" about us. Evangelical Christians have been particularly affected, both here and abroad. It has turned them against us. We've been labelled as a sisterhood "from below".*

Even so I had to press on with my travels, although it was hard to penetrate the wall of prejudice in the hearts of the listeners. The last stop of my journey was a Bible college I had fond memories of. But my heart shrank at the chilly reception. When asked to give a brief word, I was conscious of unyielding resistance on the part of the staff and students. Before I had finished speaking, I was cut short in front of everyone.

Afterwards, the leadership called me to account concerning various false rumours circulating in the college. It was a painful interview. My word was not believed and I left heartbroken. Not until several years later did I hear from someone who had been present and whose conscience was now troubling her. The students had agreed to humiliate me publicly.

About ten years after the publication of this libellous book, some of the leading brothers of the evangelical movement officially took back its statements towards me. But as the Christian world remained generally unaware of this change of heart and no public apology was forthcoming from the authors, we continued to be rejected in many circles.

Amid all the humiliation my one concern was that Jesus' love would triumph in me as I met people who maligned our sisterhood and me personally, damaging our ministry in the kingdom of God. The image of Jesus crowned with thorns had made a deep impression on me while I was in seclusion. I became aware that the foundation of His kingdom was laid as His kingship was mocked. Never was His love so evident as when His enemies insulted Him. That was how His kingdom of love was built.

To this day believers help build His kingdom when they follow in the steps of their thorn-crowned Lord, who was despised and rejected. Understanding this spiritual law helped me to endure the pain and rejection in the strength of Jesus' love. Wasn't this part of our calling as a sisterhood? Didn't we live for Christians to be one in the Lord, one in love? Painful though these travels were, I never lost the assurance that amid slander and defamation God was building His kingdom. Hidden from our eyes, bonds of Christian love were being forged. Later I would see this come true in this Bible college and elsewhere.

"Repent, for the kingdom of heaven has come near." (Matthew 3:2) This verse would soon become the motto for our life at Canaan, the land that God planned to give us for our ministry. It was to manifest Jesus' kingdom of love and be a foretaste of heaven. But how could we reflect His kingdom unless we had learnt how to love? It is amid the thorns of pain, insults and humiliation that love blooms. Love is genuine only if we love our enemies. This was a lesson I had to learn again and again during these travels and in many other situations.

But perhaps the hardest test was not rejection but pressure. Pressure was put on us to merge officially with another Christian organization. One particularly painful occasion remains etched on my memory. In December 1953 some prominent Christian men visited us in our motherhouse and urged Mother Martyria and me to affiliate with their organization in obedience to God and for the sake of unity within the Body of Christ. They insisted that we would be acting in defiance of Scripture if we continued with our ministry without the covering of male leadership. But for the sake of God's calling on us, we had to abide by our decision not to affiliate. As initiator of the sisterhood, I was accused of pride and of refusing to submit because I didn't want to give up my ministry and die to self for the sake of the whole Body of Christ. We were warned that we were calling God's wrath down upon ourselves. From their point of view my decision was beyond comprehension.

Yet I clearly knew that it wouldn't be right for me to take the step they demanded. Our sisterhood with its various ministries would not have been able to develop as the Lord had shown me. My heart was full of sorrow, for I realized what a rift my decision had caused. But God continued to strengthen me by reminding me of the spiritual truth that He delights in accomplishing His purpose through the weak and poor, which was our position as women. I knew that in this situation I had to obey God more than people. Besides, Father Riedinger had blessed me on his deathbed for the leadership of the sisterhood.

Deeply moved, I later realized the full import of this time of testing. So much was at stake. For a young and inexperienced organization it would, on the face of it, have seemed a relief to hand over responsibility to a committee under male leadership, joining an established tradition and gaining financial security. But when God gives a clear commission, we need to be true to our calling and obey Him. How could we become affiliated with an organization with a different mandate from God? Saying *no* was painful, but God abundantly rewarded our decision. In the following years we were able to develop our ministries freely under the Lord's guidance. Nothing stood in the way of our future Land of Canaan fulfilling its God-given commission.

JESUS' LAST REQUEST

Midway through my reconciliation travels in the Protestant world came my trip to Rome.

As early as August 1952 I received clear but unexpected guidance from God to visit Pope Pius XII. I was to ask for bonds of Christian love to be forged between the brothers and sisters of the main branches of Christianity. Inwardly I resisted: anything resembling pushiness went totally against the grain. While serving as national president of the DCSB (Women's Division of the German Student Christian Movement), I had often been taken aback by the ease with which some could approach leaders with their requests. To me, it smacked of over-familiarity. Nothing could have induced me to do the same. And now, though quite unknown in the Catholic world, I was to ask for an audience with the Pope?

Prior to the Second Vatican Council such an undertaking was virtually unheard of. Back then there wasn't the openness for communication within the Christian church that there is now. Barriers still separated Protestants and Catholics. I well remember that Catholic nuns living nearby were forbidden by their Rule to set foot on our property. Even years later when Catholics from Italy visited us, they didn't dare enter our chapel. Many evangelical Christians held strong reservations towards Catholicism, and some Catholics, as we heard ourselves, mentioned Protestants in the same breath as Muslims and communists.

Could anything have been more pointless in those days than a visit to the Pope? Anything more calculated to arouse hostility? Our detractors would pounce on it. In any case, everything spoke against my going. How could I, a Protestant sister, approach the head of the Roman Catholic Church and plead for unity of love within the Body of Christ for the sake of Jesus' last request in John 17? To me it seemed like unpardonable presumptuousness. I knew that as far as the Roman Catholic Church was concerned unity was to be found only within their ranks, in the "one true Church" – "the universal aid to salvation". How was I to explain that I had a different perspective? I was advised not to go. Compounding my distress, serious reservations were expressed by relatives. For the sake of peace and harmony I would have preferred to drop the whole matter.

Besides, how was I to go about it? Practically there seemed to be no way. A general audience wouldn't serve my purpose: I could scarcely hope to speak with the Pope personally in that setting. A private audience, normally reserved for prominent personalities, was essential. But how to obtain such an audience? Only if the Lord made the impossible possible, would I take it as a sign that He was really calling me to speak with the Pope.

If the practicalities were difficult, worse still was the inner torment. My intellect protested like a caged bird beating its wings against the bars. Baffled and frustrated, I felt isolated from God. This state lasted for months. It takes many blows for our fallen intellect to die. And I had seldom felt so dry spiritually – especially when giving a biblical talk to my daughters. On one occasion I wrote afterwards:

Better to let a stone preach. I am so lifeless and lacking in spiritual authority. How can I even open my mouth when my words can't touch a single heart. I am but a speck of dust, a mere nothing.

So how could I possibly deliver my message to the Pope, let alone reach his heart? *I can't do it!* I protested. *It's folly even to think of going to Rome!* reason argued. I was the last person in the world for such an enterprise. My heart was not on fire for the task: I had neither the faith nor the love to see it through. A journal entry at that time reads:

Jesus has left me to battle this through on my own. I can only walk in obedience, trusting in His love and faithfulness to stop me if I'm on the wrong track.

Why the intense inner conflict? Satan attacks whenever he suspects the significance of an undertaking. During those lonely weeks of seclusion he was relentless with his insinuations. He made every effort to deter me from obeying God – not without reason, as time would show. The 1960s would see a great falling away from God and the Ten Commandments, but also the coming together of those who love the Lord. The trip to the Pope entailed so much pain. But could it be that in the spiritual realm this pain would help pave the way for believers to become one in Christian love as the end-time Bride?

Suffering for a cause, such as Christian unity – is that biblical? The Bible seems to take it for granted. To quote Paul, for instance: "Now I rejoice in what I am suffering for you, and I fill up in my flesh what is still lacking in regard to Christ's afflictions, for the sake of his body, which is the church" – "I will most gladly spend and be spent for your souls" – "I, Paul, the prisoner of Christ Jesus for the sake of you Gentiles ... ask you, therefore, not to be discouraged because of my sufferings for you" (Colossians 1:24; 2 Corinthians 12:15 RSV; Ephesians 3:1,13).

Every call of God comes at a price. Living for Christians to be one in love was to cost intense inner conflict. Why? Because dissension originates in the human intellect. People tenaciously cling to their opinions and views. The mind is a hotbed of all strife and judging, presumptuousness and division. Our fallen mind, poisoned by self-centredness, needs to be put to death if the divine spirit of love and conciliation is to rise and live.

So mental anguish was an integral part of this commission. A papal audience seemed pointless and irrational to me. First I had to die to my preconceived opinions before I could call others to surrender their prejudices and personal opinions to God. Only when our fallen intellect is willing to die, can love rise victoriously. As the fires of inner conflict purged my mind, more space was created for the Spirit of God, the Spirit of love, to build the fellowship of love among Christians. Evidently, this was God's intention behind my sufferings.

Meanwhile my daughters had made me a little flag with a Bible verse I had received in prayer for that summer: "In addition to all this, take up the shield of faith, with which you can extinguish all the flaming arrows of the evil one" (Ephesians 6:16). They presented it to me during a brief interlude from seclusion as an encouragement to my faith. "Right! Let's raise the song of faith and victory!" I exclaimed. Singing, we marched round our inner courtyard, filled with the spirit of faith. We were inspired by the Bible reading for that day, which was about the children of Israel marching seven times around the walls of Jericho. And so began our battles of faith at Canaan, which soon caught on among our friends.

I had asked the Lord for three signs if the audience was really to be. And He answered unmistakably. Firstly, I was granted permission for a private audience, which was unusual. Secondly, my travelling expenses were wonderfully covered. And thirdly, I received an invitation to stay as a guest in Rome, where I knew no one. These were the three unlikely signs I had requested from the Lord as confirmation.

Rome or, to be precise, the Vatican City was my destination in May 1953. Almost lost in the crowds surging towards St. Peter's Basilica, I sat with Sister Eulalia on a stone bench. Looking across to the Vatican, we sang songs of faith and victory. Though our singing was drowned by the noise around us, it rose to Him who hears every prayer.

Then came the morning of the audience. My heart was heavy and anxious. But as we sat in the reception area of the Vatican, the heaviness lifted and my fear vanished. I felt as carefree as a child. Half an hour later I was able to share freely with Pope Pius XII what was on my heart. In the name of our Lord Jesus Christ I asked that His last request would be honoured and that those who believe in Him and love Him would join hands across the denominational divide. Pope Pius replied that there was unity for believers within the institution of the Roman Catholic Church. Once more I appealed to him that Jesus longs for us to love each other now. In His love He cannot wait until we are all united in one Church. After listening quietly, Pope Pius replied, "Is that what the Saviour really wants?"

Today all the world can see that Jesus really desires Christians to be one in love. Across the denominations those who love the Lord and are true to Him and His commandments are coming together. Why is this so significant? Because in both the Catholic and the Protestant churches the spiritual foundations are crumbling. Disregard for God's Word and His holy laws is widespread. Even in Christian circles biblical values are being undermined.

The dividing line no longer runs between denominations but right through individual churches. At the same time, true believers of the various traditions are discovering a oneness in their love for the Lord to their mutual benefit and encouragement. Spiritually they form the Bride of Christ, and their oneness will crystallize under the pressure of coming persecution and culminate in the Marriage Supper of the Lamb.

The trip to Rome had cost me dearly. Was it worth it? Seeds of obedience and suffering, sown in the dark, germinate later – sometimes years later. But with God nothing is in vain. We have His promise that suffering bears fruit. Yet it did seem that my trip to Rome had achieved nothing. The news spread that I had been to the Pope, and evangelicals were outraged. It was claimed we wanted to become Catholic, which was never my intention. The kind of unity I sought was spiritual. All I wanted was that believers would be one in their love for Jesus while continuing to serve faithfully in their respective Christian traditions.

Now, instead of unity, there was even more strife and divisiveness within the Body of Christ. Eventually, in God's perfect timing, new doors opened for the call to strengthen and bring together those who love the Lord. Around the world Christians of various nationalities and traditions are drawing closer to each other – the Bride of Christ at home in His heart. Over the years the Lord has enabled me to write songs and books inspiring love for Him and for one another, leading to reconciliation within the Body of Christ. For the first time, Catholic bookstores, not just Protestant ones, started ordering our literature. A growing readership sprang up in convents. Bonds of fellowship were being forged worldwide among those who love the Lord.

Nor was that all. Branches were established in England, Greece and Italy, respectively the homes of the Anglican, Greek Orthodox and Catholic Churches. So, too, in Lutheran Scandinavia and multi-denominational America. Who could have foreseen such a development? Our branches have become a meeting point for believers of various traditions, as borne out in their reports. To quote our sisters on the Mount of Olives: "Over the past few days we have had individual and group visits from Switzerland, Finland, Denmark, Holland, Japan and New Zealand, among them Messianic believers, Salvation Army members, Arab Baptists, members of Catholic orders and Anglican clergy ... Though often a colourful mix, we were one in the Lord, singing and worshipping till late in the evening."

Opening nights at our retreat centre demonstrate the same miracle time and time again, as our guest sisters share. Despite a wide disparity of backgrounds, guests soon connect and bonds of love are forged. At some retreats almost every major denomination is represented. Converging on Canaan from all directions, the guests represent a cross-section of differing views, traditions and cultures. Yet each time the Holy Spirit works a miracle of unity. With Jesus as their focus, they pray, worship, celebrate and enjoy fellowship together. A frequent comment is that it is like a foretaste of heaven when all believers will be united in love round the Lord's table at the Marriage Supper of the Lamb. Then I can't help thinking of the trip to Rome and what it entailed, and I am awed at the wonderful outcome prepared by God.

In summer 1953 my reconciliation journeys were completed and the Lord had a wonderful gift in store for me. As a birthday surprise the sisters set up the room next to mine as a private prayer room. We called it the Trinity Chapel after the stained glass window designed and crafted by Sister Angelica, symbolizing Father, Son and Spirit. There in the stillness the holy, triune God drew near to me as I prayed. In my journal I wrote:

> *The stillness of eternity rested upon the chapel. The holiness of God filled the room, and His presence was almost tangible.*

Until then Jesus had been the primary focus of my love. Now I was filled with love for the Holy Trinity, Father, Son and Spirit. Awed by God's holiness, I wrote a number of worship songs:

> Father and Son enthroned on high,
> Shrouded in holy mystery,
> One with the Spirit, the holy Dove.
> Silence majestic broods over space.
> Reverently angels ponder His ways,
> Touch but the hem of His garment.

The love of the triune God overwhelmed me. I had undertaken these journeys so that Christian love would prevail among believers. And now the Holy Three-in-One, the source and goal of all love and unity, drew near. What amazing love.

GOD'S PEOPLE ISRAEL

Plans for a further trip had taken shape during my time in seclusion: this time not to our Christian brothers and sisters but to our elder brother Israel. It all began in the summer of 1954. In those days we had neither a prayer garden nor a Land of Canaan. So we leased a small plot of wooded land, north of our motherhouse, where our House of God's Goodness now stands. There among the pine trees we could withdraw for prayer. One day my daughters gave me a lovely surprise – they had built a little hut as an ideal quiet spot for my prayer ministry during the summer months.

On my first day there, I found myself pondering the miracle of Christmas, though it was the middle of summer. *God became man!* The reality struck me with greater force than ever. From the moment of His birth Jesus lived under the shadow of the cross. Even as an infant He was acquainted with grief and sorrow. Deeply moved, I found myself writing a number of Christmas songs about the Child of Sorrows.

I couldn't shake off the impression. Persecuted, hated, vulnerable and sensitive to the evil around Him, this little child was to become the focus of our love that Christmas. By nature we flee the burden of any cross, but worshipping Him, we would be led to a deeper repentance.

Shortly before Christmas, while I was contemplating all this, the Holy Spirit suddenly quickened to me the pain God feels for His chosen people. Now as then Israel is a people dear to His heart. Referring to Israel, the Bible states, "God's gifts and his call are irrevocable" (Romans 11:29). Israel's tragic history is evidence of her calling, for God submits only His chosen ones to the refining fire of affliction. Yet as a nation Israel still hasn't responded to God's love and turned to her Messiah Jesus, even though He came to His people and gave His life for them.

To this day Jesus grieves as He waits in vain for the love of His people Israel. If we love Him, this will hurt us too. It is part of His present-day suffering. This drove me to prayer and filled my thoughts in the Christmas season. Celebrating the love of God, who gives so freely and generously, we wrote out our petitions to God for the coming year, as we do each Christmas. That year, as we worshipped Jesus as the Child of Sorrows, the Holy Spirit prompted me to make two specific requests: "Bridal souls from Israel to Your joy – and, please, a trip to Israel."

My first request put into words what God had impressed on my heart during those months in seclusion. It was the pain of God that His people had failed to receive Him – not just two thousand years ago when He came as a child under the shadow of the cross. To this day Israel has not found her way back to her Messiah Jesus. My second request stemmed from the realization that we Christians bore a large part of the blame, especially those of us in Germany, if His people were unable to perceive His love. As a nation we had committed unspeakable atrocities against them instead of showing them the love and respect due to God's chosen people. God's Word says, "Whoever touches you touches the apple of his eye" (Zechariah 2:8). Yet we dared to mock and degrade them, subjecting them to inhuman suffering in concentration camps and brutally murdering millions. Our guilt as a nation is immeasurable.

An overwhelming sense of contrition came over me as I grieved for failing His people. I had done too little to show love and kindness to my Jewish brothers and sisters in their hour of deepest need. The pain in my heart became an anguished cry, *How can we ever heal the wounds we inflicted? How can we ever make amends?*

During a week of prayer and fasting I was led by the Lord into deep intercession for Israel. In the creative power of His Holy Spirit, who calls into being things that do not yet exist, God awakened in my heart a deep love for Israel. His redemptive purposes for His people had always interested me, and even under the Nazi regime I had spoken publicly on this theme despite the risks. But now my heart was on fire.

Out of this spiritual experience came a commission that would involve the entire sisterhood. The Lord was giving us all a heart for Israel. He was calling us to serve her people. As a result of the meetings I held with my daughters in February 1955, a wave of repentance swept over them. They had lived through the Third Reich as children or teenagers. In the following fifteen years, before sisters joined us from abroad, we started the day with a small token of repentance. In memory of the gruelling morning roll calls in concentration camp, we stood in silence during breakfast, using this time to bless Israel in prayer.

With God's gift of repentance came new attitudes in day-to-day life. Shy and awkward about meeting Jewish people, we had avoided places where they lived. Now we started seeking out Jewish people in our area. At first our efforts met with marked reserve, which was hardly surprising. For us it was a sign of God's forgiveness when Jewish people began to invite us into their homes. Over the years we have also been privileged to welcome a steady stream of Jewish guests who came from many different countries to visit us at Canaan. God inspired the entire sisterhood with love for Israel. Israel had become part of our lives.

Now I was to see the practical outworkings of my times apart with the Lord. God heard my prayer for a trip to Israel. I scarcely believed my eyes one day when I saw the postmark on a letter slipped under my door. It was an invitation from Israel. In those days Germans needed this to apply for a visitor's visa, though there was no guarantee that the visa would actually be issued. Until then few Germans had been able to visit Israel. But Mother Martyria and I were granted the necessary papers without any complications. This we took as confirmation for the trip. Quite unexpectedly we also received a gift of money to cover the travelling expenses. The way seemed paved for a visit in autumn 1955.

But eight weeks before we were due to go, I fell seriously ill. My life was in danger. This was to be a time of preparation for my commission. The trip was to have far-reaching significance, so it had to be undergirded with suffering. By the grace of God I recovered sufficiently for us to venture on the trip. God Himself prepared each step of the way, as we were to discover.

It was an indescribable moment when I first set foot in the Holy Land, where Jesus Himself walked, the Son of God. There I was to come to know His people, who had returned home from many nations, and to experience their way of life. Dear to Him, they were now dear to me. Still frail when I arrived in Israel, I stumbled on my second day and sprained my ankle. As a result I could hardly walk. Had the Lord brought me all the way to Israel only to confine me to bed for the duration of my stay?

On the contrary, God used this accident to show me the whole land within a few short weeks. At a gathering Mother Martyria met someone with an extensive knowledge of Israel. Hearing of my accident, this woman offered to spend a week or so driving me round in her car, where I could recline. As a result I was able to see the key sites and the Holy Places. Thanks to my injury, we not only acquired an excellent guide but were able to visit places we could never have reached without a car.

Wonderfully led by God, we came into contact with Israelis whenever we stopped at the roadside. Because our guide was fluent in various languages, including Modern Hebrew, we were able to engage with Israelis, hearing first-hand of their sorrows, hopes and joys. It was a deeply moving experience. The Jewish people had suffered unspeakably under us Germans. Their total annihilation had been planned. But God overruled. As a result of their afflictions the Jewish people returned to their land by the thousands, as the Bible prophesies for the end times (Ezekiel 38:8).

In His Word God had promised that the desert would bloom when His people came home. For nearly two thousand years the land had lain barren and desolate. As we drove through Israel, we were struck by the fertile fields and thriving orchards. With our own eyes we were privileged to see the fulfilment of God's promises. The flourishing land, which now belonged to His people again, bore witness: soon the King will return! On that day "they will look on me, the one they have pierced, and they will mourn for him as one mourns for an only child, and grieve bitterly for him as one grieves for a firstborn son" (Zechariah 12:10).

It was impossible not to feel deeply moved. Our love for God's people and land grew. We understood better God's great love for this people and were full of thanksgiving that He gave us a measure of His own love for them. We were also thankful for the opportunity to meet leading Israelis and to express, with a weeping heart, our shame and sorrow for the guilt of our nation.

Everywhere we went I was conscious of God's leading. It was all about the new commission He had given. In Haifa a small boy came up to our car window as we stopped in the street. Cheerfully he introduced himself as Gideon and asked with a child's frankness, "Who are you? Where do you come from?" Suddenly he said, "You have to come to Israel and help us. We really need you." It was a strange feeling. Was God calling us through this child? Did He have a task for us there? We hardly even dared to admit we were from the nation that had inflicted such unimaginable horrors upon them. God gave this lad an open heart for us Germans, and we were to encounter the same openness among other Israelis as we sought forgiveness with a broken and contrite heart.

The call to Israel was repeated when we returned home, this time coming not from the lips of a child but from someone influential. "Come and help us." God was looking for deeds as the fruit of repentance. So we sent two sisters to Israel. After studying Modern Hebrew, they took up nursing in an Israeli hospital. Even though our sisters offered their services voluntarily, the fact that they were accepted as Germans was remarkable. It showed that God was behind it all and this was His commission. There is no other way of explaining it.

Much as I loved Israel, I found it hard to be separated from the sisters. For the first time we had to part with two members of our small, close-knit family, sending them out to a distant country, which even then was threatened by war. Mother Martyria and I had known them both since their childhood in Bible class days. Yet I could only regard it as a gift of God's grace when we finally saw them off to Israel in March 1957. God had confirmed that my prayer at Christmas 1954 was in keeping with His purposes. From now onwards part of our commission would be to live for Israel. Out of repentance, and for love of our Lord Jesus Christ, we sought to fulfil a concern close to His heart.

The fire for Israel that God had kindled in me still burned, prompting me to write. First came a booklet and then a full-length book, ISRAEL, MY CHOSEN PEOPLE, which was translated into various languages. Driven by a sense of urgency, I challenged people to face up to our crime against Israel, particularly as Christians. At the same time I had a burden to tell the Jewish people about their calling and election, God's wonderful purposes for Israel, and His promises, which were beginning to be fulfilled. The Lord blessed the book and it was well received by Christians, but also by Jews. Some rediscovered the faith of their fathers as a result.

Still, there was a divine restlessness in my heart. Love, especially when fuelled by repentance, is forever seeking new outlets, new forms of expression. Even before the trip to Israel, I was led by the Holy Spirit to write our first "proclamation play", a Bible-based drama with Israel as the theme. In summer 1956 we presented ISRAEL at the bi-annual *Kirchentag* (Protestant Church Convention) in Frankfurt. People came by the thousand to see it, though it had little in common with most modern drama. Such was the impact. Despite twice-daily performances the church could not hold the crowds. One night we had to put on an extra performance at ten o'clock. ISRAEL was later performed at other cities in our country, often in connection with the *Kirchentag*. As pastors told us, it helped to change the attitude towards Israel in many churches.

Thousands of guests attending our retreats over the course of the years came to see the significance of Israel in God's redemptive purposes and the seriousness of our national guilt. They took part in our Israel Prayer on Friday evenings. Many experienced a deep repentance and a change of heart towards Israel.

The Israel commission did not end there. In 1959 God showed me that a house called Beth Abraham would be established in Jerusalem in answer to prayer and faith. It would be a place where wounds would be healed, trust in God restored, and His beloved people prepared for the coming of the Messiah. It was an impossible task; yet despite enormous difficulties, the Lord gave us this house the following year.

It was all part of God's plan that the dedication took place in 1961, a few days into the Eichmann trial. Emotionally all Israel was in turmoil as old wounds from the terrible years of 1933–1945 were opened under the glare of publicity. For the first time Israel's youth became aware of the full extent of our national guilt. Many parents had been silent about the past in order to spare their children.

To begin with I was devastated at the seemingly unfortunate coinciding of dates. We feared that hardly any Israelis would attend the dedication. In this situation, who would enter a house belonging to Germans, and Christians at that? Yet over a hundred Israeli guests came, and the Lord in His grace used the occasion to bring something of His healing balm to their grieving hearts. They sensed our love and that helped to melt their natural reserve and to ease the pain.

Among the invited guests was a former mayor of Jerusalem, Daniel Auster. As he gave his address, I began to understand God's love and wisdom in allowing the dedication to fall within the opening days of the Eichmann trial.

> *Abraham rose and served his guests himself. They sat, while he stood ... I see this same attitude here. The story makes a lot of sense to me, especially now as this terrible trial is in progress. I can see the difference between this man, whose name I do not even want to mention, especially not here, and the love that I find in this place. I have heard your reasons. I also understand*

your motivation. The source, the origin, is contrition, repentance, atonement – not for something you did but for what others did. Love is the purpose, and faith, trust and hope are the means. This is what led you to open this house.

The Jewish author Shalom Ben-Chorin also spoke:

If in the course of these days we Jews are in danger of repaying hatred with hatred, you have helped us to overcome the temptation. There is only one weapon against hatred, and that is love. Thank you for saving us from hatred, from collective hatred, in this hour of temptation.

For us Sisters of Mary, so much ensued from that holy moment in 1955 when the Lord bound our hearts together with Israel. Today our house Beth Abraham in Jerusalem is a place where Jews, especially those who suffered in concentration camps, can come for a time of refreshment in body and soul. At the same time Beth Abraham is a place of prayer, a little centre of light and blessing.

Israel had become part of our life: their joys and sorrows were now ours. Our prayers intensified at every fresh incident of anti-Semitism or outbreak of war, such as the Six Day War in 1967 or the Yom Kippur War in 1973. We would send encouraging words of greeting to Jewish communities and the many Jews we have come to know over the years, both in Israel and in our own country.

Again and again I was invited to Israel, where doors opened for me to hold lectures. There was a keenness to hear "the remarkable, incredible story" of our community. I was astonished and humbled to see large numbers of Jews, some sick or elderly, some from long distances, flock to the meetings even in bad weather. Over half had heard by word of mouth. I shared, for instance, about the miracles of God we had experienced at our little Land of Canaan, and they listened with real interest, responding warmly.

The gratitude was overwhelming. People spoke of the new hope that had been sparked in them: something of the biblical spirit had been restored to their land, the land of the Bible. Some, whose faith had been shattered, had the courage to believe again. Only God's chosen people could have responded like that. And these were secular audiences. After a talk in Haifa, a local newspaper concluded that if government departments would only live by faith, trusting in the living God, the state of the country would improve.

Further invitations came from Jewish communities in Canada and the United States. I was asked to speak in synagogues, at student and rabbinical meetings, and even to hold the sermon at their Sabbath service. The call to repentance, arising from personal conviction and confession of guilt, had reached their hearts.

Still, burdened by God's grief for His people, I wasn't satisfied. For a long time what I wrote both for and about Israel reached very few in the land. At that stage there was no way for my books to be published in Modern Hebrew. Demand for the German and English copies was scant in the bookstores. Indeed, it was hardly safe to show interest in the books. At a book fair in Jerusalem we had police protection. It didn't seem to matter which topic I wrote about, there was little response, and our sisters in Jerusalem were discouraged by the situation. The spark of faith in their hearts needed constant rekindling.

Meanwhile years passed by. No branch cost me as much in terms of suffering as Beth Abraham. Practical repentance was our desire: national guilt and centuries of Christian anti-Semitism precluded normal missionary work. To this day our calling is to help heal the wounds of His people. Yet we are present in Israel as believers in Jesus Christ, who love and trust Him. And so we cannot help bearing witness by our lives – even if not in words – to the One we belong to, who means so much to us.

Even so, there were signs that a new era was dawning: the day God has been waiting for these past two thousand years. I will never forget the evening when a prominent Israeli joined us in our Hall of Zion in the motherhouse. It was a deeply moving moment. He sat facing our large crucifix. As we were singing and worshipping, I asked him if he would like to choose a song, and he requested the verse:

> O beautiful Lord Jesus,
> my heart belongs to You.
> All-loving is Your nature,
> so holy, pure and true.
> You've stolen my heart, a single glance
> has made me ever Yours,
> O King of Love and heaven's crown:
> I worship and adore.

We had first met at an important Israeli institute, where he had a leading position. On that occasion God gave me the grace of tears as I asked forgiveness as a member of my nation. Many a significant encounter followed. Now I shed tears of joy to see this son of Israel, who had suffered torture at the hands of us Germans, find Jesus shortly before his death. Something new was indeed beginning, though barely visible and only perceptible to the eyes of love.

During and immediately after the Six Day War in June 1967 a booklet I had written in Israel years earlier was suddenly in demand. Recorded excerpts from THE HOUR OF THE MESSIAH were made widely available and thankfully received. My book about Mount Sinai was suddenly popular as Sinai became a focal point for Israelis. FOR JERUSALEM'S SAKE I WILL NOT REST, which I wrote after the Six Day War, reached many hearts.

Offers were made to translate the literature into Modern Hebrew, and it was a Jew who published REALITIES OF FAITH and part one of my autobiography in Modern Hebrew. A call to repentance entitled TURNING-POINT, written for a European readership in connection with the invasion of Czechoslovakia in 1968, was introduced to the Israeli press by friends from the Netherlands. Nine Israeli newspapers printed the text in six languages. A few months later a leading figure in Jewish public life told me: "From the Orthodox Jew to the modern Kibbutz youth, one and all heeded your words. Some even carried the newspaper clipping in their jacket pockets. You have reached hearts in Israel."

As I look back on summer 1954 I can see why God called me to come apart rather than engage in active ministry. It was then that God planted in me the seed of love for Israel. So much has grown from this seed. I can only worship God for the goodness and greatness of His all-embracing heart. The cost in terms of pain cannot begin to compare with the harvest it yields.

CANAAN – A FORESHADOWING OF JESUS' KINGDOM 1955 – 1957

MAY 4, 1955 – GOD'S MOMENT HAD COME

Once before, the 4th of May had marked a new epoch in our community. That was back in 1949 when God gave me the inspiration to build a chapel, a small sanctuary, where worship and thanksgiving would rise to Him. The previous year Mother Martyria and I had made the decision to trust God for all our needs. By embarking on this faith project, we were now fully committed.

Some kinds of suffering are soon forgotten if things turn out well. But the harsh reality of those initial years of living by faith is indelibly imprinted on my memory. Financing the building project was a huge responsibility, and we frequently found ourselves on the edge of the abyss. Again and again I cried out to the heavenly Father for help, which often didn't come until the last moment. He seemed intent on drawing the utmost trust from my heart.

All my life I had been particular about having my financial affairs in perfect order – another reason why I found ventures of faith so hard. Debts were unthinkable. But these worries were only secondary. My greatest concern was that God's honour was at stake. Many eyes were focussed on our building site: government officials, workmen, firms, the press, the clergy, parents of our sisters – both friends and critics. The whole purpose of this enterprise was that God would be glorified and His name exalted in the sight of all. People would either believe that God does miracles, or doubt His power – even scoff – depending on the outcome of this project. If it all ended in debts and bankruptcy, the name of the Lord would be discredited, and it would be my fault as I was the one who had heard from God.

While we were building, I often cried out in prayer, "Lord, I believe; help my unbelief!" (Mark 9:24 NKJV). Sometimes I even sighed, "Oh, if only I were in heaven! What a relief it will be: no more believing, just seeing." This is reflected in my journal entries in those years:

> *No money. The situation seems utterly hopeless. And we're right in the middle of building. Tears are my constant companions. But I know You're going to bring us through. You will not allow Your name to be dishonoured. Hardly any money has come in for weeks now, but I will bear the suffering, for it's all about You and Your honour. One day this path will come to an end.*

And so it did – to His glory. The motherhouse and chapel were completed in 1952, and Jesus' Printshop in 1954 – debt-free! At that time I thought with relief, "No more ventures of faith! No more mountains of bills to be cast by faith into the sea!"

Then came a day in 1955 – again the 4th of May. In the early hours of the morning God gave me a vision for our future Land of Canaan. What an incredible commission! I happened to be sick in bed at the time, and Mother Martyria came in with my breakfast tray. I painted her a glowing picture of what God had shown me. Years later Mother Martyria would recall how she nearly dropped the tray in horror. This was a faith venture on a far greater scale! But God's moment had come on that 4th of May. He gave me not only the vision, but also the faith and commitment to see it through. It was all grace, for I could never have done it myself.

Inwardly God had been preparing me in the previous weeks while I was in seclusion. I had assumed that during Lent 1955 the focus would be on the Passion of Jesus. God led me differently.

One night I awoke, conscious of the very real presence of the heavenly Father. All I could say was, "My Father, my Father!" over and over again in loving tones. And as I spoke His name, a sweetness flooded my soul – the bliss of knowing I was a child of God. To be sure, I had long had a childlike love for my heavenly Father. But this was something richer, deeper – an intimate father-child relationship, far stronger than anything I had known before.

God the Father revealed Himself to me through His Spirit. He broke powerfully into our life as a community. He wanted to impact every area of our lives: all my spiritual daughters were to learn how to relate to the Father as a beloved child of His. For countless numbers Canaan was to be a living testimony, a signpost pointing to the God who is alive and active today, answering prayer and working miracles. This is the message that would sound loud and clear to a world increasingly alienated from God and to a compromised church attempting to "demythologize" the Bible by explaining away the miraculous.

One sunny day in August Mother Martyria and I set out with the sisters to view our "promised land" from the castle ruins on a nearby hill. Climbing up through the woods for an hour and a half, we paused on a grassy slope where we sat and sang our first song about Canaan, which the Lord had given me a few days beforehand.

> Canaan, O most lovely land,
> Fashioned by God the Father's hand,
> Chosen as His possession.
> Here on this land God's eyes now rest,
> His mighty hand outstretched to bless:
> This is His land, His treasure.

Reaching the castle ruins, we saw our prospective land far below: fields and meadows bordered by forests on the outskirts of Eberstadt. In every way it seemed unattainable. Yet at that moment God directed my gaze away from the circumstances and towards Himself. I was able to share with our family of sisters the wonderful plans and purposes of God. I spoke as if Canaan already existed, complete with buildings and gardens, and with people going about their various ministries.

The biblical Canaan is the land of promise – a land of God's miracles. And our own promised land will become ours only as we hold on to God's promises in faith. It will be acquired not by the usual human means but by the Father's personal intervention.

Seeing the questioning eyes of my daughters, I continued:

God envisaged the biblical Canaan as a land of joy and song. The Bible says, "They will come and shout for joy on the heights of Zion ... Then young women will dance and be glad" [Jeremiah 31:12–13]. *With drums and trumpets Israel would celebrate for days on end. So an atmosphere of overflowing joy should prevail at our Canaan. All who come to visit, on their own or in groups, should be caught up in the celebration and singing, no one leaving without tasting something of this joy. Nothing pleases the heavenly Father more than to see His children happy. Can we imagine how His heart thrills to look down and see a little land of festivals, of joyous song and celebration!*

The land that God intended for His people was a land where milk and honey flow. So Canaan too will have cows and bees. It will be a little paradise and, under His blessing, a fertile and beautiful land. And a spring must also be found.

The biblical Canaan was destined to be a centre of blessing for all nations. So our Canaan too will be a spiritual oasis for people from all over the world who love Jesus. But the more visitors we receive, the more careful we must be to maintain quiet areas where we can draw apart with the Lord. The motherhouse prayer garden and inner courtyard will be set apart and no longer open for guests. Communion with God in the stillness of prayer must be safeguarded if we are to fulfil the Lord's commissions.

The biblical Canaan is a holy land. So nothing unholy must be tolerated at our Canaan. Sin needs to be brought into the light and covered by the blood of the Lamb. Our fellowship in the light is to be kept sacred. Then the Lord will shine more and more out of Canaan and all who live here. Whatever our task, it will have that distinctive mark of being lovingly done unto the Lord.

Each new facet of God's land of Canaan was greeted with songs of faith. Joy took over, and as I continued to share, the hours flew by.

The biblical Canaan is a land that the Lord Himself watches over as Guardian. So He will also take care of our Canaan, which He has given to us as an inheritance. He will ensure that the houses are built, all costs covered. Daily He will provide the food on our table. Our part is to permeate this land with our prayers; in keeping with His word, He will pour out His blessings. And one day when Canaan is finally ours and the land developed, we will see God's promises come to fruition like a miracle before our eyes. Canaan is the land where the resurrection and ascension of Jesus took place. So we'll keep singing of victory, and people coming here will join us in waving victory banners. But they'll also learn to share in the sufferings of Jesus, for Canaan is the land of the Passion.

So at our little Land of Canaan the Passion will become more real to us, and many will be reached through the Passion plays.

From our vantage point at the castle ruins we sang and claimed the land in faith, overjoyed at what God had planned. It was a mountaintop experience. Regardless of how much or how little each of us was able to grasp at that point, we all sensed the significance of the occasion. We had received a new focus, a change of direction for the coming years.

Ever since becoming a believer, I had longed and worked for something of the kingdom of God, the kingdom of heaven, to become manifest. I yearned for Jesus Christ's rule of love to become visible here and now. Hasn't this always been the desire of God's heart, even before the world began? All His leadings with Israel point to this goal.

John the Baptist announced the coming of Jesus with the call, "Repent, for the kingdom of heaven has come near" (Matthew 3:2). It was the message Jesus Himself preached and then commissioned His disciples to take to the ends of the earth. He taught them to pray, "Your kingdom come" (Matthew 6:10). His kingdom was the theme of His talks with His disciples during the forty days after His resurrection. "The kingdom of the world has become the kingdom of our Lord and of his Messiah, and he will reign for ever and ever." (Revelation 11:15) This is Scripture's grand finale as history reaches its climax.

Could anything be more wonderful than living for the dawning of Jesus' kingship, His rule of love, wherever God has placed us? This was my dream and the goal of my life. What I cherished in my heart was now to assume tangible form. God was calling into existence a land with gardens and buildings, and a people abiding by His rule and commands.

After our mountaintop experience, the way led downhill – literally and figuratively. Leaving the castle ruins, we headed for home, down through the wooded hillside to the motherhouse in Darmstadt's suburb of Eberstadt. At the same time we were descending into a spiritual desert: the harsh reality of the many difficulties surrounding our vision for Canaan. Now it was a matter of battling on in faith, treading the dark paths that would ultimately lead to the goal God had shown me.

Difficulty upon difficulty arose as we set out to possess our "promised land". Only by the grace of God was I able to persevere all those years. The way to Canaan was barred – not least due to the flat refusal of the authorities. We also had to deal with over twenty private property owners – plus communities of joint heirs, an issue further complicated by inheritance laws. In any case, who would want to sell with inflation a real likelihood?

Other property owners were the City of Darmstadt, the Church and the State of Hesse. Obtaining a decision from these quarters meant dealing with considerable red tape and waiting from one council meeting to the next. The administrative procedure was long and drawn out. Trying to explain our vision for Canaan was almost hopeless. God was calling Canaan into existence at a time when a project was judged chiefly by its sociopolitical value. Who would recognize and understand, let alone endorse, Canaan's social significance as a centre promoting spiritual renewal?

Even if the miracle happened, against all odds, what good would it do? Supposing God did intervene and the gates to Canaan swung open … Supposing the land was suddenly free for development and the numerous property owners were willing to sell … Where would the money come from?

Wasn't all this a tempting of God? Wasn't it sheer audacity on my part to engage in a faith venture on such a scale? But God Himself had given me this commission and filled me with the burning desire that He would be glorified.

All three Persons of the Trinity, Father, Son and Holy Spirit, were to shine forth from Canaan, so that many would be inspired to love and honour God. God must be glorified! This was the driving force behind acquiring and developing Canaan. It was our biggest risk of faith so far. In terms of suffering it would prove the most challenging and costly.

DISCIPLINE – A SPECIAL MARK OF GOD'S LOVE

In the stillness of the little Trinity Chapel I had discovered what it means to be a child of the heavenly Father – before even embarking on the Canaan project. During the acquisition of Canaan I was to experience it for real in our dealings with the town authorities. Nowhere do we come to know the Father so intimately as when "the Lord disciplines the one he loves" (Hebrews 12:6).

Crises and shortages are often the Father's way of testing us. But saying *yes* and accepting His disciplinary measures works like a key. It gives us access to the treasure store of God's heart – all the blessings and favours He is waiting to pour out on us afterwards. Was it any wonder that the road to Canaan was paved with chastening?

At the time, though, it was hard. Hadn't God given us the commission? Why wasn't He standing up for us? Miracles were few and far between. I was to learn a valuable lesson: to persevere against overwhelming odds. Sometimes when God seems to be fighting against us, He is actually fighting for us. Many tears were shed in the following years, but my plight actually drove me to the Father. A helpless, tearful child belongs in the Father's arms. And I was to experience His abundant goodness in the end.

The first test of faith arose when plans were announced for a large bypass that would cut across our prospective "Land of Canaan". Our whole commission was at stake. It was either Canaan or the bypass, but not both. Things grew more and more hopeless. Typical of faith ventures, there were highs and lows. At times, victory seemed within our grasp, only to be snatched away. For ten whole minutes we rang the Motherhouse Chapel bell in thanksgiving that God had heard our prayers. The bypass was to be relocated! Then came the crushing news that the bypass was to be built right across our future Land of Canaan after all. For the top government officials in Bonn, it was the only viable option. Once and for all they turned down our petition. In my journal I wrote:

> *I know that my heavenly Father would never abandon His little flock. He would never leave us at the mercy of our opponents. Why would He give us all those promises, win over the town council, and then take it all back with thousands watching? We had been praying so hard for Him to intervene. Why would He mislead us? He would never do that.*
>
> *Father, You are all love, You are true and faithful. Nothing can shake my conviction that You have set apart Canaan for us. You are only putting obstacles in our way in order to prepare us. The greater the suffering, the greater the fruit Canaan will bring forth.*

The difficulties in purchasing the various plots of land were innumerable. One owner planned to have a filling station on his property next to the proposed bypass. Commercially it was an ideal location. Another was reluctant to sell or exchange his property, quoting family reasons – he had relatives living in the States. A third was involved in an inheritance lawsuit and thus not in a position to sell. Each case was a problem in itself, and we were dealing with roughly twenty plots of land, as well as an additional twenty which we planned to offer in exchange.

Our visits to the municipal authorities almost always proved fruitless when we enquired about buying city-owned property in our future Land of Canaan. Finally a meeting was arranged for the municipal council to discuss the matter. How we prayed for the outcome! But when the session was over, the mayor, deputy mayor and municipal council sent us their unanimous decision along with a map showing Canaan reduced almost by half. And that was final!

In tears I laid this map before the Lord and with a broad-nibbed pen I crossed out the proposed boundary. In faith I held on to God's commission and promises, trusting that He would fulfil His word. Two-thirds of the land in question was owned by the State of Hesse, and the local government flatly refused to sell or exchange this property. In those years I was greatly comforted by scripture verses the Lord gave me from time to time in my many prayer battles for Canaan. His Word bolstered my faith. Later, in thanksgiving to God, and to His glory, I had memorial stones erected at Canaan's entrance, engraved with these promises. Here are a few examples:

> Do not be afraid, you worm Jacob, little Israel, do not fear, for I myself will help you. Isaiah 41:14

> The one who calls you is faithful, and he will do it.
> 1 Thessalonians 5:24

> See, I have given you this land. Go in and take possession of the land. Deuteronomy 1:8

> No one who hopes in you will ever be put to shame. Psalm 25:3

Considering the challenges, it was nothing short of miraculous that I was able to persevere in faith. Looking back on those dark and twisting paths, I can only admit this wasn't my doing, but God's. He is the One who sustained me in those agonizing moments when I had literally no one to stand by me. However well-meaning the advice of friends, so often it was the hand of the Tempter offering an easy way out. Give up. Give in. No more battling in faith. No more struggles.

Inwardly I would cry out to the Lord, *What is hindering You from helping us? Have I grieved You in some way? Have we grieved You as a community?* Yet the conviction never left me entirely that this was the way I had to go. Nor in my heart of hearts did I want to go any other way. This was God's leading for my life, and it was His intention that I would glorify Him on this pathway. So I wrote:

I bind myself to You, O Lord,
by the power of Your blood.
I would be true to You
and to the path of faith,
in the night persevere
till I behold You face to face
and see at last what I believed.

There were a few brief interludes during those years when the Father withdrew His hand of discipline. Like the sunlight bursting momentarily through dark clouds, He would shine His love and compassion upon us and show us His heart.

Sometimes He reserved special dates for these occasions – like our tenth anniversary as a sisterhood. We had just received three flat refusals from the highest authorities in our city and state. Naturally the sisters were very upset. Yet I felt it was all the more important to celebrate the Father's goodness and glorify Him in a service of thanksgiving.

Hardly had the afternoon celebration begun when we heard that the local government had withdrawn their housing plans and were giving us first option on the territory in question! Professor Peter Grund, Senior Town Planner, came personally to bring us the news and we were able to announce it to the whole gathering. Everyone shared our deep joy. The testimony of God's fatherly love and care spread far and wide.

So we were not left without comfort: there were bright spots. In various crises the heavenly Father raised up influential people when we had no one to fend for us. For instance, there was Fritz Dächert, the mayor of our suburb Eberstadt; Professor Paul Luchtenberg, my former lecturer who had meanwhile become Minister of Education and Culture for North Rhine and Westphalia; two prominent church leaders; and, above all, Professor Grund, the Town Planner.

But the Father saved up His greatest consolation for our twelfth anniversary. More of that later.

When anyone did agree to sell, payment was soon due. We struggled financially throughout this venture of faith. And so I prayed:

My Father, You would never desert us. We're Your children, however imperfect. What's more, we're Your needy children, virtually destitute, with no one in the whole wide world to fend for us – no network, no church, no institution to back us ... We are completely dependent on You and Your goodness. We are pinning all our hopes on You. Would You ever let us down?

Father, aren't we living to magnify Your name and to make known Your love and Your pain? Surely You will provide for our needs out of the abundance of Your wealth. An earthly father would for his child ... You can't do otherwise, for You are all that a father could ever be, loving and caring. June 11, 1955

"How are the finances?" That was my number one question every day. Though accountancy was not my field, I used to surprise the sisters by being so informed. That was because I found living by faith so challenging. There were occasions when the relevant sister was at a loss to give details of the financial situation when asked with no forewarning at table. But I could reply for her. For years I had a list of the invoices due each month hanging in my room. Daily I would petition the Father for the necessary money, for so often funds were at a low ebb. When the money did come, I would cross through each amount as it was paid, writing next to it, "Thank You, Father".

Still the time of testing was not over. A journal entry reads:

I feel as though a sword had pierced my heart. We are walking this dark path of faith for the sake of Your glory. But it's having the opposite effect. Not only here in Darmstadt, all over the country rumours are going round that we receive large sums from foreign donors and don't know what to do with all our money! See my tears. It's only for You and Your glory that we want the various buildings.

Later, when Canaan was under development and we were once again in a tight spot financially, unsettling news reached us. Public institutions were making supplementary payments to previous owners to compensate for rising land prices. Though under no legal obligation, we chose to do the same, because as disciples of Jesus we wanted to live by the Sermon on the Mount. Since there were twenty plots of land, this added up to a considerable sum. It was a hopeless situation, and I'll never forget how I cried out in prayer, *My Father, we're drowning! Have mercy.*

My prayer was wonderfully answered. Yet I was very much aware that I myself needed this discipline. The heavenly Father wanted my trust in Him to be tried and tested. Tough though it seemed, this was a small price to pay to be freed from all that is not consistent with His kingdom values. And in heaven He will compensate us with unimaginable glory.

Again, why this discipline? Canaan was to be a spiritual oasis reflecting God's fatherly love and wonder-working power. Later many visitors would learn to submit to the Father's chastening and, in the process, discover His heart. The foundations could not be laid deep enough.

There was yet another reason why we had to walk these paths. Canaan was to be established in an age when riots and revolts would sweep across the western world. In spirit I often saw clenched fists raised in defiance against the heavenly Father. I heard the torrent of blasphemous accusations from the lips of many, even Christians, as they blamed God. *Is that supposed to be a God of love? – Where is God in all this? – How can He allow something like this to happen? – I can't believe in God any more.* I grieved at the bitter words, spoken or unspoken, and the shouts of rebellion openly mocking and taunting Him.

Against this backdrop, trusting God took on a new dimension. Persevering in faith had meant walking a desert road fraught with disappointments and suffering. But suddenly it all seemed so infinitely worthwhile: trusting in God's love meant showing the world that He is trustworthy. He is love itself. No one can say with all their heart, *Father, my Father,* or bear witness to His love with such conviction as those who dared to trust God when all seemed lost – and then received help from Him.

HEART-SEARCHING

If we're sure that a commission is from God – if we are absolutely convinced of its rightness – then we can take a lot. Which is why Satan tries to shake our conviction by sowing doubts. Trials and temptations are among his most effective weapons, as I was to discover for myself. The spiritual attacks intensified as our hopes of acquiring Canaan dwindled. In the winter of 1956 my lifework seemed doomed: it was like a wilting leaf about to die. Was there any point in believing for Canaan? In my diary I wrote:

> *Our Passion plays lack substance and power. Yet they are part of the reason why we are engaged in a life-and-death struggle for Canaan. In reality, the Passion of Christ has little room in our hearts. Had I known that a year ago, I would never have planned a Land of Canaan, complete with a Herald Chapel. My whole vision lies ruined ... This year we are performing to declining audiences. Numbers will drop further with so many committed Christians warned against my writings: in some circles they are actually banned. It's like staring death in the face – the end of the commission Jesus entrusted to me.* February 8, 1956

I began to ask myself whether it was sheer madness to want such a large property and to plan all those buildings. The voice of reason asked, *How long will it take for Canaan to be established, the grounds laid out and the buildings constructed? By then war may have broken out, making it impossible for Canaan's commission to be fulfilled.*

Questions were raised by sisters. Weren't we overshooting the mark? Better to limit ourselves to half the size with fewer buildings and less land and retain our family character. Life at Canaan could easily become impersonal and lose its appeal. Friends also advised giving up the plan for a grand-scale Canaan. "It's unrealistic. You're headed for disaster."

Had I really been mistaken? I was in deep turmoil. If this project wasn't of God, I wanted to abandon the struggle immediately. But I felt a compelling urgency to persevere in faith. *This project is of God,* my conscience told me. *This is His commission. If you don't see it through, you are disobeying God. He wants Canaan to be a place where people taste something of the kingdom of heaven here on earth.* As a confirmation God gave me the word, "Whether you turn to the right or to the left, your ears will hear a voice behind you, saying, 'This is the way; walk in it'" (Isaiah 30:21).

So I persevered in faith, trusting that inner conflict would only serve to humble me and prepare me for Canaan and its future ministry. I knew that if Satan attacked, we must fight back, knowing that God's weapons are stronger, and combat doubts with the audacity of faith, hoping against hope. In this spirit we sent out a newsletter in May 1956, describing everything the Lord had shown me about Canaan, the grounds and buildings – complete with ink sketches.

Yet making such a declaration of faith seemed like sheer madness. How could we send out the letter when the way to Canaan seemed permanently closed? Mother Martyria agreed it was out of the question. Still, I couldn't shake off the impression that this was a unique opportunity to honour God. If we dared to step out in faith and if, against all odds, Canaan did materialize, the Father would be glorified. Everyone would see that it was thanks to His supernatural intervention and miracle-working power that the land was acquired and developed. Human endeavour and resources had no play in it. If we now failed to proclaim in faith that Canaan would come to be, how could we proclaim His glory later?

With much trepidation we sent the letter out. The inner conflict did not abate, despite the words of confirmation Mother Martyria and I received beforehand in prayer. "Always be prepared to give an answer to everyone who asks you to give the reason for the hope that you have." (1 Peter 3:15) "He who began a good work in you will carry it on to completion until the day of Christ Jesus." (Philippians 1:6)

More testings followed. My faith in God's plan to create a little paradise among us was sorely shaken. Disappointments in my daughters reached a climax and my vision for Canaan as a foretaste of heaven seemed to be disintegrating before my very eyes. Inwardly it was so dark that I could only weep and grieve in my heart, "They are not willing." Everything I had believed for seemed to be destroyed. There was so much spiritual apathy, self-centredness, self-righteousness and lack of love among them, blocking God's commissions.

I was reminded of St. Francis of Assisi, whose life-work was destroyed by the conduct of his spiritual sons. Tears marked his final years as he faced the collapse of all that he had worked for. I, too, suffered bitter disappointment as God's commission seemed to have been wrecked by my daughters' conduct.

A number of them were unwilling to walk the way of daily repentance, although God continued to challenge us unmistakably. Some we had to ask to leave, as they had become like a dead limb; others left of their own accord. Love for Jesus had died in them, and they showed no willingness to change. Such gaps in our spiritual family caused deep wounds for Mother Martyria and me.

In those months of agonizing heart-searching I wished I could lay down the leadership of the sisterhood. God did not allow it. He helped me to overcome these disappointments by showing me His infinite patience with myself. In His grace, He filled me with fresh hope through a word of promise: "Let the earth open wide, let salvation spring up, let righteousness flourish with it; I, the Lord, have created it" (Isaiah 45:8). He strengthened me to hold on in faith.

MOUNT MORIAH – THE HOUR OF TESTING

What is the most crucial moment in the life of a Christian? Not conversion, nor a loss, nor discipline we suffer. Crucial is our response when God leads us to Mount Moriah.

Abraham is given to us as an example in Genesis 22. Offering up his son on Mount Moriah was incredibly hard; harder still because he had waited twenty-five years for this child. But hardest of all was sacrificing God's promise. All the nations of the world were to be blessed through this very son, miraculously given to him in old age. Now, at Mount Moriah, Abraham was being tested in the crucible of inner conflict. Would he lose confidence in God when God seemed to go against His own word; when His actions ran counter to His promise?

At times like these, when our confidence in God is shaken, when we are disappointed in Him, we come near to breaking point. But if we stand the test, we will be blessed with deepest union with the will of God. There is no greater gift. But such oneness comes only as the culmination of countless acts of surrender in daily life when the way is dark and we can't make sense of God and His dealings with us. During the years when the battle for Canaan raged outwardly, God was at work inwardly in my life. The hidden struggle was intense: God was laying a cornerstone.

In those years God gave me a promise that for me comprised the highest and best a person could ever receive from Him. For a long time I prepared myself inwardly. All God's leadings seemed directed towards this goal. In September 1956 the moment of fulfilment seemed close. God in His holiness drew near as never before. But I was to discover the meaning of Moriah – burying God's promise. I consider it one of the greatest blessings of my life that on that September 27, 1956, I did not lose confidence in God.

By the grace of God I was able to give Him my *yes*. This was the hardest path I had ever been asked to tread, so bitter was the disappointment. In a symbolic act I laid some pebbles on the ground, forming the words YES and AMEN at the place where I had spent so much time in prayer. Despite everything, I would hold onto His love. And though my heart bled, by His enabling I wrote in my journal, *My Father, I do not understand You, but I trust You.* Later, responses came from all over the world testifying how these words spoke into people's darkest hours. The greater the cost, the greater the impact.

The darkest day in my life became the day of greatest blessing. God's gift to me was deepest union with His will when I was least able to comprehend it. Not till much later did I realize that He had indeed fulfilled His promise, only differently. At the time, that was hidden from me. Much of what I later experienced in the way of the fulfilment of God's promises was related to that Moriah experience. It was certainly true when it came to possessing our "Promised Land".

The years from 1956 to 1959, however, were rife with disappointments as God's promises for Canaan failed to be realized. Instead of permission, we received an emphatic *no* from the highest authorities. In 1958 our sisterhood seemed to lie in ruins before my eyes, our commissions doomed, as I lay in hospital close to death. What helped me to keep faith was that first and hardest of Moriah experiences in 1956. God is love and always will be! That was my testimony during those dark moments.

On paths of suffering
When night surrounds me,
I praise the blessing that will come.

His name is Amen:
For this I praise Him,
Although I cannot understand.

God's will is goodness,
His heart all-loving,
His leading always wise and best.

Praising His will is what helped me to stand firm in those times of testing. Afterwards I experienced something of what it must have been like for Abraham who, having stood the test, was commended: "Now I know that you truly fear God" (Genesis 22:12 NLT). Times of testing are followed by an outpouring of God's blessings, an indescribable sense of His presence.

In the woodlands near Wüstenrot, where I had this Moriah experience, stands our Mount Moriah memorial with the inscription:

Moriah means God sees you
in your pain and agony.

Moriah means God tests you
as gold is refined in fire.

Moriah means God loves the soul
who yields Him everything.

Moriah – God, who gave His Son,
bears with you your suffering.

In such Mount Moriah experiences everything depends on our standing the test. The enemy of our souls takes advantage of such times, hoping to trip us up where he failed with other trials and temptations. Later I wrote about this to my spiritual daughters:

Have you ever encountered the paradoxical God? Have you ever found Him baffling, beyond understanding? Have you known times in your life when God seems to be leading you the wrong way, your faith is shattered, and everything you believed for seems to end in bitter disappointment?

If you have never faced the God of the unexplained, allowing Him to have His way in your life, then you have not proven your faith in Him. Believe me, if anyone wants to enter heaven's glory one day, they must be willing to suffer acute disappointment on earth. In this profound darkness it's like being lost in a maze. We feel far from God, we can't understand Him. He is silent: our prayers go unanswered.

If we want to taste heaven for eternity we must be willing to pass through such phases of darkness on earth. Jesus tasted this darkness on the cross when He cried out, "My God, my God, why have you forsaken me?" (Matthew 27:46). *He suffered profoundly and innocently. If we belong to Him, we should be willing, as sinners, to endure a measure of such darkness. Compared to His inner night, it is a mere shadow – and we will never be completely forsaken. Jesus is with us. In suffering, our rightful place is close by His side.*

Disappointments in our lives are the criterion as to whether we really do trust in God, surrendering our wills completely to Him. They are the touchstone that shows whether God can do with us as He pleases. Whatever He does, will we still love and follow Him as an obedient, trusting child? Will we be true to Him and committed to His leading to the end?

Then we'll discover that His heart is truly love and that He always leads us out of the darkness into the light. Times of testing are rewarded beyond anything we could imagine.

GOD'S ANGUISHED WRATH

THIS IS OUR GOD! – a testimony that would sound forth from our promised land of Canaan. It would also be the title of our 25th anniversary book. Later, the documentary film GOD LIVES AND WORKS TODAY would carry this message around the world.

Meanwhile, before we could proclaim how great God is, we had to discover for ourselves who He is. During the foundational years when Canaan was being developed, He revealed many facets of His nature. We came to know Him more fully in His mercy and forgiveness, His discipline and guidance, His wonder-working power and omnipotence, His spoken word and His silence, His patience and faithfulness – an ever-loving Father. Yet one distinctive feature of His love we were yet to experience.

In 1957 I was back in Wüstenrot for some days of quiet. I was staying in a cottage made available to us by friends from time to time. In the past God had drawn very close to me here, so I was looking forward to a time of undisturbed prayer in His presence. But as soon as I entered my room, I was struck by the altered atmosphere. This time His nearness filled me with fear and trembling. I scarcely dared to breathe. The very air seemed to be charged with God's holiness. What up till then had been head knowledge now became real to me. I was faced with the God of wrath.

I was aware that God grieves when neither love, nor kindness, nor words of warning bring us back to Him in repentance and He has to resort to judgment and wrath. Now I caught a glimpse of the pent-up anguish in His heart. It is just as Revelation describes for the age of wrath. For the first time I consciously noticed many Old and New Testament passages about the wrath of God. Most of them refer to the cataclysmic end-time events ushering in God's great day of reckoning when the earth will go up in flames (2 Peter 3:10). In the coming judgments His wrath will descend like streams of lava (Revelation 16). Trembling will strike the whole world. Instead of turning to their Saviour, people will pray for the mountains to fall and hide them from the wrath of the Lamb (Revelation 6:16). Such is their nameless terror as God's wrath is unleashed.

Something of God's anguish for His lost and erring children was revealed to me in its sheer intensity, wild and turbulent as a mountain torrent. I could almost hear the impassioned cry of His heart, echoed in Jesus' lament: *But you refused!* (see Matthew 23:37). Again today God grieves over a humanity that refuses to come back home to their heavenly Father – refuses to be saved through the sacrificial death of His Son – refuses to accept His light, choosing instead darkness and sin. And so they perish in sin and hell's torment. It was like a foreshadowing of the time when God's anguished heart will overflow, and the foundations of the world shake at the thunderbolts of His wrath. Thrice holy is God in His grief and righteous anger, which will not cease until the day comes when every knee bows before Jesus.

Never had I felt so intensely God's sorrow over us, His children. Infinitely loving, He is always there for us, but so few respond as He deserves. His pain filled my heart. Suddenly I found myself singing in the Spirit tunes of lamentation I had never known before. My voice, naturally weak, was supernaturally borne along, and for hours on end I would lament His suffering in melodies the Spirit gave me.

Then followed days which even after the passage of time I can only describe as terrifying. God allowed me to taste a measure of the force of His wrath. It was like being hurled to the ground. Nothing I had ever experienced with God could compare with this encounter. Over the years I had often felt His disciplining hand. But this time God approached me, a sinner, in His holy wrath. In His stern silence and righteous anger He was like a complete stranger. Fear befell me. I felt as though I were rejected by Him, and my heart was numb with pain. An atmosphere of death engulfed me, its grimness palpably near. During those days I felt something of God's wrath over sin in general and over me in particular as a sinner.

The wrath of God pursued me wherever I went. When I found it unbearable to stay in my room, I would leave for the woods, but there too His wrath pursued me. His fury seemed to have been unleashed in nature. A severe storm broke out, with gale winds lasting throughout my stay. Lofty fir trees snapped in two and fell to the ground. In the woods death could strike at any moment. So I did as Scripture said – "Go, my people, enter your rooms ... hide yourselves for a little while until his wrath has passed by" (Isaiah 26:20). So great did God's wrath seem that I felt it would destroy me.

In retrospect I realize why I had to undergo this. Only if I had personally tasted God's wrath could I write of the coming end-time judgments. At the time I couldn't have known that humanity's sin would be so outrageous that it would call down divine judgment. Deception would soon be rampant, and even within the church people would fall under the sway of blasphemy and immorality. A mere ten years later the crime rate would soar as the Ten Commandments were trivialized, paving the way for hell on earth. As far back as 1957 I wrote in my journal:

The message of God's anguished wrath over a sinful humanity is the word for now. We are heading for God's judgments.

Three years later I was to see more clearly how the Lord was preparing me as in spirit I tasted His wrath. As of 1960 I felt an inner compulsion from the Lord to write on the theme that "the end of all things is near" (1 Peter 4:7). Only because He impressed on me the reality of His coming judgments and His righteous anger was I capable of writing. The experience of His holiness in May 1957 enabled me to convey something of His broken heart and anguished wrath as I commented on the horrific developments in our world. If only people would be warned and saved, I was willing to suffer in advance something of His coming judgments.

Having personally come face to face with the God of wrath, I could also grasp the meaning of grace. Only by tasting something of God's righteous anger can we understand the significance of what Jesus did for us. He died on the cross as an atoning sacrifice so that no one who believes in Him need be destroyed by the wrath of God. This is why I was able to declare that God's grace is always greater than His judgment, provided we repent and bring our sins to Jesus before it is too late.

This call has lost none of its urgency. God's preliminary judgments are growing in scope and intensity, a signal that the day of the Lord is close. A day that none will escape – a day of unrelenting wrath and anger (Isaiah 13:9). If only we would hear His voice today!

A YEAR OF DEATH AND RESURRECTION, 1958 – 1959

BLOW UPON BLOW

The year 1958 was to be a year of unprecedented testings, bringing us face to face with death itself. Would I still hold on in faith to God's love in the darkest hours?

First came the big disappointment regarding Canaan. Despite our prayers and petitions and the efforts of influential friends all those years, the State of Hesse gave us a categorical *no*. State property in the area wasn't up for sale or lease. And that was final. Once again the vision for Canaan was as good as buried. Yet another opportunity to say yes to the Father's will – at great personal cost. I reaffirmed:

> *My Father, I do not understand You, but I trust Your ways. Your plans are always good and right. Just as You can raise the dead, You can revive the buried promise of Canaan.*

Then came the next blow. Seldom had we faced such financial difficulties. Construction work on our retreat centre, the House of Jesus' Joy, nearly had to be suspended for a while. Only cautiously did we continue building, anxious not to incur debts.

But the waters of tribulation reached the high-level mark when sickness and even death struck our sisterhood. Until then the Lord had graciously held His hand over us. Illness was rare among our sixty young sisters. And when it did occur, healing came through prayer and the laying on of hands; sometimes also through medical treatment.

The Father had shown special kindness in the case of Sister Angelika. Drafted as an anti-aircraft helper, she returned home critically ill once the war was over. When she joined our community, the doctor gave her only two more years to live. Yet ten years later she was still alive – truly a miracle of God. But the whole situation changed in late 1957. First, in autumn 1957, Sister Margaretha suddenly fell ill. She was diagnosed with cancer. We prayed and believed the Lord for a miracle of healing, as did Sister Margaretha herself, who was only thirty-three. But instead of seeing a miracle, we found ourselves in a crucible of trials and temptations. We kept battling through in prayer to the point of believing that God would intervene. At the same time it was clear that she was not improving but approaching death. Her condition deteriorated and in May 1958, after half a year of suffering, she was called home to the Lord.

It was the first time I had seen one of our spiritual daughters on her deathbed, and I thought my heart would break. Sister Margaretha was still so young and we loved her dearly. Our sisterhood was not a vast, impersonal organization, but a family, particularly as Mother Martyria and I had known some of the sisters since their childhood. We regarded them as our daughters in a double sense. They were dear to us, and we to them. Losing one of them to death was bitter, and it left a painful wound in our spiritual family.

With a heavy heart I left Sister Margaretha's deathbed to break the news to Sister Angelika, little realizing that the second blow would strike me the same day. "I'll be the next to go," was Sister Angelika's reply. The previous night her eyesight had deteriorated drastically, a sure sign that her kidney disease had taken a fatal turn.

This was the second young sister we were to lose within a few months. Bubbling over with life, Sister Angelika seemed an unlikely candidate for death. She played an active part in the sisterhood. Not only did she bear considerable responsibility, she was also our sculptress and the stage director of our religious plays.

Her presence would be sorely missed. Would her passing mean the end of the religious drama ministry? My daughters raised the question, and I could only reply that no one is indispensable and no commission from God is tied to a particular person. But how the ministry was to continue I couldn't imagine. Painful months followed at Sister Angelika's bedside. She suffered intensely before she was called home to the Lord half a year later in December 1958.

Yet death seemed determined to reap a harvest among us that year. Other sisters became seriously ill. One sister's life was in danger, and there was concern that the infection might have spread to others. There seemed to be no end to the bad news, and not once did God grant healing. Sick at heart, I could only humble myself beneath the mighty hand of God and amid tears surrender to His will.

Not only did our prayers for healing remain unanswered, but God's promises for Canaan were unfulfilled. Acquiring the land seemed as impossible as ever. No help in sight. And what about our retreat ministry? It seemed to have been nipped in the bud. As early as 1954 the Lord had given me the inner commission for the House of Jesus' Joy during a time of prayer. He showed me it would be a place where people would meet with Him, see themselves in the light of His Word and, through repentance, come to love and follow Jesus with all their hearts. He would lead them into uncompromising discipleship; a relationship of childlike trust and dependence on their heavenly Father.

Now, inexplicably, a mere six or seven registrations came in for one of those early retreats in the new centre. So much effort had gone into building this guesthouse with its fifty bedrooms. Previously when we had lodged guests in the upper storey of Jesus' Workshop, above our printshop, and in makeshift quarters, we often received far more applications than we could handle. Now the necessary facilities were finally available, and yet everything seemed to stagnate.

The spacious Herald Chapel, still in the planning stage, proved no less problematic. In obedience to God I had tried to explain to the Senior Town Planner why we needed such a big building. The Motherhouse Chapel was so small that the sisters were doing up to three performances a day. Yet once the plans for the Herald Chapel were underway, the Motherhouse Chapel was frequently half empty. On one occasion our sisters put on a Passion play for an audience of twenty. All these burdens weighed heavily on Mother Martyria and me, not to mention the financial problems.

IN THE FACE OF DEATH

The cup of suffering had not yet been drunk to its dregs. In December 1958 I too fell critically ill. I was admitted to hospital. There I lay, body, soul and spirit under death's shadow. It was Christmas. But unlike other years, the motherhouse was shrouded in sorrow, for on Christmas Eve came the news that my life hung in the balance.

Darkness had fallen upon our sisterhood. Mother Martyria and the sisters were facing more than just their personal grief at the thought of losing me. They felt as though God were dealing a death-blow to our ministry. In keeping with His call on my life, I had been the one to receive the main spiritual and practical initiatives for our sisterhood. Was I to die without seeing Canaan become a reality? Was I to depart this life disappointed in nearly all my hopes, the commissions unfinished and lying in ruins? Was death to part me from the sisterhood before God's promises were fulfilled?

My life-work, the Sisterhood of Mary, was still young and in need of direction and guidance along the paths God had shown. Canaan had to be developed. The future was precarious and time was needed for the vision for Canaan and its ministries to unfold.

Was my life to end before my daughters reached the spiritual maturity I so longed for them to attain? Disappointments in a number of our daughters had come to a head during the past year, causing Mother Martyria and me real pain. The difficult months leading up to Sister Margaretha's death had brought sinful attitudes to light: hardness of heart and an unwillingness to repent. Blow after blow came from the hand of God, yet a number of sisters remained more or less unmoved. What had happened to the vision to reflect something of the kingdom of heaven Jesus proclaimed wherever He went? Was God calling me home now when the vision seemed more elusive than ever? How could the sisterhood, and later the whole of the Canaan community, ever live up to the mandate God had given? This is what caused me the greatest pain and turmoil.

For weeks I lay in hospital, utterly weak and racked with pain in body and soul. I felt abandoned by God. In this inner night I agonized over the promises so far unfulfilled.

While in hospital, I wrote in my journal:

> *Ruins wherever I look, nothing but ruins. Sister Margaretha has been taken from us. Death and sickness have laid us low. The way to Canaan is barred. Nothing has come of the Herald Chapel. Sister Angelika, our stage director, has died. My strength is gone. But the Lord has given me the grace of repentance, a contrite and broken heart – the biggest blessing of all. And so the ministry will continue. Out of the ruins life will rise.*
>
> January 1, 1959

With this critical illness and the collapse of everything I had lived for, God was teaching me faith on a totally new level. He wanted to hear me say, *Yes, Father* – words dear to Him because they cost me so dearly. Ultimately it was the fulfilment of my prayer all those years to glorify Him with ever new acts of dedication. I knew that He prized the surrender of the will more highly than a thousand prayers of adoration offered in His honour. Saying *Yes, Father* in a dark moment is the most precious prayer we can offer, especially when God allows major suffering in our lives and we no longer understand Him.

Every time we tread a dark path and feel God's hand of discipline upon us, we have the assurance that the Father is watching over us in love. We can almost hear Him say: *My child, will you still trust Me? Will you still believe that My heart is brimming over with love? Will you still accept My actions and leadings when nothing makes sense? Will you surrender your will to Me this time too? In doing so, you will enter into the closest possible union with Me, for the act of yielding your will to Me is like a key to My heart and My kingdom.*

Wonderful things come from aligning our will with His. It brings us intimacy with the Lord our God, the deepest possible union. This I was to discover afterwards.

And so the foundations for the Canaan ministry were laid. God intended Canaan to be a lighthouse, a living testimony to who He is – our loving Father in heaven and holy, triune God. Later God would extend our commission worldwide. But our testimony would lack integrity unless it was backed by suffering. Deeper levels of pain had to be borne and laid in the foundation. A greater measure of surrender was needed. The testings of the last few years were not enough: neither the challenge of financing our building projects, nor the challenge of claiming our "Promised Land" in faith.

What God was looking for was a whole burnt offering. He was asking us to give back to Him all the promises for Canaan. A year of death had to be endured. That, and nothing less, was the price that had to be paid. Yet from this sacrifice, fruit would come. One day, visitors to Canaan would be inspired to persevere in faith themselves and so prove their love for God and bring glory to the Father. The greater the commission, the darker the way and the deeper the trials and temptations.

"I WILL NOT DIE BUT LIVE"

Late in January 1959 I returned from hospital, but well into March I was still hovering between life and death. Inwardly I suffered too. God was leading me through the valley of the shadow of death. Often I felt forsaken by Him, and I agonized over unfulfilled promises He had given. Physically I was so weak that I could barely speak, write or take any initiative. I felt cut off from my daughters. Much as I longed to be with the Lord, I was distressed at the thought of dying before gaining the victory in certain areas of my life. I didn't think I was yet ready. Three little phrases helped me to overcome at that time:

> Yes, Father – Your will be done.
> I'm trusting in Your fatherly love.
> I give myself to suffering.

Once more, death was almost palpably near. But at the lowest point, God chose to speak to me. Through His Spirit He gave me the unmistakable assurance that I would recover. What an incredible moment! The joy of Easter flooded my heart. *I was going to live!* I would rise from my sickbed and finish the tasks God had given me. What an amazing gift of God! True to His promises, Canaan would materialize, reflecting something of heaven to His glory. My joy knew no bounds. God would complete all that He had set out to accomplish, both in our ministry and in me personally. My life would not end abruptly like a broken thread. After standing at death's door, I could hardly grasp the wonder of His grace. My heart overflowed with thanksgiving.

And sure enough, I felt the Lord restoring my health that April. I was able to speak and write again. It was like a resurrection from the dead. What grace to fulfil the task He had given me! What grace to reflect Him as He completed His work in my soul! What joy and glory for Him!

During my illness God had clearly shown the dross that needed to be purged from my soul. Now He would do His transforming work in me by the power of His blood – of this I was certain. Change would come as I walked in repentance, under His hand of discipline, and battled in faith against sin. I prayed that I would make up for where I had failed. I asked for new opportunities to show love, a love extending even to those who had done me harm. My passionate desire was for God to be glorified. That was His purpose in restoring my life.

Along with health, the Lord granted me new strength – and new commissions. Everything I had laid on the altar in the previous months He restored many times over – purified and transfigured.

It was May 1959. I was lying in the garden recuperating and enjoying the spring with its fresh green foliage. Suddenly the Holy Spirit rekindled in me the incentive to write – in two weeks making up for the lost months of illness. Day after day I wrote almost non-stop from morning till night, producing texts for booklets and festivals.

Weeks later we were having a happy time of fellowship in the garden when some sisters wheeled in a little "harvest wagon" displaying twenty new booklets with attractive cover designs. They were singing as they came, "Harvest of writings garnered in suffering: dark days bring forth the fruit of toil." And together we responded, "Praise God for sadness, bringing us gladness now and forever – eternal joy."

For quite a while I had been praying for the scripts for festivals and celebrations in our future Herald Chapel. And now the first drafts were there. No longer would the great festivals of the church year be over with the morning service. Crowds would gather for afternoon sessions to lift up the Lord in praise, and in the evening the worship would continue in the motherhouse. These celebrations would draw those who longed for God to be glorified, and together we would exalt His name and acclaim His glory and majesty.

> Jesus, matchless Sovereign, ever reigning,
> all the shame and bitter suffering
> fade as we now honour You.
> Crowned with many crowns of glory,
> Sovereign Ruler, Prince of Victory,
> we praise Your glorious majesty.
> All of heaven the song of glory raises,
> endlessly retells Your praises.
> We worship You, the Lamb.
> To You be glory and honour,
> glory to You, the Lamb!

Such worship was to gain significance. Thirteen years later a tidal wave of blasphemy would begin to sweep across the world. Worship can help stem that tide of evil.

And I wrote to my daughters:

> *Could anything be greater than honouring and worshipping God? Worship is associated with heaven. In heaven we will be gripped by a holy ardour. Like the four living creatures of Revelation 4, we will be prompted to offer constant praise and worship to God the Father, to the Lamb, and to the Holy Spirit … Glorifying Him must be the passion of our hearts. We were made and saved to focus on God alone like the four living creatures at the throne.*

But the stream of blessings did not end there. God again confirmed my writing ministry by giving me the grace to produce a growing number of books, later available in many languages. They were to make their way around the globe, bringing glory to God and inspiring love for Him.

How thankful I was for His enabling as I wrote the book MARY, THE MOTHER OF JESUS. I was encouraged by some of the first responses. Leading Protestant theologians commented it was biblically sound and of vital importance for our Protestant world. In answer to my prayers, the book was widely read. Sadly, in some circles this book brought me into further disrepute. Even a biblical approach to the mother of Jesus was unacceptable to those who were biased in their anti-Catholicism.

About that time I also wrote REPENTANCE – THE JOY-FILLED LIFE, which led many to a spiritual breakthrough. For me, repentance was a life-transforming experience leading to true joy. So I was thrilled at the thought of others discovering its blessings.

There is a story behind this book. It all began with a letter to Mother Martyria, then Erika Madauss, in 1936. I shared some thoughts on Micah 7:18 – "Who is a God like you, who pardons sin ...?"

Repentance had impacted our lives deeply, spreading to our youth and later our spiritual daughters. Many of our guests admitted associating repentance with sadness, gloom and legalism. Now they discovered for themselves that repentance can change everything, bringing true joy. They experienced reconciliation in families, churches, villages, neighbourhoods and between members of various nations.

The wide appeal of this book shows that nothing could be more precious than contrition and repentance. This is why I encouraged the sisters to reach out in faith:

> *Are we willing to keep on praying until the treasure of contrition and repentance is ours again? It will come at a cost, especially when our hearts have been hardened. But if we lack repentance, we lack everything. If we have repentance, we have everything we need, for repentance draws down God's grace.*
>
> *Believe me, repentance is the way to a joy-filled life; it is a well-spring of joy and love for Jesus. Yes, streams of joy and love flow from a heart full of repentance.*

EASTER – A RESURRECTION FOR CANAAN

As recovery set in, the blessings simply flowed. There seemed no limit to God's goodness to me after that painful year when I looked death in the face. It was a foretaste of heaven where the Lord will comfort us and overwhelm us with good gifts after grief and sorrow.

On Maundy Thursday, March 26, 1959, shortly before our twelfth anniversary, joyful singing broke out in the motherhouse. Why this sudden jubilation? Hadn't I already buried the vision for Canaan? Didn't we hold in our hands the official *no* from the highest authorities in our state of Hesse? So what had happened? A telephone call brought exciting news. Written permission was on its way for us to purchase state property in the area marked out for Canaan. God had intervened. What a miracle! The *no* had been reversed; and now it was *yes!*

What an Easter we celebrated that year. It was a resurrection for Canaan. Physically I had been raised as it were from the dead, and at the same time the commission for Canaan was resurrected. What God had said was coming true. Dark avenues of faith would end in light, dashed hopes in a glorious fulfilment of His promises. All our struggles would pay off. Canaan would materialize and serve to herald the dawning of God's kingdom.

The sisters were overjoyed. It was like a dream – too good to be true. But personally I could only cry when the news came; the wounds left by the disappointments ran too deep. I could hardly believe that God had indeed worked a miracle. How often Canaan had seemed ours, only to be snatched away again. But now God had given us the land. Canaan was ours and this was final. Deeply moved by such a token of God's grace, I wrote in my journal:

God has kept His word. My Father, You are utterly faithful. You are YES AND AMEN, You do what You say. My heart weeps for joy, because You haven't let me down. You are so good! I just can't take it in: You are giving us Canaan, just as You promised! Loving Father, I am not worthy of such goodness.

In prayer I asked the Lord for a word, and He gave me a verse that had often comforted me in the past:

> You have heard of Job's perseverance and have seen what the Lord finally brought about. The Lord is full of compassion and mercy. James 5:11

Isn't that just like our heavenly Father! He saw my suffering over Canaan and the unfulfilled promises, but all along He had a glorious outcome prepared.

Canaan was really ours! Now we could rest assured that the Lord would take care of the next stage: development of the land – and financing. Most importantly, we could trust Him to work the greatest miracle and enable Canaan to fulfil its destiny, just as He intended.

Canaan was to be a little land where God is glorified – His fatherly love acclaimed – heaven's love and joy manifested through a life of reconciliation. He would make all this come to pass, just as surely as He gave us Canaan: His gift to us at the end of thorny paths of suffering and faith. His purpose in allowing us to go through all those humiliations was to make us humble so that we didn't steal His glory. The many paths of discipline ensured there was no room for pride. "It's grace, sheer grace!" my heart sang.

A LIFE RESTORED AND NEW COMMISSIONS GRANTED, 1959 – 1964

MAKING THE PLACE OF HIS FEET GLORIOUS

Among the new commissions the Lord gave me was one that was a great blessing personally. It concerned the real Canaan, the Holy Land. Even before I fell critically ill, the Lord had been gently nudging me about this future ministry, improbable though it seemed. But now He renewed the call to seek out the places where He had lived and suffered. He was asking me to help make them come alive again spiritually – through love and prayer.

As Christians we will feel drawn to the places associated with Jesus' earthly life, the places where He loved and suffered. Who wouldn't want to trace His footsteps through the Kidron Valley, where His tears fell to the ground? Who wouldn't feel compelled to thank and honour Him at the places where He suffered? If we love Jesus, we will be grieved to see that many coming to the Holy Land are more like sightseers than pilgrims inspired by love. Spiritual death reigns at some of the places associated with the life of Jesus. Yet these were the places where He had worked miracles, places that had heard His prayers, His inner sighs and pleadings.

How Jesus longs for us to be responsive when we visit these sites. He longs for us to recommit ourselves for love of Him and embrace our cross in daily life. From the thousands flocking there from all over the world He longs for heartfelt worship in response to what He did for love of us. I could almost hear Jesus grieving over the indifference of believers; often there seemed little regard for the sanctity of the Holy Places.

Yet what could I do? How could I make a difference? God had graciously restored my life and given me fresh energy to work. Even so, the doctor did not recommend my travelling to the Holy Land: I would be going at my own risk.

Still, I knew we can't go wrong if we are obeying a call of God, provided we have confirmation. In this case the confirmation came from Mother Martyria, among others. So for this commission too, God gave me the assurance that I would not die but live – He would enable and strengthen me to fulfil this task. And that was just what happened.

To the amazement of the doctor, I was in better health on my return than before. God had touched me as I visited Jerusalem's Old City and the nearby Holy Places in 1959. He set my heart aflame! Each time I visited one of the Holy Places, Jesus was so close that everything He had done, said or suffered there seemed to be happening before my very eyes. That's how real it was.

In spirit I was drawn into the events there. The mocking at Lithostrotos, where He was crowned with thorns. His agony in Gethsemane. His suffering in the Kidron Valley, where as a captive He was driven like a lamb to the slaughter. My heart wept. I grieved at our audacity in binding the hands of the One through whom the world was made. In the Pater Noster Grotto on the Mount of Olives, traditionally the site of Jesus' end-time discourse, the Holy Spirit prompted me to write on the last days. An excerpt from my journal at that time reads:

> *Teach me about the end times, so that I can help believers to prepare. Holy Spirit, come upon me as the Spirit of wisdom and understanding, and give me insight into Your hidden purposes. Give me books to write – for this country and our own – about the approaching end.*

Little did I realize how God would answer this prayer in the coming years.

Jesus drew near to me at each of the places associated with His life. He gave me songs and devotional pieces about His love and suffering. With crowds thronging the sites, it can be hard to find a quiet spot for prayer and contemplation. But because the commission came from God, He wonderfully opened the way.

In Gethsemane I was able to spend hours in the church by myself, grieving for Jesus' pain in melodies spontaneously given by the Spirit of God. Even when the church was closed, I was allowed to stay. The Franciscan priest-in-charge, hearing me sing about Jesus' Passion, allowed me in at any time, even giving me access to the rocky area behind the church.

At Calvary, where the noise and commotion usually make it difficult to kneel and pray at the site of the cross for more than a few minutes, I was able to remain undisturbed for a long time. What happened long ago at Calvary came alive in a new way.

A powerful inner compulsion from the Holy Spirit drove me, though physically still weak, to retrace Jesus' steps through the Kidron Valley and along the Via Dolorosa. After every few steps I would pause to kneel in prayer. With a humble but joyful heart I gave thanks for the privilege of walking where He once walked.

I could continue with many more examples. At each Holy Place I had a living encounter with Jesus. This had nothing to do with accumulating knowledge or mentally taking in what had happened. I could feel the foundation being laid for this new ministry as Jesus revealed His presence at the Holy Places. Everything else would follow naturally. A seed had been planted, from which fruit would grow. And so it was.

Next I was shown what to do. Out of the songs and meditations, mainly composed during this trip, evolved a handbook for pilgrims: THE HOLY LAND TODAY. Thousands of booklets containing excerpts in various languages were distributed at the Holy Places and placed in hotels. People applied for our Holy

Land pilgrimages. The first, which I led personally, was followed by many others led by sisters.

As God worked in the hearts of the pilgrims, others were inspired. Someone wrote, "At the Sea of Galilee several other groups paused to hear the spiritual message. At the Mount of Beatitudes we were joined by hippies, obviously searching. At Calvary many were moved to tears by Jesus' suffering. At Mount Carmel everyone spontaneously joined in singing our songs. We ran out of our literature supplies in no time. Here and there at the Holy Places I saw people reading and praying from the Holy Land book. And as we sang songs of worship, others knelt with us ..."

But for the Lord this was still not enough. He wanted tangible, more permanent, tokens of His love that would still speak to people's hearts when a church was closed or no guide was present. So we produced Holy Land plaques with texts about the love of Jesus and His Passion to remind people of the real purpose of their visit amid all the attractions and commercialism. When human voices are silent, the very stones will speak.

> *Jesus now looks upon us with that same sad gaze. He sees us in our guilt and failure, He sees our tears of repentance. The more we weep for grieving Jesus, the deeper our love for Him will grow.*
>
> CHURCH OF ST. PETER IN GALLICANTU,
> COMMEMORATING PETER'S DENIAL

> *The glory of God shall be seen by those who put their faith in Jesus in times of greatest distress and hopelessness; they are certain that He is greater than any distress, even greater than death itself!* LAZARUS' TOMB

> *The hour of Transfiguration came for Jesus when He was about to enter the night of suffering and death. As members of His Body, we can only receive the grace of transfiguration, which He won for us, by following the same path – the pathway of humiliation and purification.* MOUNT TABOR

Such a project angered the evil one, as subsequent events showed. There was quite a disturbance in the Old City when we mounted a plaque on a house wall in the Via Dolorosa, although we did have the owner's permission. The crowd was in uproar, and the police led us off while the plaque was removed. The governor of Jerusalem, after interrogating us, forbade us to mount plaques in his district again. The Holy Places themselves were under protection as heritage sites. In addition, they were under the jurisdiction of the Roman Catholic and Orthodox Churches which, understandably at that time, were not in favour of Protestant nuns cementing plaques on the walls or entrances of their shrines.

Despite all this, just a few years later our plaques were mounted at many of the Holy Places, including the Garden of Gethsemane. God Himself opened the way for the commission He had given and enabled us to obtain the necessary permissions. As we later heard, the plaques helped many pilgrims and tourists to have a vital encounter with Jesus.

This was all part of God's plan. Pilgrims described the impact: "Cold and lifeless stones come alive through these plaques." – "They formed the golden thread running through my visit, linking up the Holy Places." – "A life-changing experience." Guides would point out the plaques and, where there were none, guardians of Holy Places would sometimes request plaques and care for them.

Ever deeper grew the longing to bring joy to Jesus at the Holy Places. How about a base on the Mount of Olives, the scene of His Agony and Return in glory? A few of my spiritual daughters could live there, singing and praying at the Holy Places and ministering to pilgrims. And how about a permanent memorial to Jesus' love and Passion at our future Land of Canaan? I'll never forget the moment God laid this on my heart as we drove through Samaria. Indeed, Canaan would one day have a prayer garden commemorating the Passion. For many it would be an opportunity to reflect on His amazing love and respond with heartfelt praise and thanksgiving.

Everything came to pass, just as the Lord had said. Years later the Garden of Jesus' Suffering and Resurrection was created as a place of prayer conveying the loving cry of His heart. The promise for a house on the Mount of Olives also came true. In 1962 the first sisters moved in. With its panoramic view of Jerusalem, it soon became a spiritual hub where pilgrims from various nations and traditions joined our sisters in prayer and in celebrating the Lord. All this was His doing.

After my return from the Holy Land in 1959, the Lord fulfilled yet another request close to my heart:

Give me something for my daughters for Holy Week – something that will help them to walk closely by Your side year after year. Give me something that will inspire us to worship You and bring comfort to Your heart.

Next year, in 1960, I recorded a meditation on Jesus' sufferings from Gethsemane to Calvary. It lasted several hours, and all the time I was aware of the Holy Spirit giving me the words to make it come alive. Love is what He seeks in response to His suffering for us; love which He has every right to expect. Year after year during Holy Week we come together as a community to relive the Passion story. The recordings, interspersed with songs and prayers, have helped my daughters grow in understanding of what Jesus endured for us. Over the years, countless retreat guests have joined us to share in the experience.

All this was the answer to my prayer that Jesus would reveal to believers more of His suffering heart, whether at the Holy Places in Jerusalem or in our motherhouse and retreat centre. And the more He revealed His Passion, the more love and thanksgiving He received.

With each new commission I made the same discovery: times of desolation when God seems far away are followed by times of grace. Acute pain gives way to deep joy as we sense His presence enfolding us. New life flows after debilitating illness. It is God's nature to reward. For months, hour by hour, I had surrendered my will to Him when everything seemed pointless. Now I saw that all the time He had been opening the way for an outpouring of His grace.

FILL ALL THE WORLD WITH SONGS OF PRAISE

For me, some of the most moving passages of Scripture are those where Jesus speaks of glorifying God or, as in His prayer in John 17, of having glorified Him. If there is one thing I wanted to live for, doing my small bit, it was to glorify God. All our commissions are sparked by the desire for God to be loved and honoured.

One day in May 1960 when spring had burst into glorious green and the air was filled with songbird chorus, I found myself composing song after song of praise to the Maker, recording the tunes as they came to me. Yet I felt God was asking for something more. So for love of Him I started putting up visible signs calling people to love and worship the One who alone is worthy. In 1952, at His prompting, we had already put up a crucifix in the woods behind our motherhouse, at a spot we call "Jesus' Resting-Place".

In 1956, while staying in Aeschi in the Swiss Alps, I was stunned by the sheer beauty of the alpine meadows, lakes and snow-capped mountains. Again I was seized with a passionate longing somehow to thank the Father for the glories of His world. If only I knew how!

In a letter to the sisters I wrote, "I would like nothing better than to build chapels and reminders of God everywhere." Practically there seemed no way. So nothing came of what the Lord had laid on my heart. Now, after He had restored my life, I was gripped with a fresh longing to glorify Him. I felt the Lord was asking, *Where are the signs you wanted to set up for Me?* Before destruction overtakes the world, I wanted to do all I could, calling people to praise God.

One day in 1960 a sister surprised me with a small kiln-fired clay tablet engraved with the words "God is love". Holding her gift in my hands, I had a sudden inspiration: What if we were to produce plaques like these on a larger scale? Bearing a Bible text or perhaps a song verse, they would serve as pointers at scenic spots, reminding people of their Maker and inspiring worship. The next step had now been shown!

What a special day it was when Mother Martyria and I set off with some sisters for the very first praise trip, our car "a praise chapel on wheels". As we drove through the magnificent Bavarian countryside, our constant refrain was a song given to me on the trip:

> Come, celebrate in song
> the awesome works of God,
> Creator of all things.
> No higher task than this:
> to glorify our God.

Improvising song after song, I sang my praises to the Father.

As Canaan's first praise singers we headed for places where God had earlier revealed to me the majesty of His creation and given me songs acclaiming His glory as the Maker. There we hoped to mount praise plaques as a token of our thanksgiving to God. But, as with almost every other commission the Lord had given, we soon ran into apparently insurmountable obstacles. This is bound to happen. God-given commissions are to glorify Him alone; and He is glorified most when we reach the end of our resources. So many practical issues arose that the praise ministry seemed to be over before it even began.

The most beautiful places were seldom private property. Some were even protected areas. Obtaining permission from the appropriate authorities was hopeless, I was told. Even with permission it wasn't all plain sailing, and some of our first attempts were highly dramatic. What an uproar ensued when we mounted plaques – with permission – at a popular tourist destination in Switzerland! In the storm of protest someone let the air out of our car tyres to make their point. It was a discouraging start. Our mission seemed doomed from the outset.

But faith breaks through all barriers if we are on fire for God and His kingdom. For Him, nothing is impossible (Luke 1:37). That I knew. Besides, I was asking in the name of Jesus. Could anything be dearer to His heart than seeing the Father glorified and people saved?

This is what the praise ministry was all about. It included outreach in the form of the printed word. People could help themselves from wooden "herald boxes" next to a number of praise plaques. What an opportunity to reach out to the hundreds, if not thousands, at popular tourist destinations in summer. The sisters' imagination was fired. Together we sang many songs of faith and impromptu verses as we brought our specific requests to the Lord.

We aimed high in faith. In Switzerland, for instance, a land of such outstanding natural beauty, the prospects were not encouraging. Not that this stopped us praying and thanking the heavenly Father for what He was going to do. In faith we claimed forty praise plaques at Switzerland's most beautiful scenic spots. Later we discovered we hadn't set our goals high enough! Within a few years over a hundred praise plaques in the Swiss Alps were calling people to glorify God. The plaques found their way to some of the highest and most spectacular mountains, their inscriptions acclaiming the Maker.

Our praise trip took us to Bavaria's Rossfeld Alm above Berchtesgaden. From here we had a view of the Obersalzberg, a mountain associated with a God-hater who allowed millions to deify him – Adolf Hitler. What if a monument glorifying the true God could be put up here at the Rossfeld Alm? Later, much to my joy, it became possible. From the Rossfeld Alm I saw the majestic Austrian mountains rising range upon range beyond the border. A song I had written earlier at this spot now rang in my heart:

All creation pays You homage,
Lord of life, King of the ages.
Mountains flee at Your rebuke.
High above earth's lofty regions,
High above the highest heavens,
Lord, there is no God like You!

On that day God burned into my heart the conviction that He was waiting for praise singers who would spend themselves to see Him glorified. By setting up visible signs and offering Him praise and worship, they would help defeat Satan's purposes. Impending disaster would be deferred.

Who could have foreseen that just a few years later the God-is-dead theology would penetrate churches? Or that God would have no option but to abandon humanity to shameless passions because we trod His holy laws underfoot and refused to honour and obey the Maker (Romans 1:18ff.)? Or that Christian audiences would applaud stage productions showing Jesus in a distasteful light? And who could have imagined that environmental pollution would become such an issue, with contaminated lakes and rivers, diseased forests, endangered species, and smog alerts in our big cities?

Even then God brought home to me the far-reaching significance of Revelation 14:7 for the end times: "Fear God and give him glory, because the hour of his judgment has come. Worship him who made the heavens, the earth, the sea and the springs of water." *Give God glory!* was the rallying cry God gave me for the dedication of the "Glory to God Chapel", our second praise chapel in Switzerland's Bernese Oberland. Part of this Bible verse is inscribed in mosaic on the chancel wall.

In those days relatively few grasped the importance of the call to give God glory. Yet I felt a stirring in my spirit. God was challenging us to make the best use of time to glorify Him. One way to achieve this would be to set up praise places and hold praise trips. Back then I wrote:

> *These praise outings will also serve Christian unity, as Protestants and Catholics unite in praising and worshipping the Maker.*

A few years later, that was exactly what happened.

Not that I was spared doubts. Would the plaques be worth the time, money and effort? Would they have any real impact on people's lives? All of a sudden everything seemed so pointless. Literature boxes were destroyed in various places. And what about volunteers? Would the necessary numbers be found to make it work? An entry in my journal reflected the urgency I felt:

> *We need to launch a campaign and encourage friends to put up plaques and literature boxes everywhere. What our sisters have so far accomplished is too little. Help me to write an inspiring letter to our friends so that they catch the vision for the praise ministry.*

Soon afterwards the newsletter was sent out, but the response was disappointing. It was hard to arouse interest in something as new and unfamiliar as the praise ministry, and here and there we encountered outright opposition. People expected us to engage in charitable works. This was a hurdle we had faced from the beginning, when we were building the Motherhouse Chapel. The issue resurfaced in 1962 at the building of the small praise chapel in Aeschi, Switzerland. Even friends objected. *Why build chapels? Why not hospitals? Wouldn't that make more sense?* Spending money on people's needs is guaranteed to earn approval, but not investing in projects solely for the glory of God, as I was to discover. Committed Christians were asking, *Why this waste?* – and that in spite of what Jesus said about doing "something beautiful" for Him (Mark 14:6–9).

In my journal I wrote:

> *Whether it's plaques at the Holy Places or plaques in the beauty of nature, we keep running into obstacles. It's always a battle. In the eyes of many, our ministries seem foolish and pointless, all because they are God-oriented rather than people-oriented –*

born of the desire to honour and glorify Him. You can go through the whole list of our ministries: they are all foreign to the average Christian. But how can the church's almost forgotten legacy of praise and worship be revitalized? How can it regain its appeal if no one is willing to risk opposition or look foolish?

In 1962, plans were underway to build the Praise Chapel in Aeschi, overlooking Lake Thun in the Swiss Alps. Did the evil one suspect the potential significance of this chapel as a place of never-ending praise? Did he guess that it would be visited by individuals and groups from many countries? Every imaginable obstacle cropped up.

Amid fierce opposition and speculation that we were a sect, we were refused building permission. Ascension Day, May 31, 1962, had been publicized as the dedication date, which now seemed impossible. But God spoke powerfully to me through His Word: "As for you, be strong and do not give up, for your work will be rewarded" (2 Chronicles 15:7). Hoping against hope, I trusted God for a miracle:

Because the flow of tears for the Aeschi chapel seems never-ending, it will be a chapel of never-ending praise, the flame of praise enduring beyond coming destruction. You will fulfil Your glorious work, for suffering always ends in glory. And that goes for this project.

God intervened in the nick of time. Three and a half weeks before the dedication date, building permission was granted. That was the first miracle. The second miracle followed. Construction progressed at record speed: by Ascension Day the chapel was ready for dedication.

Since then this chapel has been a testimony that God is always greater. Hell may rage when God is to be glorified. But God will win through in the end. No human refusal can stop or deter Him from sovereignly completing His work. Small, unpretentious and out of the way, the Aeschi chapel is a much-visited place. Here people are inspired to give God glory. Some have found relief through confesssion, and joyful worship has risen from hearts set free from sin and guilt.

Sacrifice, suffering, faith – including believing for finances – everything that went into this chapel has brought rich dividends. Once more we have seen that when it comes to glorifying God we should not skimp or hold back.

But where were those who for love of God would help fill the world with places of praise? It was a long while before the praise ministry made headway. Only by ignoring the voices of opposition and listening solely to God was I able to persevere. God's thoughts are higher and different from human thoughts. His commissions may seem humanly foolish. Yet I knew I had to obey Him even if I had the whole world against me.

As a spiritual legacy to my daughters I wrote:

My dear daughters,

For each God-given commission, each revelation, each time God graciously draws near, there can be a high price to pay. Don't let hard times shake your confidence in God. Don't be put off when huge obstacles arise and you agonize whether the commission is really from God.

The very fact that you are agonizing could well be a sign of authenticity. Spiritual attacks are bound to occur when you receive a God-given revelation, inspired by His Spirit. The unmerited favours of God need to be spiritually digested and worked through in order to be fruitful. A ministry from God needs to be undergirded with trials and temptations.

God always works on us first before using us as a channel of blessing for others. Being blessed ourselves is not enough. How many believers have become an offence instead of a blessing? Why? Because they didn't process the blessings but exploited them for their own benefit. They didn't want to walk the path of discipline, inner conflict and testing, which would have made the blessings fruitful. Walk this path, and the blessings will be increased a hundredfold.

Because this praise ministry was of God and carried the seed of divine life, it eventually made headway – first among our Canaan Friends, then the wider public. When God gives a commission, He will also open doors and raise up people to support the vision. Subsequent events bearing His signature of YES AND AMEN will demonstrate this. God does what He says, and we will see a glorious fulfilment of what we believed.

A city park official in America commented: "Why, it's a privilege and an honour to have such plaques in our park!" A forest ranger in the Odenwald gave permission for several praise places at once. Having seen them in Switzerland and the Black Forest, he was enthusiastic about the idea. A tribal chief in Ghana helped mount a praise plaque himself and promised to make it known and protect it from vandalism. A shopkeeper in Heligoland, for example, had a postcard made of the plaque in response to the many requests.

Coming across a plaque unexpectantly "almost takes your breath away", wrote one Canadian. "They are filled with love for Jesus." An Argentine missionary recounted: "We made an excursion to a tourist attraction, a 'natural window' at an altitude of 1200 metres. Fifty Christians gathered below, while thirty-five climbed to the top in order to mount the plaque. Afterwards we spent time praising God for all His works. We hope to go on together and fill the national parks and other scenic spots in Latin America with the praise of God."

"Wherever I go – whether it's Gethsemane, La Verna, Assisi, Switzerland or the Odenwald, I discover plaques praising God," wrote the sister-in-charge of a deaconess house. And a forest ranger in Arizona was so keen to have plaques in his territory that he not only gave the go-ahead. He promised to have his staff bring rocks for plaques to be mounted on if there were none at the site.

Hundreds of plaques in many different languages now place a divine seal on scenic spots and tourist destinations from the Norwegian fjords to the Pauline sites in Greece; from the stillness of the Himalayas to the Grand Canyon, which draws up to 20,000 visitors daily in the summer months. Every time a letter arrives reporting of a new plaque, my heart rejoices that yet again a sign has been raised pointing people to God.

Our friends increasingly caught the vision. In faith they launched out, sparing no effort to see God glorified. They persevered even in the face of huge obstacles, and if plaques were dismantled they resumed the challenge, nothing daunted. Such was their passion for God to be praised and worshipped that by 1973 approximately 600 praise plaques had been mounted in Germany and over 120 in Switzerland.

For many years, open-air devotions were held regularly during the peak season at the site of a plaque on the Baltic coast of Germany. At a notorious suicide spot in England the local town council erected a plinth for a praise plaque near the cliff edge to counter the culture of death and promote worship of God. Word sometimes reaches us that praise plaques have indeed prevented people from taking their lives.

Worshipping God and giving Him glory is the true purpose of our lives. Living and working for Him to be praised in the splendour of His creation is a wonderful privilege. In doing so we focus on the Maker of the universe, the all-powerful, all-wise, sovereign God, whose purposes are beyond comprehension. All things come from Him and to Him all things will return. That's why the praise ministry has been such a blessing, enriching my life more than words can say.

CALLED TO WARN OF IMPENDING DISASTER

A new lease on life brought new commissions from God, plus a fresh set of challenges as a result of living in the end times. By the early 1960s a new era was dawning, though at first it remained shadowy and indistinct. In the following years the rise of revolutionary movements, the brushing aside of God's laws and the sapping of the church's moral fibre were cause for concern. But who could have foreseen that we were witnessing the onset of the great falling away among Christians of all traditions? At the time the situation was relatively calm.

In the winter season of 1960–1961 I withdrew again to the small Trinity Chapel for some weeks of quiet prayer. Suddenly – I don't know how or why – I was gripped with a burning sense of urgency. Critical times lay ahead, and people needed to be alerted. Under the prompting of the Holy Spirit I worked continually on a new book entitled Lo, He Comes, published in German in August 1961. Our loving Father in heaven knew what the future held. So this book was also intended as a challenge for Christians to make the most of the time. Jesus is coming again, and He wants to welcome His Bride to an eternity of unspeakable joy and glory. To those who call Him Lord He wants to come as Bridegroom, not as Judge. He is loath to pronounce those devastating words, "I don't know you." He wants to spare them the pain of standing before a closed door and realizing it is too late. No cry of desperation can then reverse God's verdict (Matthew 25).

In my spirit I could see all this unfolding. More than ever I felt compelled to sound the warning: *Time is running out. An avalanche has been set in motion that will lead to the great falling away and usher in the anti-Christian era. Divine judgment will descend in an attempt to turn people's hearts back to God. We are rapidly approaching the Day of the Lord.*

Long, dark weeks followed as I faced the implications. Alone with God, I began to write about the coming end. First I had to taste something of God's anguished wrath over a humanity made in His image and now sinking in a cesspool of iniquity. The previous experience of God's wrath in 1957 enabled me to write about it. This time the agony was no less real. The full horror of impending judgment weighed on me as did the rising tide of sin worldwide. From my journal:

> *I am overcome with grief. It's like mourning the loss of someone you love. My heart is burdened by the harrowing events of our times and God's pain over a world lost in sin ... Despite my frailty, I am driven to complete the book* Lo, He Comes. *The perverse anti-Christian spirit of the end times, the terrors that lie ahead, fill the innermost recesses of my soul with intense pain ... Never before have I written in such inner anguish.* November 1960

I continued to write, though logically it made no sense. Who would read this book? Those who had always opposed my chosen path and my calling would object all the more: *Look at the religious fanatic, the doomsday prophet, with her sweeping black-and-white prognosis of an imminent end of the world.* More than ever, people would be warned to steer clear of my books. But God's love overcame my reluctance. I caught a glimpse of His heart aching for His children. At the Spirit's prompting, I continued to reach out, sounding the warning for believers to prepare for the coming times.

It was a difficult message to deliver – one that I sincerely hoped never to have to bring again. But this was not to be. Christmas 1960 made that evident. The corridors of our motherhouse rang with the triumphant words of Isaiah 9:6 set to music – *Unto us a child is born, a son is given, and the government is upon his shoulders.* That year the mystery of Christmas would have a very special emphasis, as the Spirit showed me while I was in seclusion. The coming King of kings was already present in the Child Jesus. From the moment He entered this world, the government was upon His shoulders, His future majesty only hidden from our sight. What a joyful, victorious message in an age when Satan is extending his sphere of influence. When Jesus comes again in glory, He will have dominion over all the kingdoms of the world.

On the Second Day of Christmas our Hall of Zion resounded with songs of adoration as we worshipped the Infant King: "Crown Him, crown Him Lord of all ..." After the last strains of the hymn faded away, we discussed various ways of honouring Jesus. The conversation turned to the forthcoming dedication ceremony of the Herald Chapel in May 1961. "We simply must have a Herald Play about Jesus coming again as King in the end times. Please, Mother Basilea, write one. We'll pray!" – "Well, I'm afraid you will have to forgo the evening celebration and come together in small groups to pray. Tomorrow I will withdraw and see if the Holy Spirit will give me the first draft for a script." It was the right moment. I could feel the prompting of the Spirit.

The following evening I returned to the Hall of Zion. Our hearts were filled with thanksgiving as we listened to a recording of the first draft, given in answer to prayer. From morning till night I had sensed the Holy Spirit's inspiration as I recorded both words and tunes on tape. For me, receiving all this in a single day was truly remarkable.

Together we rejoiced. At the same time I felt a great weight of responsibility resting on me. The book LO, HE COMES and the Herald Play on the same theme were only the beginning of something new. From then onwards I was led to write pamphlets on contemporary issues. A prophetic ministry entails a foretaste of the suffering and judgment that will come as a result of the sins of our nation and the whole world, including the sins of the church. It entails foreseeing the coming events and experiencing them in advance. Only at the cost of such priestly suffering can the pain and sense of urgency in God's own heart be conveyed.

The new ministries entrusted to me after my recovery brought me conflict from within and without. Foolish in the eyes of the world, they invited antagonism and humiliation. The pain and sense of burden intensified. Spiritually, a price had to be paid for each new pamphlet on contemporary issues. Having to study material that documented vice and apostasy was particularly distressing. I came face to face with sheer evil.

This was a ministry that left me feeling particularly isolated and misunderstood in the Christian world at large. In general, our churches had neglected the end-time message. The tendency was to regard the book of Revelation as mere symbolism rather than biblical truth. Granted, the Pietist tradition had long respected and upheld end-time teaching, continuing to attempt to interpret the signs of the times. Many Christians, however, had been lulled into a false sense of security by misconceptions regarding conversion and the Rapture. With the rise of the charismatic renewal the gifts of the Spirit regained their biblical place. This included the gift of prophecy. Still, there was little understanding for the message: The end is near! "Too gloomy," was the general opinion. "Out of touch with today's mindset."

Even among friends and guests at our retreats, I struggled to get through with this message. With other topics it was so much easier. Whenever I talked about the end times, I was aware of resistance. Barriers had to be broken down, even though it is an important theme in the Bible, one that Jesus often preached on. So I had serious reservations, particularly as a woman, whenever the sisters suggested doing a mass mailing of one of my messages on contemporary issues. For me, it went totally against the grain. But I sensed that God wanted it.

And now this commission was to become an integral part of my life. How was I to meet this challenge? Only equipped with a greater love for God and a glimpse of His anguished heart (Genesis 6:6). Only a greater love for a world running headlong into disaster could prompt me to keep on warning, pleading, reaching out in love, regardless of the flak I would take.

In answer to prayer, God increased my love for Him and for people. This alone stopped me from yielding to the cry of despair from my heart: *If only I didn't have to know, hear or write anything more about these terrible matters!* However, the burden of this ministry remained. And since the Lord had entrusted it to me, He saw to it that I was almost better informed than the sister who daily read the newspapers to keep the rest of us abreast of current events. It was as if the Lord had turned my heart into a receptor for the issues of the day.

While writing TODAY, A TIME LIKE NONE BEFORE, I noted in my journal:

> *Disaster is inevitable. I clearly see it coming. We live in the era of God's wrath, the end times, when people's hearts will fail with fear and foreboding at what will happen to the world ... The air is pregnant with doom. Destruction threatens on a scale never seen before ... It is a race with time to carry out our ministry before disaster strikes.*

My great concern was that the sisters would not close their eyes to reality but be ready for the trials ahead. I wanted Jesus to be so real to them that they could approach the future with confidence, strong in the Lord. Embracing the cross is the way to overcoming in suffering. With my daughters in mind, I copied out many words of encouragement from the Bible, later writing a book on overcoming fear and growing in trust.

This was to set the tone for the Christmas celebrations in 1961 and 1962. Christmas 1962 in particular ministered comfort to our hearts through the awareness of Jesus entering this dark world to save us and defeat the powers of darkness. Again and again we sang songs specially composed at that time.

Dearest Child, You came to darkness,
Shining brightly in the night,
In a world now ripe for judgment,
Sinking in its hopeless plight.

Yet Your radiance shines the brighter
O'er our sinful misery,
And You lead our world in triumph
Out of death to victory.

Later these songs were published, as well as various books with encouraging messages such as HIDDEN IN HIS HANDS and FATHER OF COMFORT. God was calling me not only to warn and alert people but also to offer encouragement. What a privilege. Having tasted something of the pain and misery in advance, I could point to the source of help for times when comfort is scarce. Among us there was a deep sense of peace, born of the assurance that in times of testing we would experience the loving care of the heavenly Father as never before.

Hard as this task was, it was not in vain.

SONGS AND FESTIVALS OF HEAVEN

Was I really a "doomsday prophet", as my critics claimed? Surely not. All God's leadings in my life, in both practical and spiritual matters, taught me that ours is a God of hope and love. With God suffering is never the final outcome. Light follows darkness, joy follows sorrow. What He begins, He completes. The fury of hell signals the triumph of heaven. At the height of the Antichrist's wrath, the cry of jubilation will resound throughout heaven: "The kingdom of the world has become the kingdom of our Lord and of his Messiah, and he will reign for ever and ever" – "The wedding of the Lamb has come" (Revelation 11:15; 19:7). Every pamphlet in the series on current issues contained this joyous perspective. One reader wrote: "I have highlighted the places referring to heaven, the return of Christ and the coming glory in bright yellow. Some of the pages in your messages on contemporary issues are all yellow! My heart soars in joyful anticipation ..."

After the "year of death" the Lord granted me a foretaste of heaven. It was a renewal of the blessing I received after my Moriah experience. Now I was able to convey heaven's reality as never before. Till then I never had the feeling that my songs and booklets about heaven really got through to my daughters or to friends and guests. When I first started writing about heaven in 1956, I wrote in my journal:

It is my prayer today that heaven will come down when these songs are sung. Please work this miracle and let the words come to life. You know how hard I often find it to write these songs. Sometimes they seem like a waste of time and not even particularly good. But heaven's presence is very real today, and I sense the songs are from You, just as You promised. So hear my prayer and speak Your YES AND AMEN, fulfilling Your word.

After that difficult year of 1958 the Lord began to answer this prayer. Heavenly joy flowed, carrying the sisters in its tide. We celebrated festivals of heaven like never before. Who can help celebrating when heaven comes down! As the Bible says, "You have come to Mount Zion, to the city of the living God, the heavenly Jerusalem. You have come to thousands upon thousands of angels in joyful assembly, to the church of the firstborn, whose names are written in heaven" (Hebrews 12:22–23). Celebrations and festive gatherings are integral to heaven, where praise and worship fill the air.

A deeper spiritual cleansing in our community probably contributed to this new responsiveness among the sisters. Under His hand of discipline, they too had learnt to love and revere the holy God at a deeper level after tasting something of His wrath. This gave our festivals of heaven a firm foundation. To quote a pastor from abroad: "It seems to me that to 'feast the Lord' is a special charisma He has given you at Canaan. This is why I feel especially drawn here. Joyous festivity is what makes heaven heaven. And as I have discovered, the greater the repentance, the greater the joy."

Festivals of heaven don't follow a set programme. We simply come together, acclaiming Jesus, the crown of heaven, in song after song. Caught up in worship, we never tire of proclaiming His glories. He is the King of Heaven, the Lamb enthroned on high. Singing in the Spirit, we find ever new ways of expressing our worship. Then the focus turns to what awaits believers in heaven.

Joy is diffused, and even the sad of heart are uplifted. Soon our Hall of Zion lights up with the glory of heaven. As we invite heaven into our midst with the song "Oh, that we were there!", we often end up singing the many verses all over again. It is impossible to give full expression to heaven's joy.

I wrote this song at a time of intense darkness. It was shortly before the death of Sister Angelika, who was suffering acutely as she lay in bed. I longed to comfort her but didn't know how. Leaving her bedside, I went into my room to pray, and as I prayed, the Lord gave me a glimpse of heaven's glory. One verse after the other flowed from my pen, and I hurried back to sing the verses to her. All of a sudden her pain seemed to vanish. Sister Angelika's face lit up, and despite her weakness she sang along. Heaven had come down.

Years later many others were singing this song too. I remember one festival of heaven we celebrated in our Herald Chapel with retreat guests. There were a lot of young people there. I went with some trepidation, as I had not spared them the harsh reality of our times during my Bible talk that morning. I referred to "the age of death" into which they had been born, with destruction threatening body, soul and spirit. Referring to the powers of darkness, I warned them of coming persecution, which might cost some of them their lives as martyrs. But I also encouraged them. They were a chosen generation who might live to see the final outcome – the coming of Jesus in glory. Our times herald the soon-coming King. If they were counted among those who love the Lord, the overcomers, they might well be privileged to witness what generations of believers had longed for these past two thousand years – the Rapture, that day of supreme joy and glory when Jesus will come for His bride.

That night there was an outpouring of joy as we celebrated our festival of heaven. We had seldom experienced anything like it. During the Bible talk in the morning the young people had been confronted with the hard times ahead. They had heard the call to repentance and had responded with open hearts. Now they were blessed with a joy that matched their commitment, for the greater the pain, the greater the joy. They were gripped by an overwhelming longing for heaven. With all the love of their hearts they joined in our songs of heaven, raising palm branches in honour of Jesus, King of heaven. Singing about heaven actually brought heaven down. Those who just that morning had been under a cloud of apprehension, struggling to come to terms with the future, couldn't stop singing that night. All of Canaan rang with songs of heaven. And it wasn't to be the last time.

How thrilled I was that festivals of heaven became a regular feature in our community. When a festival of heaven first appeared as an annual item on our printed programme, someone wrote: "We would love to come, but could you please explain what this is? We're not sure what to make of it." The festivals went on to be the highlight of our retreats and a long-standing favourite with the summer youth community. On one occasion we didn't initially invite the boys as space was limited. Hearing of this, one of them prayed that God would put it into my heart to include them after all. He kept praying and that was exactly what happened. Another time someone phoned to say, "Tonight we are celebrating a festival of heaven, just like we had at Canaan."

Then there was the pastor who came with a busload from a thoroughly traditional church. He commented that even weeks later the congregation were still enthusiastically singing "Jerusalem, O City High and Fair" – the festival of heaven had lost none of its lustre.

I once wrote to my daughters:

Think of heaven, and your suffering will pale in comparison with the eternal glory yet to be revealed in you. When you hear the word "heaven", know that the future joy is everlasting and that one day your suffering will be over. Live more in the awareness of heaven; focus more on the things above! It's worth it. Heaven is where you will be at home for ever. This will help you to see things in perspective and distinguish between what really counts in eternity and what doesn't. Sing about heaven. Celebrate festivals of heaven when life is at its darkest. Only heaven can banish hell. Heaven is stronger than hell, for Jesus is the Lord of heaven. "Blessed are you who weep now, for you will laugh." (Luke 6:21) *So give yourself to suffering if you want to taste heaven.*

I would often remind the sisters that there is great power in thinking and singing about heaven, focussing on what is to come. Our suffering dwindles before the glory of heaven that awaits us. And whenever heaven draws near, as has been my experience since 1956, our longing for heaven will grow. With it will come an ever greater yearning to be made fit for heaven, reflecting the glories of His nature. Only overcomers will reach the goal of glory.

It's hard talking on themes like judgment and suffering, the reality of sin and demonic powers in our times. So I was thankful for the privilege of focussing on the heavenly glory and declaring, *Jesus is coming soon – as the heavenly Bridegroom!* He had entrusted me with the two-fold message that had been His own: "Repent, for the kingdom of heaven is at hand" (Matthew 3:2 NKJV). In this I saw His great love.

YOUR KINGDOM COME

One of my bitterest experiences during my critical illness in 1958 and 1959 was burying a vision dear to my heart. Since the earliest days of our community I had prayed for something of God's kingdom of heaven to become real among us – here and now. But so far nothing had come of the vision God had given.

Now things were to change. This was a time of blessing, of restoration, when God delighted to shower me with goodness as if in reward for my time of illness. Not only did He give back what had seemed lost: He multiplied it. And He made good His word in Romans 5:20: "Where sin increased, grace increased all the more". What a mighty Saviour we have in Jesus! Canaan began to take shape before our eyes. But it was not the grounds and buildings that defined it or gave it its distinctive character. There are more beautifully situated pieces of land, and we were not the only ones to undertake building projects by faith. No, what really glorified Jesus was the atmosphere. Here were people living in reconciliation because they knew God's forgiveness. What Paul said of the church in Philippi I could now say of my daughters: "my joy and crown" (Philippians 4:1).

From our earliest beginnings at Steinberg House I had longed for God's promise to come true among us: "The LORD has chosen Zion, he has desired it for his dwelling, saying, 'This is my resting place for ever and ever; here I will sit enthroned, for I have desired it'" (Psalm 132:13–14). To me that would be like the dawning of the kingdom of heaven. Now, after many disappointments, I was privileged to see something of this come true among us. By walking in the light, admitting where we've grieved the Lord and one another, we invite God's presence. God chooses to dwell in the contrite and broken of heart (Isaiah 57:15).

I still remember my feeling of joy and thanksgiving upon my return from a long trip. As I walked into our Hall of Zion, where the sisters had gathered to welcome me, I thought I was in a brightly lit room. Yet it wasn't the good lighting but the radiance of the sisters that I saw. Jesus was shining out of them.

But now the Lord was showing me something new. His desire was for a foreshadowing of heaven not just at Canaan but in other countries too, starting with Jerusalem, the centre of the world. The Lord wanted multiple Canaan centres emanating love, peace and joy. Visitors would have a glimpse of heaven, a foretaste of the grand finale of God's saving purposes: the Marriage Supper of the Lamb.

The Bride of the Lamb will form the new Jerusalem (Revelation 21:9ff). So it follows that, wherever she is, she will live and pray for something of the heavenly Jerusalem to be manifested here and now. This was a vision I had carried deep in my heart for Canaan, and now it was to characterize our branches too. The shining transparency of the City of God would be reflected when we as a community walked in the light, facing the truth of our personal sins and failings. God's gracious shining presence would descend, consuming everything that stands in His way, and transforming everyone willing to come into the light.

Each Canaan centre would be a place of happiness, song and celebration, reflecting the City of God above and demonstrating the joy arising from tears of repentance. Father, Son and Holy Spirit would be the focus of every heart, as with the living creatures at the throne of God. Sisters living in the unity of love would impact others. The very houses would breathe peace and harmony, touching everyone who came. In my spirit I could already see it happen.

The more the nations of our world resembled a turbulent sea churning up filth, the greater the significance of "islands of God's holy presence". From sanctuaries such as these, God's light and power would shine forth. Life-lines would be thrown out to draw people to their Saviour Jesus for an encounter with the love of God. Souls would be rescued from the brink of disaster and believers strengthened in their faith.

Such sanctuaries, if grounded in repentance, will not be destroyed when the waves come crashing down. Though the forces of evil may rage and inflict suffering, they cannot destroy these islands of holiness. It is just as Jesus said of the church, "the gates of hell shall not prevail against it" (Matthew 16:18 KJV).

Though mere dots on the map, our Canaan centres would have a far-reaching impact so long as the flame of love burned in them. Of this I was sure. And in every country those who share the vision of His coming kingdom will gravitate towards each other. People will be inspired to live by the laws of the kingdom of heaven. Daily they enter the gateway of repentance and willingly die to self, so that God's kingdom, His rule of love, can dawn.

Thanksgiving filled my heart for what God had planned for me in restoring my life. Truly His plans are "for good and not for disaster" (Jeremiah 29:11 NLT). Soon everything began to materialize. In 1961, in the still-divided Jerusalem He gave us Beth Abraham in the New City, and then in 1962 the Moriah House, the predecessor of Beit Gaudia Dei, on the Mount of Olives – our first two foreign branches and both in His Holy Land!

MOUNT SINAI – THE CLIMAX OF MY LIFE 1963 – 1969

WEEKS OF SOLITUDE AT MOUNT SINAI

The year 1963 stands out in my memory. It was the year I visited Mount Sinai. In response to God's summons, I had long considered seeking the solitude there to receive further directives from Him about our ministry. Now, as the plan began to take shape, I found myself asking, "Is this really a call of God? Is it His will? Couldn't I receive His directives just as easily in my prayer room at Canaan?" Doubts plagued my mind. I felt myself resisting the call, even though the Spirit of God kept reminding me of the verse, "My thoughts are not your thoughts, neither are your ways my ways" (Isaiah 55:8). God's plans are different from ours and beyond the scope of our human understanding.

Why shouldn't God meet me in the solitude of the desert if He should so choose? Why shouldn't He call me to such a remote location as His holy mountain? Why not indeed, if He intended to give me a new commission that would extend to the nations? I gave Him my yes. Joyful anticipation began to grip me.

Then came a traveller's account of Mount Sinai, and my doubts returned in full force. By all reports there was no chance of quiet prayer. No single rooms. Noisy tourists within the monastery precints, and venturing out alone unadvisable. Quality quiet time seemed more or less ruled out. Yet this was the main point of the trip. As if that wasn't enough, seasoned travellers rated the trip to Sinai as highly strenuous. That summer I was struggling with serious health issues: I felt disqualified from the outset. The high travelling costs seemed hardly justified. Inner conflict raged, wearing me down.

Still, I was afraid that I might be opposing God if this really was His will. Often enough I had seen how seemingly pointless, irrational leadings result in great commissions of God. I knew that the foolishness of God is wiser than human wisdom (1 Corinthians 1:25). I felt buffeted on all sides by waves of turmoil. Yet inner conflict seemed to be part of God's plan. An encounter with God is always preceded by dark times of testing when we are reduced to nothing. Then His light, which cannot blend with our fallen human intellect, will break through. Figuratively speaking, there was only one way to His holy mountain: through the wilderness. How else could I meet the great and holy God? Times of testing would prepare me, bringing me to a place of humility. But then a Bible verse received in prayer was such a confirmation of His call that it took my breath away. "I am God, the God of your father ... Do not be afraid to go down to Egypt, for I will make you into a great nation there. I will go down to Egypt with you, and I will surely bring you back again." (Genesis 46:3–4)

Remarkably, I received a visa for Egypt – no matter of course, since I had authored a book entitled Israel, My Chosen People and founded Beth Abraham in Jerusalem.

On October 8, 1963, I set out, though in poor health, and on the very first day I experienced the healing touch of the Lord. For me it was miraculous. I felt new life coursing through my body, soul and spirit. Imbued with His resurrection strength, I was able to manage the journey – three days and nights with almost no sleep.

From Suez we embarked on the drive through the desert, which lasted many hours. I was greeted by the sight of the mountains with their striking rock formations and varying hues glistening in the sun. Eternal silence reigned in the desert. Not a sound to be heard, not a person to be seen, except at the oasis of Rephidim.

When we finally reached our destination, St. Catherine's Monastery, I was overwhelmed by the sheer majesty of God. There stood the desert mountains, giants of granite and gneiss, as solid and unchanging as the Ten Commandments God delivered to His people here.

St. Catherine's Monastery, a miniature city with chapels and houses ringed in by a high wall, lay at the foot of Moses' Mountain, in the imposing Sinai massif. Since the sixth century the monastery has been home to Greek Orthodox monks. One wing is set aside for guests. As we entered the monastery precincts, one question was uppermost in my mind. Would the Lord miraculously provide me with a single room where I could pray in peace and quiet? Sister Benedicta approached the guest brother on my behalf: he shook his head at the very idea. Only shared rooms were available in the guest wing. But in the course of the conversation the Lord gave him a change of heart, and I was allocated a three-bedded room all to myself! My heavenly Father had paved the way for me, confirming His call to spend weeks in seclusion at Sinai. Such love touched me deeply. From my room I had a view of Moses' Mountain, glowing red at sunrise.

In His goodness God provided me with another quiet spot where I could pray – the flat roof of the building. There I spent whole days in undisturbed prayer and writing. I was almost always alone. Surrounded by towering mountains, I had a view to the west of the broad Raha Plain in the Sinai massif's hollow – the scene of God's amazing actions. This is where the Israelites camped when God made a covenant with them and gave them His laws at Sinai.

And so I was spared the noise and commotion of the monastery compound. The voice of inner conflict was silenced as I repeatedly saw God fulfil His promises in concrete ways. A strict time-honoured rule limited monastery visits to three days: in my case it was overruled. Permission was granted by the highest authorities for me to extend my stay by several weeks – yet another confirmation that God had called me to His holy mountain.

God graciously provided for our daily needs as well. It was certainly a challenge, as we couldn't buy or cook our own food, nor bring supplies for weeks, and in any case nothing would keep for long in the intense heat. We were constantly surprised by the Father's loving care. One day a monk presented us with magnificent grapes from Rephidim. The monks, in an unusual gesture, kindly provided us with bread from the monastery bakery. Tourists left us their remaining provisions. A Bedouin brought us eggs and even meat. Every day we tasted the heavenly Father's gracious provision, often quite remarkably.

God was paving the way, taking care of every detail, for there in the solitude of the desert I was to have an encounter with Him.

SINAI – the holy mountain of God, where He entered a covenant with human beings, with His people (Deuteronomy 5:2).

SINAI – the mountain where Moses was privileged to encounter the Lord and hear Him speaking.

SINAI – the mountain where God made known His will to His people, and by extension to all peoples, through His commandments.

Sinai – the mountain of divine revelation! How could I have approached Sinai without having first undergone a year of preparation, marked by physical suffering and sickness, mental anguish and spiritual trials?

In the first twelve days the Lord began to speak to me. He spoke so powerfully that I felt as if the events of long ago were happening now. First, Sinai became for me the place where God gave us His commandments as the divine standard to show us our sins and failings. The daily text for October 13, 1963, my third day, was "Love your neighbour as yourself" (Leviticus 19:18), and the verse for the week was "And he has given us this command: anyone who loves God must also love their brother and sister" (1 John 4:21). Familiar as these commands of God were to me, they cut me to the core. Heartfelt tears of repentance flowed. I wept for the times I had sinned against God's law of love and failed to act in love. I knew that before *ascending* that holy mountain, Moses' Mountain, I needed to *descend*, bringing my sins to the Lord to be cleansed by the blood of the Lamb. Deeper and deeper I descended, humbling myself in spirit for my own failings but also on behalf of my daughters. Then the Lord lifted me up.

The day came for the ascent of Moses' Mountain, a day rich in blessings. Calm, bright and not too hot, it also happened to be my birthday. At six in the morning I set out on camelback for the first leg of the journey. With its contours clearly outlined against the sky, Moses' Mountain was a strikingly beautiful sight. Waves of bliss flooded my heart. I felt as if the Lord was waiting for me at the summit where Moses' Chapel stands. How I longed to meet with Him in the stillness. In spite of my heart condition, I fairly flew up the huge, roughly-hewn granite Steps of Repentance for the last stretch of the way, a forty-five-minute climb following the camel-ride.

As I reached the top of the holy mountain my eyes were met by a sea of peaks stretching out before me in every direction. An awe-inspiring sight for sheer beauty and grandeur: range upon majestic range of rocky summits bearing witness to the elemental force of creation. Here I began to understand the meaning of God's name of Yahweh – I AM WHO I AM (Exodus 3:14). I experienced the truth of His words, "I will cause all my goodness to pass in front of you" (Exodus 33:19). He drew near as the God who enters a covenant with a sinful human being, every sin covered by the blood of the Lamb. What God now granted me on Moses' Mountain was for real. As a gift of His Spirit, who calls into being things that do not yet exist (Romans 4:17), He gave me a love I had not known before. It was a God-given love for the nations of the world, which He created to His glory. Love was the prerequisite for the new commission to the nations He was now entrusting to me.

He filled me with a spirit of compassion and pity for the nations heading for their downfall as a result of abandoning God's holy laws. From then on I was inwardly compelled to lift the nations up in prayer daily that souls might be saved from the morass of the sins typical of this age. In this newly awakened love I felt as though nothing could stop me. Whatever He showed me I would do to the best of my ability. The lifelines of God's love needed to be thrown out to the nations: His commandments, designed to save us from destruction.

From then on the nations had a place in my heart and were a part of my life as I travailed for them in prayer. Without this experience I could not possibly have released sisters shortly afterwards for a ministry in foreign countries. God had equipped me with a sacrificial, priestly love. Now I was moved by compassion to stand in the breach for the nations of the world. It was a significant day for our ministry: a day of divine favour.

God also blessed me with a new gift of faith for this new, far-reaching ministry to the nations. The sheer magnitude of the task would otherwise have been daunting. I was keenly aware of my inadequacy.

But greater than all else was the encounter with the Lord Himself on Moses' Mountain. What a day of divine grace! God Himself was present. And inextricably linked with the experience of His nearness was the tremendous commission He gave.

The heavenly Father sealed the events of that day with an impressive natural phenomenon. Late in the afternoon, as I made the descent, I paused to rest on a projecting rock three-quarters of the way down. Suddenly a magnificent rainbow formed a perfect arc over the spot, although the rainy season hadn't yet begun. God was confirming His covenant and His commission. What happened at Sinai long ago was not just for then: it was for now. This I experienced for myself. God caused all His goodness to pass before me and revealed His nature to me: "merciful and gracious, long-suffering, and abundant in goodness and truth" (Exodus 34:6 KJV).

That day when I first ascended Moses' Mountain was the highlight of my stay. Those hallowed hours set the tone for the remaining weeks with all they were to bring. As I looked back over my life in the stillness of prayer, God helped me to see my struggles in the light of eternity. Suddenly I was able to trace His hand guiding everything towards a wonderful goal. What had seemed meaningless at the time held a deep significance as part of His perfect counsels. But above all, His light shone on the future. He lit up the way ahead, indicating the ministries He had in store for us. He gave me our Rule. The sisters welcomed this short manual for applying God's commandments in the Bible to everyday situations. I wrote a similar Rule for the Thorn Sisters, a group of women closely associated with us. Finally I wrote THE JOY OF MY HEART for the Canaan Friends, men and women at home and abroad who share the vision for Canaan in their respective walks of life. These watchwords were later translated by friends into various languages and even transmitted over radio.

God alone knew how soon lawlessness would sweep through the nations. By the mid 1960s a New Morality and a New Theology were openly calling the Ten Commandments into question, presenting them as obsolete, irrelevant, no longer binding. Even churches were pushing for the old restraints to be cast off. This was why God had imprinted His mission so deeply in my heart at Sinai. I was to sound the call far and wide: the Ten Commandments stand unique and inviolable for ever.

Those were days of grace, when God revealed this commission and gave me our Canaan Rule, based on and expounding the commandments. Days of deep affliction followed. In my spirit I grieved for the nations as I saw them approaching the horrors of the anti-Christian era and destruction. What God wanted was a company of priestly souls with a burden and a passion for the nations. He was calling our daughters to embrace their priestly calling (1 Peter 2:9) and spend themselves in sacrificial love and prayer for the sake of souls. Some He would call to launch out on their own in faith. Serving at our foreign branches even under threat of war would be a lonely, challenging life. I myself had to taste in advance the sacrifices the commission to the nations would entail. God was calling me to overcome a very human weakness of mine, a tendency to be overly concerned for the well-being of the sisters. The concern was natural enough. The sisters, most of them young, would face difficult tasks in foreign surroundings, where they would be basically left to fend for themselves. In my journal I wrote:

> *Already I feel the pain associated with the branches God is going to give us in these turbulent times. In nations increasingly antagonistic towards Christianity, our daughters will be threatened by persecution. I am experiencing in advance the pain of tearing daughters from my heart and sending them to foreign countries.* St. Catherine's Monastery, November 4, 1963

I carried this pain with me wherever I went – whether on the flat roof, in my room, in the Chapel of the Martyrs, or when walking alone through the desert to Aaron's Hill, where the people of God worshipped the golden calf. And so Sinai became for me the mountain of supreme grace and joy, but also of deepest suffering and pain. All this climaxed on November 8, 1963, when I was praying in the Chapel of the Martyrs. On that unforgettable day I had an encounter with the awesome God of Sinai, who is a consuming fire. A Bible verse struck me forcefully: "It is a fearful thing to fall into the hands of the living God" (Hebrews 10:31 KJV). I tasted something of God's holiness in judging sinners. In the presence of His divine majesty I shook and trembled. This is the God before whom worlds vanish into oblivion. Before Him we human beings are but a speck of dust. In the chapel I wrote:

God of eternity, exalted on high,
holy and awesome, impossible to fathom,
God afar off, God beyond reach,
cloud and fire obscuring from sight,
mortals from Your presence thrown,
lightning flashes from Your eyes …

Who can flee Your fury,
God afar off yet near in wrath?
Who can approach Your heart,
God ablaze, a consuming fire?
Terrors of God! I shake with fear.
Lord God! – at Your name worlds expire.

November 10, 1963

Yet at the same time I grasped more fully the significance of the throne of grace. Covered by the blood of Jesus Christ, we can enter the presence of the thrice holy God without being destroyed.

As those special days at Sinai drew to a close, I made my last ascent of Moses' Mountain on November 13, 1963, the day before my departure. Would the Lord seal the events of those weeks once more? He would. Nine years later to the day, on November 13, 1972, a strange expedition set out from the base of Moses' Mountain to a spot where the mountainside rises steeply. Traditionally it marks the place where Moses raised the boundary to enclose the holy mountain. The two camels must have looked on curiously as two sisters, armed with hand drill, bolts and cement, mounted a large plaque on the face of the mountain with the assistance of an Israeli guide and two Bedouins. It was our monument for Mount Sinai. Here, almost at the end of the camel path, with a view of the summit, the following text was to be read:

The LORD our God made a covenant
with us in Horeb. Deuteronomy 5:2

Blessed are they whom God encounters here,
to make the covenant of love with them,
to unite Himself with them,
to take them into His Heart and Being,
on His path,
the path of His commandments.

For years we had been praying that a visible sign could be raised for the Lord there – and for years this undertaking seemed doomed: "mission impossible". Our requests for permission, whether written or oral, achieved nothing. Letters endorsed with impressive rubber stamps were sent off. Efforts were made by sisters, friends, pilgrims and others. But to no avail. The door was bolted shut and – as everyone predicted – would stay that way. Miraculously the door swung open in time for the ninth anniversary of my last ascent. Again it was November 13 – three times three years to the day. God has a way of lovingly remembering special dates in our lives.

The whole incident was orchestrated by heaven. Out of the blue we had received expert advice, and permission was readily granted. The flight from Tel Aviv to Sinai went without a hitch for our sisters based in Jerusalem. Willing hands assisted them in their task. Fuel for the hand drill obviously couldn't be transported in the sisters' air baggage, but amazingly the small amount purchased on arrival held out in answer to prayer. The enterprise that had seemed so impossible all those years was now accomplished with such ease that the Israeli guide helping them remarked, "That was quite something! And to think that no one came up with the idea before!" Perhaps the inscription on the plaque about God's covenant with His chosen people touches a deep chord in their hearts.

And so the Lord sealed the events of those weeks at Sinai with this plaque. But even as I prepared to leave Sinai in 1963, He gave me a confirmation. On that November 13, He affirmed through a Bible verse that He had indeed led me there and spoken with me. "You will be his witness to all people of what you have seen and heard." (Acts 22:15)

TRANSATLANTIC TRIP – IN VAIN?

Upon my return from Sinai I faced a different reality from what God had shown me about the commission to the nations. Our whole ministry seemed like a sinking ship. Newly published libel was damaging our literature ministry, with a corresponding drop in orders. Few booked to see our religious plays. Our mailing list was halved when recipients were asked to resubscribe. All this was reflected in the donations. Were we really meant to go international? The timing couldn't have been worse.

Even among the sisters, disappointments awaited me on a scale I hadn't known before. Mother Martyria and I suffered much anguish of soul. At Sinai I had pictured to myself happy times together back at home. New festivals and celebrations would fill our annual programme. All the sisters were to share in the blessings received at Sinai. For this special time of celebration the sisters at our Jerusalem branches were to come home so that they could receive everything first-hand.

But that Christmas it all turned out so differently. The gift God had given at Sinai lay shattered in pieces before me. Inwardly grieving, I held the planned Sinai week with my daughters. In what was supposed to be our best ever festive season I found myself wringing every word from my lips. It was night in my soul.

Nor was this the only disappointment. Already surrounded by opponents, I was now seemingly forgotten by friends. Even God Himself was silent, despite the amazing things He had done at Sinai. Yet His hand, at work in this situation, kept me from sinking. At the time I was unaware of any tangible comfort. But soon His promises began to materialize in real life: in concrete facts, which spoke for themselves. This was the most powerful confirmation of all. During this new phase, which began in Lent 1964, I wrote:

> *A consuming fire burns in me to spread the call of the end times worldwide: Get ready, Jesus is coming again!*

Midnight hour was striking. Darkness would soon cover the whole world. Gripped by an overwhelming sense of burden, my heart cried out for more souls to be saved. In anguish of spirit I began writing the book HOPE FOR MAN IN A HOPELESS WORLD, which conveys the message of Sinai. "Back to the Ten Commandments" was the call! Depending on its attitude towards God's laws, a nation will either stand or fall. With this book the Sinai commission began to materialize.

It was spring of 1964 when an unexpected call reached me from God. "You are to go to America. The time is ripe." It took me by surprise. We had hardly any connections in America back then. But His thoughts are higher than ours. His Spirit continued to prompt me, urging me to carry out this commission of God. When Mother Martyria and I asked the Lord for a confirmation, we received the verse, "you will be my witnesses" (Acts 1:8).

In the following weeks God granted a visible confirmation that a speaking tour in America would be the first phase of the commission to the nations. Suddenly, one American visitor after the other called at the motherhouse. This had never happened before. Most of them spontaneously extended an invitation to speak in their church or fellowship. As we were almost totally unknown in America, it was like a miracle unfolding before our eyes when an itinerary for an eight-week speaking tour came together in the course of the summer. The Spirit of God was moving. He lit a fire in my heart. I wrote:

> *The flame of prayer is consuming me. I keep pleading with the Lord for America. It is my constant prayer.*

Humanly it was inexplicable. The commission didn't make sense to me. Not only did I feel inadequate for long overseas speaking tours, but I lacked the stamina. Was this what the following years held for me? Travel to other countries and continents may be a dream for some, but for me it was a cross. We are given a cross, however, in order to die to self. When I was in my late forties and in my prime I had entered seclusion for Jesus' sake. Now on the cusp of sixty, my energy spent, I was to embark on a series of long, strenuous journeys. Why? Only when we minister from a place of utter weakness does God receive all the credit.

Spiritually drained and physically weak, I set out on my first overseas journey, conscious of my inadequacy. I am not gifted linguistically. I had studied classical languages at school and only taken a brief course in English. So there was no way I could deliver my talks freely in English. But would I find the right interpreters? Nor did I feel equal to addressing college students influenced by liberal theology. As a sister, it was doubtful I would get through to them. But deep down inside I knew that God wanted me to go. He reveals Himself through those who are aware of their nothingness. It was fitting that this journey would be a dying process. Out of death, streams of life were to flow and bless others.

In late October 1964 I set out for Canada and the United States. This first overseas journey was rife with disappointments. In general there was little openness for our message. Our religious garb was unfamiliar, especially for evangelicals. Understandably, people also had reservations towards us as Germans. And our coordinator for Canada was obviously not up to the task. Some of the promises about meetings proved unrealistic.

In the big cities where I held lectures night after night I was burdened by the dark and oppressive atmosphere. The speaking tour commenced in Toronto, Canada. From there we travelled to America's East Coast and then across to the West Coast, stopping on the way at New York, Washington D.C., Philadelphia, Baltimore, Richmond, Minneapolis, St. Paul, Chicago, Dubuque, San Francisco, Los Angeles and elsewhere. My lectures were arranged for colleges and churches of various Christian traditions, including Lutheran, Episcopalian, Presbyterian, Free Church and Roman Catholic. Arrangements were also made for me to speak at ministers' conferences, youth events, synagogues, the headquarters of the Union of American Hebrew Congregations, groups of Hebrew Christians, deaconess houses, Christian retreat centres and abbeys. The itinerary included prayer breakfasts, a "Christian fashion show" and television interviews.

The schedule was tight with no breather in between, partly due to inexperience in coordinating meetings and partly due to last-minute additional requests. Audiences were used to having a varied programme. Penetrating the medley of impressions was challenging. Generally people weren't expecting an in-depth spiritual talk, merely a closing word. Then there was the time factor: everything took twice as long due to translation. None of this had been clear to us in advance. Time constraints did not allow for hearts to grow still and focussed, receptive for God. There was little scope for the message to unfold, evoking a response to the Lord.

Again and again I asked myself whether the message had come across. In my exhaustion I could barely collect my thoughts, though the Lord graciously hid this from others. To be sure, people expressed themselves warmly enough afterwards. But louder still was the voice of doubt. Futility trailed me like a shadow. Wouldn't it make more sense if the journeys were undertaken by younger, more competent sisters with more energy? Fluent in the language, they could communicate without an interpreter. So I reasoned.

Even so, many did take copies of our literature at the meetings in the States. Making the literature available was in itself a big venture of faith. In those days we had no American publisher. Apart from a few titles published in England, most of our literature was produced at Canaan. The poorly translated manuscripts were formatted and printed at Canaan and then shipped in large quantities to various addresses in the USA prior to the meetings. It was a costly undertaking and made no sense financially. Some American visitors had cautioned us, saying there was little demand for such literature in the States. We still went ahead with the project. But now, seeing the interest the literature generated, we were thankful that we had dared to take that risk of faith.

In the big cities I felt a special burden to fulfil the commission God had entrusted to me at Sinai. Deeply concerned, I noted in my journal: "Darkness covers the nations and cities. God counts for nothing: a high standard of living is all that matters." At the end of each day I sensed how little I had achieved. You could hardly say there was widespread interest in our message. Amid all the disappointments in this journey, I was encouraged by Mother Martyria's supportive letters.

It was a sad journey home, for I felt that I hadn't served the Lord well. Feeling downcast, I asked Him for a word in view of the past weeks. Once again it was Genesis 46:3 – "I am God, the God of your father ... Do not be afraid to go down to Egypt, for I will make you into a great nation there". How amazing to receive the same verse He had given me for the visit to Sinai, where I had received the commission to the nations!

"Make you into a great nation" – but how? Only on the foundation of suffering and dying to personal desires. What I couldn't have foreseen back then has since come to fruition: a branch has been established in Phoenix, Arizona, called Canaan in the Desert. Year after year Americans cross the Atlantic to join us for our English-language retreats in Darmstadt, sampling our way of life for two weeks and then taking the message back home. Nor did I suspect at the time that a well-known American publisher would open up for my books. A second publisher followed, producing six of my titles in a single year.

Now God heaped blessings upon blessings on us, just as had been my experience while recovering from my critical illness. If we want to know what His heart is like, we just need to look at the facts. When at times God seems to be hard on His children, it is only because He has our good in mind. Once His objective is achieved, His blessings flow more freely than ever.

Who could have imagined that our current issues booklet series would be distributed in thousands at colleges or at a big international student conference in the States? Or that American radio stations with a potential audience of millions would broadcast our songs and messages? Or that across the country Americans would be singing from our songbook WELL-SPRING OF JOY? How could I have possibly known that a few years later Americans would be among the first members of our Canaan Franciscan Brotherhood? Or that Sisters of Mary would join us from the United States and Canada, working tirelessly on translations and radio programmes for their countries?

An American lady speaking at our Love-Jesus Festival at Canaan in 1972 put it like this:

> *There are about twenty-five or thirty of us from the United States, but we represent many hundreds who longed to be here with us today at Canaan. Through the visits of the dear mothers in the States and through the many published books, the song of Canaan is being sung in our country from coast to coast... In really a very few years the Canaan commission, which is a new way – and yet a very old way, because it is the way of Jesus – has been brought to us in America.*

Even in Canada, where my journey seemed especially futile, the seed germinated most wonderfully years later. The sisters at our branch in Phoenix, Arizona, reported after a two-week speaking tour in Canada: "We reached 4500 people. The 2500 books and 10,000 booklets and leaflets weren't enough. More literature had to be sent by special delivery, because we ran out of supplies."

Looking back on my trip to America, I can only worship God in awe for so wonderfully fulfilling this commission. It is a spiritual law that meaningless paths followed in obedience to God will prove to be especially meaningful. Hidden acts of dedication, faith and obedience will yield a rich spiritual harvest in the land God has laid upon our hearts. This has been my experience all my life.

Between trips in the following years I would renew my dedication to the Lord.

Gladly for You, dear Lord,
I'll follow where You will,
Whate'er You ask I'll do,
And never rest until
Your work is all completed.

Gladly for You, dear Lord,
Whate'er the cost may be,
My heart and will I give,
For You are all to me.
I give You all I treasure.

WELL-SPRING OF JOY, no. 229

UNDER THE SHADOW OF OUR NATIONAL GUILT

How could we approach the sorely-stricken people of neighbouring countries now lying behind the Iron Curtain? How could we share the message of repentance as the gateway to heaven; the significance of the Ten Commandments; the signs of the times; God's pain today; the joy of loving Jesus; the call to glorify God? How could we, with Germany's crimes from 1939–1945 hanging over us? God knew. Ever since my stay at Sinai I had cherished the plan of visiting countries like Poland and Czechoslovakia. As in Israel, I wanted to express my deep sorrow for our national guilt whenever God gave me the opportunity.

For such a journey I knew I needed the support not only of Mother Martyria and the sisters, but of our Canaan Friends. In a sense I was representing many Christians in our country. And so I wrote in a letter to our Canaan Friends:

Burdened by our immeasurable national guilt, how can we enter such countries without reopening wounds? People will see us as representatives of the country that inflicted terror and misery upon them. Only if our hearts weep for what we did, can we reach their hearts. Only an attitude of contrition will give us any credibility as we share the word the Lord gave us ... How could we ever make up for it if we fail ... to share the comfort and help of the Gospel with the victims of WWII now suffering under new oppression?...

We are asking you to accompany us in spirit during this trip ... Please pray that God will be moved by our repentance and yet grant forgiveness for the horrific crime of our people: the massacre of defenceless women and children and of Poland's intelligentsia and the Jewish people... Without His mandate we wouldn't presume to enter these countries with the message He has entrusted to us. Nor can we carry out the task without your prayer support.

Only under the shadow of the cross could we undertake this journey. Inevitably perhaps, it turned out to be a painful dying process. Back then visas for these countries weren't normally granted to Germans, let alone Christian sisters in religious garb. Yet at the very time war clouds were gathering over the Middle East, the visas for Poland and Czechoslovakia arrived. This we took as a clear sign to travel despite the threat of war. On June 5, 1967, exactly one hour after I crossed the Czechoslovak border with Sister Eulalia, the Six Day War broke out in Israel.

Now I was behind the Iron Curtain, cut off for weeks from news of the war. I didn't even know whether our sisters in Jerusalem were alive or how our many friends in Israel were faring. Suspense was the sacrifice I consciously laid into the foundations of this trip. It was fitting, though painful. I was reminded of all those who waited, some for ever, to learn of the fate of their loved ones because of what we Germans did in WWII.

Rarely had a trip seemed so pointless. Meetings were even smaller than usual because of the political situation. There was little sign of spiritual interest. Our attitude towards Israel, which was not appreciated, actually endangered us. Only one big meeting was planned, but that fell through due to an administrative error. A few hundred Catholic nuns keen to hear us waited for us on the wrong day because of a mix-up about dates. Afterwards all I could say was, *My Father, I do not understand You, but I trust You.* Hour by hour I surrendered my will to Him. I was feeling exceptionally run down, and only with great difficulty could I keep going. I felt abandoned by God and man.

Bloodguilt, unforgiven national guilt, confronted me at every turn. Mass graves, monuments honouring the dead, sites of massacres, chilling statistics, eye-witness accounts by survivors of torture, lists of the missing, at times comprising entire extended families. Wounds, still smarting, haunted me day and night.

If God had not graciously led us on the path of repentance ever since the revival, I could not have made this painful journey to these sorely afflicted people. Seeing myself as a sinner in the sight of God and man helped me to discover the secret of the all-transforming power of repentance. This in turn led me to see our guilt towards Israel and our neighbouring nations. Now as I visited the sites of atrocities and met survivors of that era, I was able to witness yet again the power of repentance. Heartfelt repentance transformed deeply-rooted bitterness into forgiveness. The expression of our grief helped soothe wounds. I saw many eyes fill with tears – but this time in response to our humble confession of guilt as we visited their memorial sites. At some places we laid tokens of our grief with texts such as the following:

> *Have mercy upon us, O God.*
> *Deliver us from bloodguiltiness.* See Psalm 51
>
> *In deep shame and grief we remember*
> *all the victims who suffered*
> *and died here in torment*
> *at the hands of the German people.*
>
> *The Evangelical Sisterhood of Mary*

At a historic synagogue in Prague, now functioning as a museum, I was deeply moved when the Jewish custodians gathered round me to hear my opinion about the situation in Israel. A new spark of hope was evidently kindled in their hearts.

We visited the sites of the Warsaw Ghetto, Pawiak Prison and Auschwitz. At Theresienstadt and Lidice we were moved by the response of well-known public figures to the reasons for our coming. As at Auschwitz they placed our tokens of grief in their museums, which are visited by thousands.

On my return trip Mother Martyria met me at the border to update me on the situation in Israel. The Six Day War was over, the sisters in Jerusalem had emerged unscathed, and our two houses in Jerusalem were still standing. One mortar shell that hit our house on the Mount of Olives was buffered by a trunk full of blankets, and no one came to harm. Before my departure I had written a letter to our Jewish friends, focussing on God's promises for His people, and it arrived in time to bring comfort to many. The letters were delivered on the first night of the war by schoolchildren standing in for postmen.

Only those who have known the pain of laying everything on the altar during weeks of total uncertainty can rejoice when the sacrifice is given back.

A few years later the seed sown during this trip germinated. A lecture I held in Freiburg for Roman Catholic mother superiors appeared in a Polish magazine. It was accessible to far more nuns in Poland than those who had waited for me in vain because of the mixed-up dates. As long as the borders were open, friends from Czechoslovakia often visited us. Canaan has become a spiritual home for them, a place to reconnect with God.

Further trips of reconciliation were undertaken mainly by sisters serving abroad. In the awareness of our national guilt, plaques of reconciliation were mounted in Denmark, Norway, Finland, Yugoslavia, Greece and at the site of a former concentration camp in Germany. Northern Norway was widely devastated through the scorched-earth retreat of the German army in 1944. In Karasjok, where only the old church was left standing, a memorable speech was given at the dedication of a reconciliation plaque. "We promised to give the plaque a worthy place and could think of no better site than next to the old church. Here we ourselves have received forgiveness and here we wish to stand together as brothers and sisters in the light of love that comes from heaven." As a sign of reconciliation, Christian and secular newspapers in Norway carried articles on the dedication ceremony, featuring photographs of the bishop and other leaders who were present.

At St. Catherine's Monastery, Mount Sinai, where I had written our Rule, I little realized that one of these brief texts would have a bearing on our relationship towards nations we had sinned against.

Be reconciled. Don't be on bad terms with anyone.
Have you got something against anyone, or they against you?
Go to them and let love be victorious.

FURTHER TRAVELS FOR THE LORD'S SAKE

Sure enough, invitations to further countries followed my stay at Sinai. A bishop of the Church of South India was the main initiator for a trip to India. He had spent three hours at Canaan. In 1969 I set out for India with Sister Pista and visited Protestant and Catholic colleges and seminaries. Meetings were held where I was able to reach hundreds of young theologians, as well as pastors and Church workers, college girls and women's groups, Christian communities, and even thousands of Hindus.

Months in advance of the trip, this bishop organized a big prayer campaign. They were expecting great things of God. A public reception was planned in order to reach the civic leaders, one of whom was a Hindu, as well as other leading personages. God acted upon the bishop's faith. Over a thousand, including many Hindus, filled the hall. The reception had come as a total surprise, but God gave me the message, and many hands reached out for a Tamil copy of my book GOD IS ALWAYS GREATER, printed just in time.

In addition to worship services and various private meetings, the bishop organized a big open-air meeting with 2000 seats placed in the grounds. It was minutely planned, complete with an extensive PA system and fluorescent lighting. Widely displayed placards invited the whole city. Much to the joy of the Christians, over half of the 3000-strong audience were non-Christians. Some 300, including many Hindus, came forward in response to the altar call. Renouncing sin and Satan, they committed themselves publicly to Jesus, the crucified Lord. Joy and gratitude shone out of their eyes. My heart was touched by the spiritual hunger of these Indians, the frank, innocent faces of the young, and the shy, childlike radiance of the women coming forward to receive a blessing.

The heavenly Father had blessed our finances before the trip, and our friends filled our hands with gifts of money to provide material aid where most needed. The bishop's wife was especially devoted to the cause of destitute widows and homeless women. At her and her husband's express wish, I took part in the foundation-stone-laying ceremony as patron of their care home.

My stay in this region of India was deeply moving in various respects. I saw the blessing released when believers honour Jesus' last request "that all of them may be one" (John 17:21). The spiritual openness was no coincidence. Previously there had been strife, even among Church workers, but now an atmosphere of love and oneness in the Lord prevailed. I noticed it from the moment of my arrival at the airport where a group of about forty met me – ministers, co-workers and their wives. Something more was in play than hard work and efficient organization. Here the soil had been prepared by Christians living in reconciliation. This is what empowered their outreach in a polytheistic environment. At the same time I was encouraged to find so many hearts receptive for the commission God had entrusted to me at Sinai.

Even so the India trip was physically strenuous, partly because of the intense heat; and speaking did not come easily. I also caught something of the pain of God's heart for this vast country. I was deeply distressed by the abject poverty and the bondage of pagan idolatry. What hurt most was seeing how disunity, indifference or the influence of liberal theology hindered many Christians from being light and salt for their pagan environment.

All the more wonderful is the way the Lord has since raised up a number of keen, influential Christians as Canaan Friends. They have made the message of daily repentance, reconciliation and first love for Jesus their own. Passionate for the Lord and for their people, they live to spread it wherever they can. Hindi, Kanarese, Malayalam, Tamil and Telugu editions of my books, leaflets and bookmarks have appeared in India. And the work continues. The response to our English-language radio programmes in Asia has perhaps been nowhere so great as in India. Moving letters have reached us even from non-Christians. Broadcasting in Indian vernaculars has meanwhile commenced.

MORAL LANDSLIDE – MOUNT SINAI QUAKES

The age of Satanism dawned in 1966. So declared the founder of the Church of Satan in America. A dam had burst, unleashing a massive wave of demonic activity across the nations. Inhibitions were thrown to the wind. Self-gratification, hedonism and a life free from all restraint were proclaimed the ideal. The values of millions were undermined by the media. Television programmes, often masquerading as art or research, schooled viewers in brutality, murder, perversion and callous disregard for the sanctity of unborn human life.

Evil activities once prohibited and punishable by law became mainstream. Behaviour once limited to the fringes of society was encouraged and celebrated. Qualms of conscience were regarded as symptoms of unhealthy inhibition. Society was to be "liberated" from human responsibility, any conviction of sin. No one, it was argued, can be blamed for what drives them or for acting on their natural impulses. Scientists, lawyers, doctors, theologians and politicians agreed: law and justice must adapt to contemporary ethics.

There was no stopping the moral landslide. The avalanche of sin and evil would roll on, burying individuals and whole nations. Sin is always destructive, as the facts would prove before long.

A cry of desperation burst from my heart. We are raising a generation of criminals! Crime and violence will soon be the norm. Illness caused by sin will result in damaged minds and bodies, fragmented personalities bearing the imprint of death.

Inwardly I saw the avalanche of sin growing in scale, speed and force as it hurtled downward. It was a horrific sight. In my heart I wept and grieved. Sin! Spewing poison to deadly effect. Sin!

Stamping out joy and peace. Sin! Blighting young lives naturally vibrant and creative but now listless, drifting, prone to crime. Sin! Wreaking havoc inspired by Satan in his desire to destroy people and nations.

Following my visit to Sinai I became more sensitive to the terrible nature of sin in my own life. This was brought home to me as I reread one of my earlier books intended as an aid in the battle of faith against sin. I was dismayed to see how ineffectual it was. Having become more conscious of the extent of Satan's influence, I realized I had to rewrite it.

God is holy. I now knew how vital it was to live in this awareness. Our sinning always provokes God's wrath. Why else did Jesus suffer such agony on the cross? This is why sinning after Calvary is so serious. Having paid such a high price to save us, Jesus urges us not to give in to sin, but to take drastic measures against it. Figuratively speaking, "If your right eye causes you to stumble, gouge it out and throw it away. It is better for you to lose one part of your body than for your whole body to be thrown into hell" (Matthew 5:29).

Jesus knows that sin brings us hell on earth and for the unrepentant an eternity in the kingdom of darkness. There "the worms that eat them do not die, and the fire is not quenched" (Mark 9:48). There the soul suffers the second death, ever dying without attaining death. Jesus only makes such frequent reference to the terrors of hell because He loves us and wants to warn us.

At a time when God's laws were being declared invalid, I wrote this new book entitled THE CHRISTIAN'S VICTORY (American title: YOU WILL NEVER BE THE SAME), essentially to replace my earlier book on this theme. God was grieving over the sins of humanity and their terrible consequences for time and eternity, and my heart ached for Him. His pain, seared upon my heart, continually flared up. Sickened by all the perversities, I sometimes felt I couldn't bear hearing any more. Indescribable anguish filled me at the thought of people made in God's image sinking deeper and deeper in a morass of filth, hate and depravity.

My cry of lament intensified over the years. I grieved for those laid low in the prime of their youth, dying not as heroes defending their country but as victims of lust, sex and drugs, having poisoned themselves. Sin and Satan lured them down the path of destruction, ruined their personalities and drove them to crime. Thousands upon thousands sick in body and soul and doomed to die…

With the prophet Jeremiah I learnt to lament, "Is there no balm in Gilead? Is there no physician there? Why then is there no healing for the wound of my people?" (Jeremiah 8:22). Yet balm was available – in the person of the Lord Jesus. But where were the believers who weep and mourn, sharing His grief? With addictions spiralling out of control, where were those who unite to plead with God and seek ways of rescuing the victims?

From the beginning of this new era I asked myself daily what I could do to help save souls. *Lord, show me how I can prove my love for You in this hour. Bring me together with others who share Your pain for our nation, our young people, and who are ready to give the task their all.*

In the autumn of 1964 I wrote about the moral landslide in the first issue of our annual magazine. This article resulted in a flyer for distribution at showings of obscene film productions. Another leaflet followed, as well as a petition in the form of an open letter to be submitted to influential people and organizations.

Every morning in our sisterhood we prayed the PRAYER FOR THE TIME OF DISTRESS, which I had written in 1962. Friends were praying the same prayer.

In autumn 1964 Mother Martyria and I approached the Christian women's organizations in our country for the purpose of stemming the tide. The Lord wonderfully guided us. One contact led to the next as if planned by heaven. A group called the White Cross, specializing in sexual ethics and counselling, invited us to a conference. Contact was made with other groups sharing our concern at recent trends. While touring Bavaria and northern Germany with our plays on biblical themes, we collected signatures for our open letter. Canaan Friends assisted in other places. The following spring we were able to submit 50,000 signatures to Heinrich Lübke, the German Federal President.

Eventually this led to a meeting in our retreat centre Jesus' Joy, convened by Mother Martyria in early December, while I was still in America. Influential leaders and others who expressed interest were invited.

Out of that gathering grew the initiative Concern for Germany. The aim was to supply the public with relevant information while engaging in prayer and issuing alerts – all in the context of a prophetic warning ministry. The executive committee arranged for every Protestant bishop in our country to receive a copy of the book HOPE FOR MAN IN A HOPELESS WORLD. They encouraged its widest possible circulation to help expose Satan's hidden agenda in the light of God.

An appeal based on our open letter was sent by the executive committee to leading personalities, requesting their endorsement. Some, including church dignitaries, expressed their willingness. The appeal was then distributed in large numbers and submitted to the press in an effort to reach the whole nation:

> *... Today we are witnessing the collapse of all moral norms due to the blatant disregard for God's will ... This dire situation calls for all who feel a sense of responsibility to take a stand together. The tide must be stemmed, a rampart built. Acting in obedience to God, we can indeed build a dam. We need to make every effort to oppose the destruction of our nation before it is too late ...*
>
> *God's eternally valid laws shine forth in Holy Scripture amid the uncertainty and confusion of our times ... When people look daily to God's Word for orientation, there is clarity and renewal ... May everyone longing for the renewal of our nation join us in the initiative Concern for Germany ...*

Within weeks thousands of signatures came in. The initiative Concern for Germany was expanding. Volunteers offered their services, soon to be followed by full-time co-workers. Circular letters were written, alerts on specific topics sent out, lectures held. People signed up for conferences convened by organizations with similar goals, and a medical conference was arranged. For all who were interested, retreats were hosted at Canaan under the movement's umbrella. They featured Bible talks on the priestly ministry of intercession for church and nation. Yet I sensed that the universal scale of the rebellion against God and the Ten Commandments called for still more – a public affirmation of our faith before the visible and invisible world. So we convened Witness-and-Worship Services to declare who God is and to exalt Father, Son and Holy Spirit. Similar events followed in other cities. Cell groups of Concern for Germany sprang up in various places.

Admittedly, overall success was not evident. The situation was too far advanced, and evil too entrenched. But the many leaflets, posters and flyers against porn shows and sex expo events were not in vain, nor the numerous prayer meetings. Every single prayer and sacrificial effort helps to deter the advance of the powers of darkness, break the power of sin and rouse people from their sleep.

But there was no stopping the avalanche. With sin crying out to heaven, God would be compelled to respond with judgment such as the world has never seen. The age of God's anguished wrath was coming. Soon He would see nothing but sin wherever He looked. And the God of love would have no option but to act in holy wrath. Divine judgment, consuming fire, widespread death would ensue. In my spirit I saw it happening. Sinai will collapse upon us, because we have dared to attack all that it stands for – God's moral code, the Ten Commandments. An English theologian wrote, "The sanctions of Sinai have lost their terrors." Immediately I saw where this would lead. Sinai would come crashing down upon our human race, for God is holy. What could be harder for His loving heart than to vent His wrath in judgment because we resist His Spirit? In my heart I grieved and mourned.

O the pain, the anguish of our God!
Soon the time will come
when He who gave His Son for love of us
must stretch forth His arm in righteous anger
and lay waste the earth.

How it breaks His heart not to show mercy
but to send judgment,
falling like shafts of lightning
on the earth He made and loved.

Stern and strange dealings of our God,
so foreign to His nature!
Yet once before, in the days of Noah,
the God of love and mercy judged the world,
sent the Flood, its waters covering all land;
then caused the rainbow to shine over this earth,
a seal and pledge of grace.

The end times have begun,
the world a Babylon of sin,
the spirit of rebellion defying the King of heaven.

And He, the God of love,
cannot but respond in wrath unequalled.
Judge He must, or earth be given over,
becoming a perpetual state of hell.
He who would sustain must now lay waste,
He who desires our best must discipline. [Isaiah 13:9,11]

Then the ground will not yield its fruits,
nor the forests provide refreshing shade and timber,
for they will cease to be.
Gone will be houses and cities
meant for human habitation.

Death and decay will cover the earth
as sin upon sin was heaped up to heaven.

O worship God in His stern love!
In holy wrath He acts, heedless of His own pain,
till born of judgment a new world emerges,
a new generation rises from the ashes.

What hour of grief and dread is now approaching!
Who will stand by our God,
feel with Him the agony?
Who will bow to His will
as a world laid low
reaps what it has sown,
judgment takes its course –
devastation upon devastation.

The eyes of God now scan the earth.
Who will heed the depths of anguish
welling up in His heart?
A child will understand –
a child who loves the Father.

God's hour of utmost anguish has now come.
Is there any sorrow like His?
Do not turn away.
The One you call Father is in agony.

In my spirit I had a foretaste of the judgment our human race will call down upon ourselves with our flagrant sinning. God will act to prevent evil entrenching itself permanently. The prophet Isaiah asked, "Why are your garments red, like those of one treading the winepress?" In response, the Lord said, "I have trodden the winepress alone; from the nations no one was with me. I trampled them in my anger and trod them down in my wrath" (Isaiah 63:2–3). At such a time the Lord longs for someone to stand with Him. "The LORD looked and was displeased that there was no justice. He saw that there was no one, he was appalled that there was no one to intervene; so his own arm achieved salvation for him, and his own righteousness sustained him." (Isaiah 59:15–16)

To stand by Him was what I wanted to live for, and later He gave me opportunities to do so.

As the tidal wave of sin and lawlessness invaded more and more territory, Concern for Germany faced a rapidly changing situation. The student protest movement had started. Providing biblical orientation for students caught in the crossfire was now Concern for Germany's priority. The first youth conferences under this umbrella were held at Canaan at the initiative of the executive director Horst-Klaus Hofmann. It was amazing to see the numbers that came and the impact on young lives. The conferences multiplied, and soon in terms of time and resources our retreat centre was stretched beyond capacity. But God wonderfully opened the way for Horst-Klaus and Irmela Hofmann to start an independent organization in nearby Bensheim. God had given them a special burden for young people.

The Concern for Germany movement soon morphed into the Young Christians on the Offensive (today known as the Reichenberg Fellowship). At its Bensheim centre, young people were trained and equipped, while spiritual backup was provided by Canaan and the Canaan Friends through prayer and literature. At the heart of our public ministry of proclamation was the priestly ministry of sacrificial prayer and intercession.

If God was grieved to the heart by human depravity in the days of Noah (Genesis 6:6), how much more must He grieve today in view of the widespread apostasy within the church? The God-is-dead theology was proclaimed and then duly promoted at the *Kirchentag*, the bi-annual Protestant mega-event. In 1965 as I was studying the promotional material for the Cologne gathering, I wrote: "The *Kirchentag* is becoming a platform for Satan." The question was whether we should still go and perform our religious plays as in the previous years. My heart sank when I thought of the thousands of Christians flocking to the event, spiritually hungry and with high expectations, little suspecting what would be on offer. God, however, gave us the assurance that we were to go one more time and present our plays there.

Yet in Cologne, Mother Martyria and I were shocked. Young people were present in large numbers as full licence was given to sin. God's laws were watered down and sexual permissiveness was condoned in complete disregard of the Bible's warnings of judgment. Typically, one night's programme featured readings from Bertolt Brecht with a female vocalist singing how sweet sin is. We left the hall in protest, for this was a symptom that Satan's penetration of the Protestant Church was not merely tolerated but welcomed. At the same event the theologian Dorothee Sölle earned applause for her lecture on the God-is-dead theology. It seemed to me that Cologne sounded the death knell for our Protestant church, as I shared with the sisters upon my return home. Indescribable pain seared my heart, and I was consumed with the fire of prayer. I wrote:

> *Night has fallen. Instead of Jesus being proclaimed, satanically inspired notions are promoted. All I can do is lament and grieve for what we are doing to Jesus. The great apostasy has begun. The years are numbered and judgment will follow, for people won't listen. They prefer sin. They are leading astray the youth and all those who are still wavering.*

One thought gripped me: This calls for a counter movement. Now is the time to sound a warning. It was clear to me that we could never participate in a *Kirchentag* again. But staying away was not enough. So I wrote a circular letter to friends commenting on the *Kirchentag* in Cologne. In our current issues series a new booklet dealt with the dangers of a false tolerance, an "anything goes" mentality. In 1970, as the downward spiral in our church continued, I wrote a further booklet at great personal cost: NEVER BEFORE IN THE HISTORY OF THE CHURCH.

How thankful I was to God that my booklets could serve as beacons in an age of deceptive lights. With so many people coming under negative influences, it was a privilege to share God's light and truth. Knowing this was a great comfort amid the pain and conflict that ensued. And it was my prayer that those who love the Lord would raise their voices with ours in lamentation.

God eternal, God alive,
Maker of heaven and earth,
God who sustains all living things,
breathing into us the breath of life,
now declared dead and obsolete,
Creator though He be, and we merely the created.

We've cut the cord that binds our souls
to the one and only Source of life.
Now we ourselves must pay the price as the living dead;
dead in sin; divorced from life.

In Gethsemane Jesus' disciples failed Him in His hour of greatest need, forsaking Him when the powers of darkness attacked. In the longing not to fail Him today I wrote a prayer entitled JESUS FORSAKEN ONCE MORE. We often pray it on Thursday evenings, and seek to minister to His grieving heart with songs of love and devotion. Friends and retreat guests who joined us in such times of worship introduced the prayer to their own circles.

Lord Jesus,
We grieve with You for the pain You feel today. Your church, commissioned to bear witness to the Gospel, is falling apart. We grieve with You as it becomes a platform for ungodly debate and blasphemy. We grieve that Your commands are declared invalid and the authority of Your Word is undermined.

Let us rise, Lord, from our slumber
and with tears make supplication;
live to soothe Your bitter sorrow,
bringing You our hearts' devotion.
Gladly let us sacrifice,
share Your shame, kneel at Your side.
My whole life I lay before You,
at Your feet I worship and adore.

CANAAN – FINAL FOUNDATIONS AND COMPLETION 1960 – 1973

ONE LAST BUILDING PHASE

The vision for Canaan, our own Promised Land, had been alive in my heart ever since God first gave me the commission in 1955. Named after the biblical Canaan, it was to glorify God. The Lord was to shine forth from Canaan as the living God, who answers prayers and works miracles. Everything at Canaan – the people, the buildings, the grounds with their plants and animals – should demonstrate, *Who is like God!* Here He was to receive the love of many hearts. He would shine out of the lives of those living here. As His Word says, "If we walk in the light, as he is in the light, we have fellowship with one another" (1 John 1:7).

In the spiritual sense Canaan was also a battleground. Battling in faith for our Promised Land turned out to be a challenging experience, testing us to the limit. Some victories proved short-lived, while the defeats seemed final. Gains were often reversed even after we had celebrated a victory with thankful hearts. The promises had to be buried again and again before we saw a resurrection and all of Canaan was ours!

1960 to 1966 now saw the completion of Canaan. The land was enclosed, buildings were erected, trees and shrubs planted, the bed of the lake was paved, the fountain built, the entrance area and prayer garden took shape. At the time it seemed like an impossible undertaking. Yet the whole purpose of Canaan was to make the Life and Passion of Christ come alive for us today. This was the vision God gave me.

We wanted to provide a peaceful environment with walks and quiet corners for reflection. Everything was to be conducive to prayer: the Garden of Jesus' Suffering and Resurrection, the Bethlehem Grotto, the Mount of Beatitudes, the Sea of Galilee, the Jordan, and Jacob's Well.

For love of Jesus I wanted everything to remind people of Him. To quote Luther, "Would to God I could persuade the rulers and the wealthy to have all the scenes of the Bible painted, inside and outside, on the walls of the houses, for everyone to see. That would be a truly Christian deed."

Words fail me when I try to describe how wonderfully the Father undertook for us during those six years. Without a skilled landscape gardener and the right firms, such an enterprise was challenging. Coming on top of other building projects like the spacious Herald Chapel, it was way beyond our means. The cost estimates left us reeling. How could we afford the buildings, the kiln for firing the sculptures, the hiring of earthmoving equipment and operators – and much more?

Perhaps harder still was the question: Are such investments justified even if covered by donations? This caused me endless heart-searching. As the initiator I bore the brunt of responsibility. *Had I been mistaken? Was I bringing dishonour to God?* Nor was I spared attacks from without. *Wasn't Canaan a waste of resources?* There was an acute housing shortage. So was it right to use prime property for park-like grounds, including a prayer garden?

In all these onslaughts I resisted the devil and he fled. I drew near to God until I sensed His closeness again and heard His reassurances. Money, I realized, need not be an issue when it comes to glorifying God. After all, we were creating a place with scenes depicting His Passion in order to inspire love and thanksgiving. Had I forgotten Mary of Bethany and her extravagant outpouring of love? She anointed Jesus with costly oil before His Passion. The uncomprehending disciples objected: the money would have been better spent on the poor. But Jesus was refreshed and comforted by Mary's sacrificial gift of love. And wasn't that my intention for

Canaan and its grounds – to inspire love and thanksgiving for Jesus? My doubts were silenced. Canaan was to be.

If only I could have seen what the future held just years later: summer for summer thousands passing, singly or in groups, through the prayer garden, with many lives wonderfully impacted by God. What a comfort that would have been in those hours of inner conflict. I wouldn't have worried about the costs – still less if I had been able to foresee the sums that would be poured into unwholesome entertainment soon to flood the world.

Yet even then there were solaces. I was humbled by the Father's provision, and my heart was warmed to see Him acting on our behalf. Sand and earth were donated from adjoining building sites for the landscaping of our grounds. At no cost to us they were transported and shaped into hills on our property. We were not even charged for the use of the earthmoving equipment. And many of the shrubs and trees for the prayer garden were donated.

Our sculptress Sister Myrrhia created the art for the Garden of Jesus' Suffering and Resurrection. Quarry stones were donated, with transportation provided. Mr. Hottes, our foreman, selflessly gave of his time to oversee the sisters at work. The bed of the lake was paved with disused cobblestones supplied by the city authorities, as streets were being resurfaced with asphalt. Even the cement for sealing the cracks was provided free of charge by a firm. Literally everything came together. We suffered no lack – though normally these materials would have cost us a small fortune. It was as if God had made it a point of honour to take care of everything down to the last detail. After all, this property was to be to the glory of His name. Through it the Passion of Jesus would come alive for people. So tears turned into laughter, petitions into thanksgiving, and believing was rewarded by seeing.

The Lord had taught me a valuable lesson. By all means economize, but not when it comes to glorifying Him. Give generously of your time, energy, money and resources, sparing nothing.

AT RISK FROM POLLUTION

Imagine a piece of land dedicated to God and existing solely for His glory. Is it any wonder that Satan will rage? He is the enemy of human happiness. He cannot bear to see people living together in harmony on pleasant, fertile land where the soil produces its fruit and the air is filled with jubilant birdsong praising the Maker.

So it was clear to me that it was the work of the enemy when Canaan was affected by various pests. It was so easy to resort to pest control, forgetting the harmful effects on the environment as beneficial species of insects, fish and birds go into decline, and soil and water are contaminated – ultimately to the detriment of human health.

But when Satan attacks, we need to counter-attack by declaring war on sin in our lives and claiming Jesus' victory in faith. Admittedly, I knew nothing about agriculture, and back then environmental pollution was not such a hot issue. But one day the Holy Spirit created in me a feeling of uneasiness. Calling the sisters together, I shared the insight God had given. Poison has no place at Canaan. God has other ways of eliminating pests than by chemical insecticides, which kill life He created. This is a call to walk in faith. As we trust God to deal with the sin in our lives, victory will be ours in the battle against harmful insects invading Canaan. He will act and we will see His wonder-working power, just as He says in His Word: "I will prevent pests from devouring your crops" (Malachi 3:11), provided we keep His commands and obey His will. I was convinced that God was giving us a new opportunity to honour Him with our faith. An exciting prospect.

At first our daughters, especially the garden sisters, were reluctant. Stop using toxic sprays to combat pests? Why, that went right against their experience. The Lord convinced them in the end, and we abandoned these methods. Afterwards we were severely tested. Typically, things get darker when you first launch out in faith. Situated at the edge of the forest, Canaan was invaded by swarms of bugs – various species of plant lice that thrived in the dry weather, as well as Colorado beetles, grubs and caterpillars. The whole harvest was endangered.

God was clearly disciplining us in allowing Canaan to be afflicted with garden pests. That meant sticking it out until God had achieved His objective with each one of us. He wanted to increase our reliance on Him and help us to grow in an intimate father-child relationship, rather than evade His discipline by using insecticides that disrupted the balance of nature. Once again we were to discover that repentance leads to a fresh experience of His mercy and help. With repentance came the realization where God was waiting for us to change. We learnt to see these plagues from God's viewpoint. Satan's plans backfired and he accomplished exactly the opposite of what he intended: we were more alert than ever in the battle against sin.

In the evenings we often came together to sing songs of faith. God's honour was at stake in the sight of all the visitors at Canaan. But the bleaker the situation, the more Mother Martyria and I encouraged our daughters to keep up the battle of faith against sins God had brought to light. We urged them not to give up even when disheartened. Singing, we made a procession across our afflicted land. Individually and together we brought our personal failures to God. Wherever He laid His finger on a sore spot, we claimed the victory of the Lord, determined to battle on till release came. Through times of fellowship in the light and personal counselling, many hidden faults painfully came to light during that "summer of unmasking", as we called it. God in His holiness revealed the canker in our lives. Some, by nature easily discouraged, came out as winners as they learnt the secret of claiming victory over sin, which is what the battle of faith is all about.

At the same time they learnt that the battle of faith is also about the fruits of repentance – good works, in the New Testament sense, all in response to God's grace. This has nothing to do with "earning grace". It is about showing we're sorry in practical ways – as a token of our willingness. As the situation worsened, everyone pitched in to help. In their free time sisters scoured the grounds for grubs, inchworms, potato bugs and other harmful insects, digging them from the soil, picking them off the leaves, and hosing down crops and roses. During a rabbit plague they were up early in the morning for the chase. It was like catching the little foxes spoiling the vineyard (Song of Songs 2:15). Sin has to be dealt with radically. To be sure, our efforts couldn't end the plague (just as our battle of faith cannot free us from sin). They were merely a sign of good will.

God alone could end the plague. As with all further plagues, the turning point came in His good time. In His abundant goodness the Father responded to our faith. Our battle of faith against sin and Satan culminated in the victory of the Lord. After gruelling months of drought He sent us rain at the right time, ladybirds to feed on the greenfly, and flocks of birds to devour other harmful bugs – plus volunteers to help with the weeding. At the last moment the heavenly Father turned the situation around and blessed us with a bumper harvest. At the harvest festival our garden sisters went from house to house at Canaan singing songs of praise with thankful hearts for the overwhelming goodness of God. On their shoulders they carried poles with wonderful specimens of harvested fruit and vegetables – just like the Israelites sent out to scout the Promised Land. That was our first "harvest of grace", as we called it, for the Bible verse we received for that summer was, "where sin increased, grace increased all the more" (Romans 5:20).

Time and again since the late 1960s this has been our experience. How often the Father had to be stern with us in order to shake us out of our apathy and prompt us to take up the fight against sin. Having chosen to rely on God in this way, we have experienced so much renewal spiritually. We cannot thank Him enough for it. Subsequent harvests were often so abundant that we had enough and to spare: guests and needy families in our town shared in the blessing.

Only later did the full significance of this leading dawn on me. Pollution was a growing problem worldwide, and there was no turning the clock back. The existential threat to our planet only highlighted our dependence on God's grace, leading us to repentance. As we take sin seriously, we will enter a purified and deeper relationship with God. In 1972, after several years' experience of combating pests without toxic pesticides, I was able to write the book POLLUTION – BUT THERE IS AN ANSWER as part of the current issues series. Yet this was not the last battle we faced. Canaan's foundations were laid deep.

EPHESIANS 6 – COMBAT WITH THE UNSEEN

Meanwhile Canaan was becoming a land where God's presence could be felt, as visitors commented. Something of His gracious promise was coming true: "Here will I dwell" (Psalm 132:14 KJV). Isn't that enough to provoke Satan to even greater onslaughts? And sure enough we came to feel the heat of his attacks. A big celebration was planned for July 10, 1966, to give thanks to the heavenly Father. As we were gearing up in prayer and practical preparations, Satan struck – less than a year before the event. It was a major attack by the powers of darkness.

One of our young sisters confided that she had suffered horrific harassment by demons since childhood. Her grandfather had sold her to the devil, and the demons constantly taunted her. She had hoped to become free in the sisterhood, though she had said nothing of her experiences before joining.

After a long talk with her, when she brought everything into the light, I was overcome with grief and horror. Earlier I had read about Johann Christoph Blumhardt's intense prayer battle for the deliverance of Gottliebin Dittus. The mere thought of confronting the powers of darkness filled me with dread and revulsion. From Blumhardt's description I knew that nothing could be more horrific than engaging with demons, especially when they are oppressing a human soul.

Personally I felt this was a task for a group of men like Blumhardt and his brothers in the Lord. But now God had entrusted this young sister to my care. I couldn't walk away from her plight. God was calling me to take up a battle I would have preferred to avoid: combat with demonic forces.

Nor were my fears groundless. It turned out to be an extremely severe case, as confirmed by others with experience in spiritual warfare. Harrowing months followed. During that time I wrote battle songs and prayers. One song in particular I sang regularly:

There's only One who has such might.
It's Jesus Christ, who won the fight
And Satan's power defeated.
And still He puts the foe to flight
And takes from Satan every right,
Our living, glorious Saviour.

Our ransom has been fully bought.
All Satan's wiles must come to nought,
His claims on us are cancelled.
Our souls to Christ alone belong,
Who gave His life to right all wrong
And rescue souls in bondage.

SONGS AND PRAYERS OF VICTORY, p. 29, adapted

The fight was on, and so I called some of the sisters to form a small prayer group for reinforcement. We prayed and we fasted, but seemingly to no avail. The powers of darkness only raged all the more. It was a horrendous experience. I could relate to what Blumhardt said about his own intense suffering in the battle for a human soul.

Seldom had I carried such a burden. From my anguished heart arose the cry, *Where is Jesus, the Prince of Victory?* Over and over again I battled through in prayer, taking my stand on scriptural truths. *Jesus did win. Jesus did save us. His power has brought us victory – His mighty power in battle! It's true: Jesus holds the keys of death and Hades. It's true: Jesus has crushed the head of the serpent. It's true: Jesus came to destroy the works of the devil.* (See Psalm 118:16; Revelation 1:18; Genesis 3:15; 1 John 3:8.) Again and again we made these proclamations of faith, reminding the Lord of His promises and claiming Jesus' victory. Because of Calvary, Satan had lost all right to this soul.

How could I celebrate the Thank-You-Father Festival with this burden on my heart? Yet God willed it so. I wrote:

> *This shall be my gift to You, loving Father. Implicit trust, my unconditional "yes" when the way is hard and nothing makes sense ... But how can Canaan live up to its name and be a land of God, a place where the Lord dwells, a foretaste of heaven, if Satan exercises such power over a human soul? If Satan will not yield, this is a sign that he is winning. But that can never be. Jesus' honour is at stake.*

I kept on praying, refusing to give up: *Because You've won, Lord, Your victory will be seen.* "And though I wait all night long till break of day, never shall my heart fret or doubt God's power." (Luther)

Acquiring Canaan had been one long test of faith. A hundred times over I learnt to believe, even if my faith was unrewarded by visible results. I learnt to believe when my hopes were dashed, the other side winning, the vision for Canaan ruined. With a heavy heart I struggled through till I could believe again. But now I prayed as if my heart would break. This was more than coming to terms with a difficult leading. I had to deal with the demonic. It was all about praying free a soul entrusted to my care: free from Satan's clutches and safe from an eternity without God.

What kept me from succumbing to battle fatigue? I found what Blumhardt shared about his experiences very helpful. Significantly the evil spirits admitted they were forced to abandon the struggle because of his "loathsome persistence" in calling on the victorious name of Jesus. That showed me: *Never give up the battle of faith. Keep on proclaiming the victory of Jesus, even if you seem to experience nothing but failure.* Then the miracle happened. Jesus proved beyond all doubt that He is the Lamb of God, who has destroyed the devil's power. Satan was forced to yield. Our sister was set free. After a year and a half she knelt weeping at the feet of her Lord, whose name she had profaned – against her natural inclinations – while under demonic influence. Now she brought Him tears of repentance and tokens of her love and dedication. She grew to be a bride of Jesus in the truest sense of the word, utterly devoted to Him.

But that summer the fight was still on. So I had to go through with the Thank-You-Father celebration with this heavy burden on my heart. This was a big disappointment. So far the Lord hadn't answered my many prayers.

In this situation God wanted me to thank and praise Him – not with a rejoicing heart because He had intervened, but with an aching heart. It was a song in the night, but I knew it would give depth to our celebration.

A song is ascending,
A song celebrating
The will of the Father, so holy and wise.
In loving devotion,
In humble submission
We worship the Lord for His counsels divine.

Though not comprehending
What God now is doing,
One day we will see how His word He fulfilled.
In worshipful silence
We bow in deep reverence,
Until the Lord chooses His plan to reveal.

IN PERFECT LOVE?

It was January 1966. I was in seclusion for a week of prayer and fasting, seeking the Lord for the spiritual renewal of our sisterhood. During those days a book came into my hands called KRÄFTIGE IRRTÜMER [Powerful Delusions], warning against fanatics past and present. The author, Richard Ising, had founded his own Christian fellowship in Berlin. I did not know him, nor had he ever visited us. As I read what he wrote about our ministry and myself, I felt the waves of shame and devastation breaking over me. Though various ministries were negatively critiqued, we took the brunt of the attack. There and in a further report I read that my life was of a "diabolical nature"; that I was "splitting and destroying the church of God"; that I "profaned and blasphemed the name of God". Reference was made to heresy and "Catholic tendencies". A false spirit had crept in, it was claimed, because I had given way to pride, the root of all apostasy.

The book was the culmination of a long history of antagonism since our founding years. This was not merely a newsletter with a limited readership. All the accusations were presented in a single volume for the wider public. As well as circulating the book among preachers, pastors and Christian organizations, the author and his team sent it to Christian bookstores, along with promotional material.

Such a book, without the backing of a publishing house, would surely have little effect in Christian circles? Not so. An order was cancelled for 25,000 copies of my booklet on false tolerance and of my letter on the Cologne *Kirchentag*. The literature, though packed and ready, was never dispatched. The minister who ordered it for distribution at an evangelical conference withdrew after receiving copies of Ising's book from various quarters.

My week of prayer became a week of tears. The book was circulating in groups where my writings had previously been well received. Readers mentioned experiencing a deeper love for Jesus and a closer walk with Him through repentance. It was agonizing to think of the confusion of those who genuinely wanted to follow Jesus. Perhaps they were now having doubts about whether they were on the right track.

Believers, incredulous that such defamation could be published, reassured us that no one would take such outrageous statements seriously. They assumed the libel could not cause any real damage. The last twenty years had taught me differently. Lies and slander, however unbelievable and bizarre, poison the mind. Inevitably a residue remains. Libel can discredit a ministry or even damage a reputation permanently.

From our founding days I had seen how false reports, whether in newsletters or talks, spread like wildfire. But Richard Ising's book signalled the start of a large-scale attack. He and his team felt duty-bound to distribute it extensively. Key personalities at home and abroad were targeted as part of a deliberate move to marginalize me and ruin our ministry. Of all the slander I had been exposed to over the years, this was the worst. Whenever excerpts from my songs and writings appeared in daily readings, calendars or elsewhere, editors faced angry criticism. Publishers risked losing clients if they continued to print my words. It was humiliating to realize that anyone having dealings with me or our ministry would be tainted by association.

Richard Ising's book continued to penetrate the Christian world, reaching new circles. Many of our friends received warning letters. Better sever connections, don't read another book of hers, was the advice – *she's demonically inspired, the greatest heretic ever.* Repeated calls came to burn my books. Even in places like East Germany, where Christian literature was scarce, my books were consigned to the flames.

News kept arriving of the damage caused by the book. Heartbroken, I wrote:

I've been labelled as demonic. Once again, our ministry is effectively dead and buried: character assassination has done its work. My heart is broken by all the insults. I am sick with grief. People against us wherever I look. Not a bright spot anywhere.

But with each new wave of libel I would renew my dedication to the Lord.

May this serve to make me more humble and help me to mature in priestly sacrificial love. I'm crying to the Lord that all these wounds will help put to death everything in my soul that is not love.

It was a major attack of the evil one, but the Lord graciously enabled me to remain at peace and to humble myself beneath His powerful hand. It was hard to believe that ultimately our ministry would not come to any harm. But again and again I would battle through to the point where I could trust God that all would work out for the best.

This shadow was hanging over us as we prepared for the Thank-You-Father Festival in 1966, which was to be a celebration of God's goodness. As the Lord stressed, it wasn't about the festival *per se* or the various ministries. It was about Canaan's calling. The land had been developed and houses built for one purpose alone: to be a place where God's love reigns. And as God had given me the initiative for Canaan, everything depended on the influence I exerted. It all boiled down to my spiritual attitude. Would I respond with love and compassion to these attacks? That was the issue. In my heart the words were ringing: "Adorned with love for friend and foe alike, brimming over with compassion, you will be fit to take your place at Jesus' side for all eternity" (Paul Riedinger). Only then can we qualify as belonging to the kingdom of love. Only then would Canaan become a spiritual powerhouse, a place where heaven becomes real to people. For what makes heaven heaven? That everyone is governed by love.

Love is what would give the residents of Canaan their radiance and Canaan its atmosphere of joy. God evidently had a clearly defined plan to awaken love in my heart. That year as we approached the final stages of Canaan's development, God had raised up someone who would work against me with serious allegations. But he was merely a tool in God's hand. Love was God's goal for me. That was His purpose in this painful time of discipline.

Personally I had come full circle. The struggle to love had marked the beginning of my Christian life. In my youth I was compelled to own myself beaten when it came to love. And ever since then, I had prayed for love. The first breakthrough came in the 1930s. For a while I shared a home with a very difficult person, liable to over-react and become hysterical. At that time I was bitter over the wrongs I had suffered. When the Lord convicted me, I repented of my resentment, and, claiming the blood of the Lamb, I experienced release. As I overcame my bitter feelings, love flowed into my heart, and the broken relationship was restored.

Later, by the grace of God I was free from an unforgiving and bitter spirit – and that despite the defamation that had hounded me since the founding of our sisterhood. Even so, I sensed I was still far from the goal of perfect love. As the granddaughter of a lawyer, I found lies and injustice very hard to take. And so the flow of merciful love was stemmed.

This I noticed three years before the book by Ising was published. We had been invited to present one of our religious dramas in Berlin, but many were put off by the libel spread about us and didn't come. The next morning at church some left in protest when I was asked to give a word after the sermon. In the midst of this humiliation I rejoiced. This was disgrace for Jesus' sake. Back in the motherhouse, I learnt of further incidents and fresh opposition. It upset me to see committed Christians spreading such falsehoods.

When the matter kept me awake at night, God showed me very clearly that it was sin. And why did I find it hard to take injustice? Because my tender ego was bruised. This is why I was so wound up and couldn't sleep. Yet Jesus explicitly prepared us for such situations. "If they have persecuted me, they will persecute you also." – "I am telling you this now so that your faith in me may not be shaken." (John 15:20; John 16:1 PHILLIPS)

So I asked the Lord to help me to remain calm in the face of defamation, though I knew lies were poisoning minds, dividing the Body of Christ and hindering the spread of the Gospel.

This was my constant prayer during those three years: a prayer that God answered. But He wanted something more for me: perfect love was His goal. During the 1960s the prayer for perfect love pervaded my diary entries and songs. Love is the greatest gift we can receive from God. God is love. We were created and saved to love. A love that extends to our enemies – real love. I knew that this love will become ours only if we keep asking for it and firmly believe that on the cross Jesus redeemed us to love. Again and again I sang in faith:

I am redeemed! To love, You set me free.
I am redeemed! You won the fight for me.

I remember walking up and down a certain path in those years and pleading for love, every step a cry from the heart:

Father, as Your child I am called to reflect Your nature. So I know You will answer my prayer to become loving. Lord Jesus, I want to belong to the Bride of the Lamb, Your bride. So I know You will make me like You. This is why You shed Your blood. Holy Spirit, You are the One who works in our souls, and so I know You will transform me into the image of love.

Conscious of my lack of compassion, I kept praying to God. And as I prayed, I was aware of Jesus standing there, His heart overflowing with love. On the cross His first prayer was not for His friends but for His enemies. "Father, forgive them." His very nature is mercy and loving-kindness.

Couldn't I trust Him to create in me what is dear to His own heart? How He longs to see His children reflect His compassionate love. This is a love that embraces their opponents and shines upon the quarrelsome and opinionated. It extends to those who insult us, giving us a bad name. A stream of compassion straight from the heart of God, this love knows no limits or barriers, taking trouble and shame in its stride. Was it so hard to believe that Jesus freed us by His sacrificial death to show forth His perfect love? Time and again I had seen how God stands by His promises.

Naturally, we have to be willing to accept the discipline of the Lord. Faith alone can't achieve such love. Faith and divine chastening go hand in hand, as I had learnt on the road to Canaan. The Bible tells us that we are cleansed through faith in the blood of Jesus. But it also teaches that God disciplines us so that we can partake of His holiness (Hebrews 12:10). Believing in Jesus' victory and praising His blood is not enough. If we are unwilling to accept God's discipline, we will experience little victory and our lives will bear no fruit. But those who are sincere in claiming the blood of Jesus will also allow the Lord to discipline them. God used Richard Ising's book to answer my prayer to become more like Jesus, the King of Love.

In the following years (1968–1969) my love was tested in new ways. Mother Martyria and I suffered painful disappointments, similar to Paul's. People who had been close to him and worked alongside him later turned against him. This was our experience at home and abroad, especially with those dear to us. Every time a wound was inflicted, I felt the Lord was waiting for my reaction. Would I be full of mercy like Him? Would I love as He loved? Would I suffer patiently as He did? It's all about love.

This is what the Lord seared into my heart. He showed me that love was the only thing that counts in my life. All our works are worthless if they do not bear the hallmark of love: they will perish. Only love never ends (1 Corinthians 13:8). Love is eternal and immortal, because it contains the seed of divine life.

Reconciling love born of love for Jesus was the message the Lord was especially calling me to proclaim at our retreats, through our magazine INTO ALL THE WORLD and my writings. And now I was to carry it overseas, to Christians and the unreached alike.

The message of reconciling love had become the very fabric of my life. Time and again I would hear after giving a talk: "Just what we needed. There is so much strife and disunity. Everywhere hearts are embittered." Because the message wasn't theoretical, but born of personal experience, people were moved to seek reconciliation.

As Canaan was supposed to be a land where the love of God would reign, this had to be its primary message. Those who love Jesus are compassionate. If we love God we will love our neighbour and even our enemy. Unity of love with God leads to unity of love with others. Even if a fellow believer turns against us, we will continue to offer the hand of reconciliation for love of Jesus.

All these struggles to attain perfect love were thus laid into the foundations of Canaan before its completion and consecration.

THANK-YOU-FATHER FESTIVAL

On July 10, 1966, there was to be a big gathering to give thanks and praise to the heavenly Father for fulfilling His promises for Canaan. It would be the crowning event celebrating God's goodness, and a milestone in the history of Canaan.

On that bright, festive day, our Land of Canaan was a glorious sight. Over a thousand friends joined us in praising God. Twenty national flags were displayed on our little Mount of Beatitudes, representing the multinational assembly of guests. With our own eyes we could see the wonderful works of God. His promises had come true. By faith and prayer alone, without human influence or resources, we were able to enter and possess our own Promised Land. The "immovable" bypass and the sites designated for a housing estate and American officers' quarters had been relocated – once and for all. By the grace of God the money had come together for the acquisition of the various plots, for the buildings and landscaping.

What God had done here was a revelation of His loving heart, a lavish outpouring of His fatherly goodness. He was indeed worthy of honour and glory for His marvellous acts. People travelled long distances in order to join us in singing praises to the "Father of Goodness". A large and diverse festal congregation had gathered between our Mount of Beatitudes and Sea of Galilee. Yes, Canaan even had its own miniature lake. Who can imagine what a miracle that was, or the disappointments and trials of faith endured before the water came! In an area of low rainfall Canaan had resembled a wasteland with its poor, sandy soil.

By faith alone did we venture to have the bed of the lake dug out and did the sisters pave the lake bed. Drilling for water on our property wasn't worthwhile – or so the water authorities informed us. At the best we could only expect a daily supply to cover the needs of a household of four or five. An adequate water supply for a property as big as Canaan would require a biblical miracle. In that bleak situation God gave us a ray of hope in a virtual stranger – Karl Erdmann, a wine wholesaler in Lützelsachsen. The Lord wakened him at night to pray for water at Canaan. He also put it on his heart to fund a drilling.

Now on that festive day a trumpet blast rang out. Every head turned in the direction where the sound of rushing water could be heard. Jets of water spurted high in the air from the sprinkler system and descended upon the fields and meadows. On the other side was the sound of splashing water from the Fountain of the Father's Goodness, while in front of us the Sea of Galilee sparkled in the sun. Everyone joined wholeheartedly in singing the hymn, "Holy God, we praise Your Name".

Why were people so moved? Among the guests were some who earlier on had difficulty believing in a water miracle. Mother Martyria and I had seriously considered whether we should even share with our friends our goal of faith for "water at Canaan" before anything was in sight. As a confirmation, we asked for a Bible verse containing the word "water" – and received Isaiah 12:3, "With joy you will draw water from the wells of salvation".

This verse headlined our 1960 newsletter as we asked our friends to pray and believe with us for water at Canaan.

Now, six years later, on July 10, 1966, our friends did "draw water from the wells" while we sang the words set to music. They drank fresh Canaan water from the fountain taps. After the humbling years of waiting and preparation God really did the water miracle in 1964. Our well produces over twenty-five times more water per hour than at a hundred similar drillings in the area. Impressed, a leading official from the local waterworks affirmed, "This is nothing short of a miracle."

Yes, we have a God of miracles! This was the refrain echoing from the Mount of Beatitudes, our outdoor stage for the afternoon session. From here the mighty deeds of God were proclaimed, as our sisters testified in various ways what the Lord had done in the past years. Canaan's residents, young and old alike, came forward, vying with each other in thanking God for His goodness in giving us Canaan for an "inheritance". And the festive gathering responded with songs of praise, thanksgiving and celebration. Three hours sped by unnoticed.

For me, the Fountain of the Father's Goodness with its constant flow of water symbolized the heart of God constantly brimming over with love and goodness. I had experienced for myself that His heart is indeed a fount of loving-kindness. Seven names of the Father adorned the fountain's rim and had been beautifully set to music. All day long we sang, with the congregation joining in: "Father of Goodness – Love – Grace – Comfort – Faithfulness – Mercy – Patience."

During the intervals guests roamed the grounds, delighting in what God had brought into existence. What had been, three years earlier, a patchwork quilt of untidy sandhills and parched fields, was now an oasis with its lake, fountains, lush meadows, colourful flowers, and graceful shrubs and trees. A prayer garden with sculptures and inscriptions invited reflection, while debt-free buildings bore mute testimony to God. What amazing goodness of the Father!

Yet another proof of His goodness was the weather. We were completely dependent on good weather, because most of the celebrations would be outdoors at the Fountain of the Father's Goodness and the Mount of Beatitudes. Heatwaves and thunderstorms were normal in mid July. But the Father gave us glorious weather. It was a mild, pleasant day so that everyone could sit outside. It could not have been more perfect. And not until the last guests had left did it begin to rain.

The festive worship service was held in the morning in the Herald Chapel. In my longing for God to be glorified I felt led to ask our spiritual daughters in the presence of God and the congregation:

Did God provide for us all these years,
spreading our table each day with good gifts?

Did He keep His promises concerning Canaan?

Has He proven Himself as a Father?

The sisters rose to their feet and answered with a resounding, "Yes, amen." They had personally witnessed the many impossibilities and hardships, the impasses and crises. So their affirmation was a powerful testimony to God's goodness and omnipotence. A mighty anthem of praise and thanksgiving rose up to God in response.

A row of memorial stones outside the Herald Chapel was a further tribute to God, our personal thank-you in acknowledgement of His help. Engraved with Bible verses He had given us over the years, they recounted the challenges in acquiring our Canaan land, and His gracious intervention.

Wherever my glance fell that day, I couldn't help feeling amazed at the wonderful acts of God. I could only worship Him in awe. Truly, our God is a God of miracles! He is a Father of goodness, who not only gives promises but fulfils them – true to His name of Yes and Amen!

I PRAISE HIS NAME OF YES AND AMEN

From the beginning of our sisterhood I would often play the harmonium in the evening, with the door ajar, as I sang our daughters songs of love for Jesus, songs about His Passion, the Father's goodness, and heaven's glory. They would listen, waiting for my favourite songs, which they knew so well. In the years following our Thank-You-Father Festival there was one particular song I would sing time and again. In a dark moment I had written it in faith, giving thanks in advance that we have a God who leads everything to a glorious conclusion.

> I praise His name of YES AND AMEN,
> for paths ordained for me to walk in,
> for blessings yielded by the night
> and choicest fruit in darkest places.
>
> I praise His name of YES AND AMEN,
> His will of loving-kindness leading
> onward, upward to the goal of heaven …

Why did this song mean so much to me? Because in various areas of my life it was no longer necessary to sing it in faith. Over and over again I had seen that when God entrusts us with a commission He sees it through. Many of the promises He had given me were now fulfilled: He had honoured His pledge of YES AND AMEN.

The road to Canaan had been paved with agonizing doubts and heart-searching. It had been one long test of faith. Seeing how God led everything to a successful conclusion, many believers were encouraged to take a step in faith themselves. A missionary couple in the Far East were inspired by REALITIES OF FAITH: THE MIRACLES OF GOD EXPERIENCED TODAY. Almost in passing, they mentioned receiving a copy at a critical point in their life. A flood had destroyed the huts in which they had been housing children, and now they had stepped out in faith and were building a permanent children's home. – A pastor in Africa wrote: "I am in the process of creating a Canaan, a faith ministry for indigenous children." – An Anglican minister said, "I would like to help build such a Canaan in England." – A sister serving in India informed us, "I already have a plot of land for a Canaan." Here and there God was prompting people to launch out in faith to help make the rule of Christ become more visible on earth.

While some were applying the principles of Canaan in their own setting, others helped in practical ways to make the vision for Canaan a reality. After testing the faith of His children, God loves to show kindness. True to His word, He blesses a hundredfold even amid persecution (Mark 10:30). He doesn't save up the reward till we get to heaven. Here and now He pours out His goodness, as we literally experienced. He gave us friends who assisted in various capacities: a caring doctor always there for us, a dependable foreman, and a senior town planner and mayor to stand up for us. He sent professionals to advise us in our multi-faceted ministry: religious dramas, printshop, radio studio, vegetable gardens, livestock and beekeeping, the production of praise plaques and ceramics. He gave us donors who by their sacrificial giving supported us as we built Canaan. Finally He raised up people who took the vision of Canaan further afield, becoming "ambassadors" for Canaan in their own part of the world.

In addition, the Lord fulfilled beyond all imagination the promise I had held up before Him since 1945: "My dwelling-place will be with them; I will be their God, and they will be my people" (Ezekiel 37:27).

For all our shortcomings, God made His presence real at Canaan. How often we heard visitors say, "It's a foretaste of heaven." God met with them; and like us, they tasted the joy and renewal that comes from repentance. Year after year people came from near and far and went their way rejoicing. Jesus' forgiveness became even more meaningful for them through the experience of repentance and confession. Leaving their burden of sin at the foot of the cross, they were free and happy. All this generated a deeper love for Jesus and the desire to follow Him and even suffer for Him. Believers of various traditions and nationalities were flocking to Canaan. In these end times we also had the joy of seeing many, including the young, give their hearts and lives to Jesus. Again and again I would sing, "I praise Your name of YES AND AMEN …"

Yet the Lord hasn't only sent us numerous guests and visitors. Not a day passes without my thanking the Lord for giving us spiritual daughters whose lives demonstrate that it pays to fight the good fight of faith against sin. Mother Martyria and I have invested much in their spiritual development, daily lifting them up in prayer. But God Himself brought about the transformation. It was a supernatural breakthrough leading to an outpouring of joy. Those easily despondent became cheerful, the tense grew relaxed, and those who seemed to be fighting a losing battle against sin experienced release. Certainly, they have caused me disappointments. But greater still is the joy they have given me. Each one is a gem, close to my heart, saved and won by the precious blood of Jesus to be His bride – all belonging to the Bride of the Lamb. No prayer, no effort on their behalf was wasted.

The close relationship Mother Martyria and I have had with our daughters from the beginning, as a spiritual family, has deepened from year to year. The bond of love, constantly renewed through mutual forgiveness, is the strongest bond there is. Aware of my own failure, I have not found it hard to forgive. How often I have failed in love, patience and kindness, not making it easy for my daughters. So I thank them for their love and affection.

The love and spiritual oneness within our family of sisters have grown in the same measure as our love for Jesus. The self-absorption and indifference towards the Lord's kingdom concerns that had often marred our fellowship in earlier years has for the most part disappeared. Our daughters fully share in the joys and sorrows of the commission God has entrusted to us.

Mealtime fellowship is a happy time of sharing, often sparking fresh initiatives. Faces light up with joy at every victory won for the kingdom of God as we hear reports from the branches about lives touched by God and new ministry opportunities. Special highlights are morning Bible studies and evening sessions. At prayer meetings everyone joins in wholeheartedly claiming the Lord's victory in various areas of ministry.

I especially treasure the monthly personal talks I have with individual sisters, giving me a precious glimpse of what the Lord is doing in their lives. What blessed hours I have spent with small groups of sisters, sharing about the glory of heaven awaiting us, or singing songs about the heavenly Father or the love of Jesus. We meet as a happy family in the Lord, children of God, all children of one Father, part of the Bride of the Lamb, led by the Spirit, one in love and in joyous expectation of the day when with the hosts of heaven we will worship the Lamb of God for ever.

Ever since I became mother of the sisterhood, this shared life with my daughters has been deeply meaningful for me. It's only natural to want to be with those we love. That is love's way. Because the sisters are so dear to me, I find it particularly hard not to be with them. Yet over the years this is a sacrifice God would ask of me again and again. First it was the call to seclusion as of 1952, then the many trips He later called me to undertake. But I always knew I had to be faithful to my prayer ministry. Half the time I would spend alone with the Lord; the other half with the sisters as I fulfilled my responsibilities. My daughters did not miss out as a result of this arrangement, for God blessed the times we had together all the more.

God's pledge of Yes and Amen was coming true not only for the motherhouse but for the sisters serving in the branches. For love of Jesus they were willing to leave behind them Canaan, their spiritual mothers and sisters, and to live for the dawning of His kingdom abroad. The specific ministries God has entrusted to them in their respective countries have become part of their lives.

In these uncertain times I have always found it hard to send out sisters to other countries. But the Lord not only required daughters from us: He gave us new daughters – this too in fulfilment of God's pledge of YES AND AMEN. In recent years Mother Martyria and I repeatedly inspected the motherhouse to see if more living space could be arranged or whether we would have to build again. As it turned out, we did have to build again – and urgently. Within a span of six years over fifty sisters of ten different nationalities joined us. On the day they join it is always moving for the community to hear how they heard the call, sometimes in far-away countries, as Jesus drew near as the Bridegroom of their souls, breaking powerfully into their lives.

The same goes for our Canaan Franciscan Brothers, whose fellowship was founded in 1967. It all began with an unforgettable moment during my trip to the United States. A pastor in Minneapolis was driving me to a speaking engagement when I suddenly became aware of a divine summons. The Lord wanted us to open the way for young men to share in our life of discipleship and ministry at Canaan. The conviction was stronger than the many questions Mother Martyria and I had. Shortly afterwards the Lord called the first brothers from America and our own country.

He planted them, and those who came later, into our spiritual commission as Canaan Franciscan Brothers. On the one hand they are able to develop in healthy independence as a small brotherhood, on the other they are true spiritual sons of Canaan. They are involved in various areas of ministry, like garden maintenance, tape production and youth work. Above all, they draw upon the same spiritual sources God has granted us over the years.

Not everyone associated with Canaan actually lives here. Early on, a group of mainly married women we have known since the revival formed a satellite fellowship. For decades the Thorn Sisters, as they are called, have faithfully borne with us the trials and burdens of our ministry. With many hidden sacrifices they have put all their energy into the task. Some, though well on in years, later heard the call to a shared life at Canaan. Single or widowed, they gave up careers and family ties and banded together to form the Sisterhood of the Crown of Thorns. Their House of Jesus' Comfort in the south of Canaan also became a home for Thorn Sisters.

In recent years both groups have been blessed with spiritual renewal – a special point of thanksgiving for me. This was yet another sign that God has honoured His pledge of YES AND AMEN. They too went through a time of testing and spiritual maturing. For me, it is always a comfort to see their dedication in standing up for the Lord, whether behind the scenes with their prayer support or on the front line as the battle rages in our dark world.

I am also full of thanksgiving to the Lord for raising up so many faithful Canaan Friends at home and abroad. They are on fire for the Canaan ministry and live for the dawning of the kingdom of heaven here and there in our world.

In addition, the Lord has linked me spiritually with many others whose countries and languages are unknown to me – friends, readers and listeners. Humbled by their spontaneous, heart-warming responses, I give all the glory to God. Truly, His Word is faithful. He does what He says.

GRANDPARENTS FOR CANAAN

The Lord blessed us at Canaan not only with friends and benefactors but with something else that was a special gift for me personally. He gave my daughters spiritual "grandparents", as the sisters fondly called my parents, and as they in turn signed their personal greetings to them.

Canaan and the sisterhood had grown very dear to my parents. They knew each one of their "granddaughters". The sisters, in particular those serving abroad, had a special place in their hearts and prayers. Even as they approached their nineties my parents attended all our festivals at Canaan, whenever health permitted. Despite a failing memory towards the end of his life, my father vividly recalled the specific needs of Canaan day by day in detailed prayers.

My parents' affection for Canaan and the sisterhood was so evidently of God. This was something new, and again and again I would sing, "I praise Your name of YES AND AMEN ..." It hadn't always been like that. My parents understandably found it hard to accept the direction my life took as of 1935, especially when I chose to share Jesus' path of poverty. My father, a professor and long-time rector of the technical university, had financed my studies to doctorate level, only to watch me turn down all suitable positions shortly after obtaining my PhD.

Nevertheless, after the founding of the sisterhood, my parents selflessly welcomed our large family of sisters into their home at the cost of peace and quiet and living space. Being little involved in our community life, which fully preoccupied me, meant yet another sacrifice on their part. Certainly, I learnt to make time for my parents so that they could share in the concerns of our young organization. But since it wasn't possible for me to put their demands above God's call, pain and disappointment were inevitable. Later, in their old age, my parents feared they might pass away while I was on a ministry tour abroad. This weighed heavily on me and I was saddened for their sakes. Yet Jesus says, "Anyone who loves their father or mother more than me is not worthy of me" (Matthew 10:37).

For my family, some of God's leadings were problematic and initially hard to understand. Take the call to live by faith. As a physicist and professor for mechanical engineering, my father regarded this as highly unusual and questionable. He was used to having a solid financial plan with detailed cost estimates and funding all worked out in advance. Actually, by nature I'm the same. But now my parents were being surprised with one adventure of faith after the other. Each time, they felt the honour of the family was at stake. I'll never forget my father's dismay when I first shared with him God's commission for our Land of Canaan.

For my parents' sake I was deeply thankful for God's faithfulness during the acquisition and development of Canaan. It was a special token of His loving-kindness. With their own eyes they saw God validate the commissions, proving they were indeed of Him as they came to pass. My father's amazement grew from year to year as he heard of the miracles God did at Canaan. His prayers overflowed with thanksgiving. His face would light up every time I shared a new answer to prayer. Now my father praised the "heavenly mathematics" God used to bring about our Land of Canaan. After all the difficulties of the past, this was a wonderful outcome and sign of fulfilment.

This loving fellowship with my parents, which deepened immeasurably over the last ten years of their lives, was another instance of God's faithfulness in keeping His pledge of YES AND AMEN. After all the struggles, suffering and tears of repentance, He had granted victory. The dawning of His kingdom of love was manifested, which is what Canaan is all about.

LAST HOUR FOR CARRYING OUT THE COMMISSION

During my weeks at Sinai God had given a commission for the nations. In the following years radio programmes based on my writings were put together in German and a few other languages. They were simple, basic, and produced without the proper technical expertise. When we approached various radio stations with this material, only our Russian programmes were accepted by one station. Still, we couldn't help rejoicing at the thought of reaching our persecuted brothers and sisters.

Much to my sorrow, this transmission was cancelled in spring 1966 as a result of Richard Ising's book. In late 1969 we once again sent material to radio stations around the world. This time we received positive responses from the Philippines, Indonesia and India – all stations of FEBC (Far East Broadcasting Company) – as well as from Addis Ababa, Ethiopia, from Monaco for Czech programmes, from the Russian department at BBC, London, and from Rome for German broadcasts to Siberia.

Our production methods, amateurish and time-consuming, soon proved inadequate. To keep up with the demand we urgently needed a radio studio. But how to start such a major enterprise without funds, experience and trained staff? And once a radio studio materialized, would there be sufficient time to carry out the ministry? Dark clouds of persecution were gathering on the horizon and natural disasters were increasing. God gave the go-ahead, despite the risks. Amazingly all the money came together for this costly enterprise. Unexpected talents came to the fore. The Lord raised up sisters and brothers among us and gifted them in the area of sound technology, as well as providing co-workers with the necessary expertise. So in February 1971 our Canaan radio studio was up and running.

Now we were far better equipped to produce quality material. The programmes were interspersed with songs and instrumental music recorded in our own studio. There I could also read the radio scripts in German and sometimes in English. And thanks to God, the unimaginable became reality. Various foreign-language versions of our programmes (one, two, five, fifteen and thirty minutes in length) were soon being transmitted daily or weekly in all five continents with a potential audience of millions. Truly, God's thoughts are higher than ours.

Responses came from the jungles of Indonesia, Vietnamese war zones, schools and colleges in India, American big cities, the wilds of Burma, and from remote missionary stations in New Guinea and Malaysia. I couldn't help feeling awed by God's incredible purposes. The speed with which God opened doors and paved the way seemed to confirm that time was short. Manifestations of sin, evil, filth and perversion were flooding our nations.

For years I had cherished the idea of producing a film credibly demonstrating that God is alive and real. Accessible and relevant, it would be an ideal medium for reaching every age group and nationality. For this enterprise God gave us a word in prayer: "Therefore, my dear brothers and sisters, stand firm. Let nothing move you. Always give yourselves fully to the work of the Lord, because you know that your labour in the Lord is not in vain" (1 Corinthians 15:58). Undoubtedly it would be a challenge, since we lacked even the basic requirements for film-making.

Yet now, in 1972, God's moment had come to produce such a film about Canaan. We were recommended a film company on the strength of its technical competence and sensitivity for the project. Everything dovetailed perfectly. A film schedule was set up, and under the Spirit's guidance a film script soon came into being despite our inexperience. For the two-week filming period the Father gave us glorious weather and orchestrated a number of unplanned shoot-worthy incidents. Financially He also provided: sufficient donations arrived to cover the expenses. The enemy, however, seemed to be enraged by the film and tried to destroy it in part during its development and later stages. But to no avail. God fought for the Canaan film GOD LIVES AND WORKS TODAY. Even before the German original was completed, work began on the English version.

The impact of the film showed God's burning desire to reach the seeking, the spiritually hungry, the indifferent and those who have given up hope, to draw them back to His heart, the source of life, and to reignite the passion of those who love Him. I had waited so long for this film. For years I had prayed that it would succeed in drawing a big haul for His kingdom like a fisherman's net. Again and again I had asked the Lord to extend the time of grace so that we could help rescue many more souls. At Canaan we've been so privileged. On a daily basis we have experienced what an all-powerful, all-loving Father we have in God, and what a wonderful Saviour we have in Jesus. We have seen what the Holy Spirit can do. If only many others could experience the same for themselves. But up till then we lacked the ways and means of sharing our experiences with others worldwide.

Undoubtedly, much had already been achieved, thanks to the devoted efforts of our Canaan teams. On fire for the Lord, they distributed our bookmarks and literature, mounted praise plaques at popular scenic spots, provided "Dial-a-message" phone bases, displayed posters, formed house groups to listen to audio tapes, travelled through the country with the Canaan sound-slide-series… and much more. But the lament in my heart was not stilled. "What is all this in view of the millions out there?" Tangible proof is what they need of who God is and what He is like. This is the living Lord who can deal with every sin and predicament in our lives. Nothing is too big for Him to handle. If only I could paint a picture in glowing colours of what He is really like. Joy is what people need to see – the joy that comes from repentance and the forgiveness of sin, from reconciliation with God and with one another. He's the one who resolves our problems and helps us conquer our fears. Beyond all else, He is worthy of our love.

Meanwhile the Canaan film had made its debut and was being shown in various cities across our country. Nor was that all. Shortly after its release, an offer came from Canada for it to be carried on the newly developed cable television. In the USA, dates were immediately set for it to be shown at big conferences and on TV channels, while lending libraries took over its distribution nationwide. Even before its release, pre-orders were placed by Australians and New Zealanders visiting Canaan. Offers reached us from other television stations abroad. More foreign editions were made. Even as far afield as India, Taiwan and the Philippines ways were explored for producing versions in the vernacular.

With this rapid, global development of our ministry the Lord showed me why He had curtailed my foreign travels, which had been part of my life since the stay at Sinai in 1963 – right up till 1969. In 1970 I was invited to speak in Indonesia, primarily in the Timor revival area and at a faith conference in Batu. I had already accepted the invitation and all the arrangements were in place when God intervened. My life suddenly took a 180 degree turn. I became so ill that the doctor did not permit me to make the journey to Indonesia. God had other plans for me. The main thrust of my ministry was to be through radio programmes, later the film, and the unexpectedly rapid publication of my writings in many languages and countries. With this development the Lord relieved me of my travels abroad, which would have been beyond my strength. But that was not all. He had a new commission lined up for me.

THE SHADES OF NIGHT ARE FALLING 1970 – 1973

"PUT YOUR HOUSE IN ORDER" 2 KINGS 20:1

About the time I cancelled the trip to Indonesia, someone was shown by the Lord that, quite apart from my illness, I was to withdraw and spend more time in seclusion. It was time to prepare for heaven, put my house in order, equip our daughters for the future, and, along with Mother Martyria, prepare our successors for their task. Uncharacteristically our doctor expressed similar sentiments.

Almost the moment I entered seclusion, the Spirit of God came upon me, prompting me to write extensively for when I was gone, as a spiritual legacy for the next generation. In that outpouring of grace the Lord gave me an abundance of messages for our sisterhood and the sisters who would later lead it. They covered various areas of ministry as well referring to a future time of disaster. Writing of the coming times inevitably caused me pain and anguish:

My heart is in turmoil. The atmosphere is pregnant with disaster. It is sheer agony to think of what awaits them.

I felt the urgency of not only preparing for heaven but also having everything ready for my daughters by then. All those weeks a tune was ringing in my heart like a soft undercurrent: "heaven's glory beckons". Amid the sadness at the travelling ministry being cut short, a secret bliss welled up. "Going home! Soon I'll be going home to Jesus!" I was consumed with longing to be with the Lord for ever.

A holy atmosphere rested over those weeks spent in seclusion away from the motherhouse. Joy at going home to the Lord mingled with the pain of parting as well as concern at what awaited those left behind. Eternity had drawn near, and with it the shining goal of the City of God. As never before I sang:

> There is a city bathed in light,
> Far, far from grief and weeping.
> And as we glimpse this city bright
> All earthly longings fade from sight.
> A secret yearning fills us; a secret yearning.
>
> ANON.

The closeness of eternity brought me face to face with the reality of death in a new and deeper way. Up to this point death was for me synonymous with going home to the Lord. The mere thought filled me with indescribable joy. "Soon I will be going home! Soon I will be with the Lord for ever!" One of my favourite Bible verses was Philippians 1:21, "For to me, to live is Christ and to die is gain". Over the years I had experienced something of what Paul writes: "I die daily" (1 Corinthians 15:31 KJV). This is why I was so happy at the prospect of going to be with Jesus. Our longing for heaven corresponds to the suffering and spiritual dying beforehand.

Now I became deeply aware of the terrors of death. Death, perhaps our greatest enemy as it will be the last to be destroyed (1 Corinthians 15:26), is indeed to be feared. It inspires dread. At Lazarus' grave Jesus "groaned in the spirit, and was troubled" (John 11:33 KJV). He wept at the heartache death causes and the power it can wield, instantaneously transforming a living being, full of vitality, into a lifeless corpse, rigid in death.

Confronted with this stark reality, our fathers in the faith and traditional hymn-writers often sang of death and its terrors. They prayed in words that will resonate with all who have faced the truth about themselves and know that they will one day have to give an account of themselves before God's throne:

When I am in the throes of death,
When I must draw my final breath,
Lord Jesus, hasten to my side
And help me past the stormy tide,
Shorten death's hour of agony.

PAUL EBER, 1511-1569

Before me stood death, grim and relentless. The hour we die, a line is drawn under our lives. No more opportunity to repent, to make up for anything. It's all over, every chance forfeited. Death is ruthless in stripping away our masks.

Was it any surprise that my life was laid bare before me, stirring up painful memories? Memories of wrong things done and good things left undone. Opportunities neglected. My lack of love and patience for those who caused me distress and, most painful of all, the consciousness of having failed Jesus. The missing tokens of love. The missing sacrifices in response to His love and forgiveness. Where was my thanksgiving for His supreme sacrifice? Various incidents came to mind, along with attitudes, actions and words better left unsaid. Names and people rose accusingly before me. In subsequent months and years God took me through periods of deep regret and contrition. But amid it all ran an undercurrent of profound thanksgiving. Because Jesus shed His blood for us, we have access to heaven as penitent sinners saved by grace. No word was so dear to me as "grace", for looking back I could no longer see anything good in my life.

Out of this deep and lasting conviction of sin was born a heartfelt prayer: "Help me to love where I have failed to love. Prompt me to make sacrifices where I have sacrificed too little. Help me to prove my dedication in times of suffering and divine discipline. In the time still left to me, grant me the grace, in all weakness, to spend myself as never before for Your kingdom and the commission You have entrusted to us."

Now, as my life was drawing to a close, I was reminded of those words of Jesus that had impacted me deeply during my critical illness in 1958. "I brought glory to you here on earth by completing the work you gave me to do." (John 17:4 NLT)

To complete the task God had given me was the longing of my heart: *Help me to fulfil my ministry to my daughters. Help me to fulfil the ministry to the nations, though differently than before. Now, as my life draws to a close, help me to continue unabated the ministry of warning, hard though I find it. Help me to fulfil each task out of the place of stillness and the fellowship of Your sufferings. Help me to feel Your pain over a lost humanity, whose sins are crying out to heaven. Above all, let me fulfil my primary task since 1952: helping to gather the Bride from the ends of the earth and to prepare her for the day of Your return. As my life draws to a close, keep me from growing weary. Help me to persevere, despite the libel spread by our opponents, which is destroying everything I have lived and prayed for: the unity of believers.*

In the light of eternity one acts differently than before. God doubtlessly made us that way. He wants to encourage us to use our time wisely and make amends where we can. So those years were a time of contrasts. Older and frailer, I found myself accomplishing more than ever. Seldom had my working hours been so long. In my exhaustion I drew new strength from the Lord and lived solely from His miraculous touch. I spent much time apart with Jesus and yet I was also able to do so much for our sisterhood, the branches, the Thorn Sisters and the retreat guests, alongside the literature and radio ministry.

So I cannot thank the Lord enough for this major change of direction in my life in spring 1970. Through my illness heaven stopped me in my tracks: "Get ready. Forget about travels abroad. Set your house in order." Even though I couldn't understand why the ministry to the nations should end so abruptly, here too God had a specific purpose. His counsels are more wonderful and far-reaching than we can ever imagine. Without my needing to travel, the ministry entrusted to me at Sinai was to be carried out on a much bigger scale. At the same time I was able to set my house in order and equip the sisters. The commissions, rooted in spiritual suffering during times alone with the Lord, grew and branched out. Tears over my failings enabled me to speak with greater conviction of God's holiness, His coming judgments over sin, repentance as the only way to deliverance, His loving overtures, and the blessed hope of our soon-coming King.

The latest pamphlets on contemporary issues were now written in the light of eternity. A further product of those years was the book on the battle against sin (The Christian's Victory, American edition: You Will Never Be the Same), as well as The Unseen World of Angels and Demons, and Setting Our Hearts on Heaven.

OUR TWENTY-FIFTH ANNIVERSARY

Putting your house in order means above all checking for cracks and other damage and making timely repairs. A thorough spring cleaning is needed, and this is what the Lord laid on my heart for our sisterhood. How else can any house stand in years to come and retain its value?

With our twenty-fifth anniversary only months ahead, I knew that without spiritual preparation we weren't in a position to celebrate this event, let alone face the future. Over the years we have practised walking in the light together as a community, with the opportunity for private counselling and confession. And we have seen God working in each one of our hearts. Yet even though I couldn't quite put my finger on it, I sensed indifference, lack of love and a tendency to be overly busy. These and other habitual sins had taken root, squeezing out first love for Jesus.

Our house, which was meant to be a "temple of God", urgently needed a spring cleaning before we could celebrate. This burden weighed heavy on my heart, and inwardly I struggled. Nothing would have made me happier than calling my daughters home from abroad for a family reunion. Together we would worship and celebrate, receive fresh impetus for our ministry and be strengthened in our faith for the days ahead. But first, I knew, there had to be cleansing. I was ready to go through with it, I told the Lord, even if it took days, though I hoped we could soon move on to joy and celebration.

But it went differently. There was a holy sense of God's presence throughout those ten days of preparation at the end of 1971. Jesus was among us as Lord and Judge. After I finally let go of my cherished plans for joyous times with the sisters, I was resolved that Jesus would have the space and the right to deal with everything displeasing to Him – even if it took up the whole time. He must have the right to cleanse His temple, for didn't He promise in His Word, "Here will I dwell; for I have desired it" (Psalm 132:14 KJV)?

As the Lord worked in our midst, I sensed how concerned He was for each one of us. He was submitting us to the refining fire now so that we could stand firm in the coming trials. That also went for our ministry in years to come, when we, the founders, were gone. He wanted to prepare every one of us for the heavenly destination, the Marriage Supper of the Lamb.

During those days the Lord gave the sisters the grace to open their hearts and minds for His light. Over our Hall of Zion rested the Spirit of Truth. No one held back from sharing in the light of God whatever the Spirit put in their hearts for someone else. There was an almost total absence of people-pleasing or fear of what others might think. True Christian love prevailed, the love that cares enough to challenge others instead of leaving them a captive of sin. Hourly I sensed the Lord sustaining me during the times of fellowship in the light with various groups of sisters. Mother Martyria happened to be ill at the time.

Coming together on the last day to celebrate and worship in His presence, we were blessed afresh by an outpouring of divine grace. Never before had we experienced anything like it as a community. Our hearts were literally overflowing with praise and thanksgiving. Some sisters were changed almost beyond recognition. Afterwards, warm letters came from the branches thanking for the spiritual renewal gained from this "cleansing of the temple". So the Lord had already laid the groundwork for our forthcoming jubilee.

My one desire was for Jesus to be exalted in an outpouring of love and devotion. Back in 1966 a Thank-You-Father Festival was held in the Father's honour at the dedication of Canaan. This time it was to be a Love-Jesus Festival. Jesus was to be greeted by the love of many hearts. He was to be celebrated as Lord and heavenly Bridegroom for revealing His great love. His glories were to be praised in every imaginable way, for He is truly beyond compare. No one is like Him. For all the contempt and shame He is made to suffer in today's world, He must receive love upon love, as never before.

As I came apart for some days to pray about the Love-Jesus Festival, the Holy Spirit gave me the inspiration for the various celebrations, the texts and songs. At the suggestion of Sister Agatha, the Jesus Pathway was created at Canaan. Lined with large plaques proclaiming who Jesus is, it was to be a lasting memorial of our jubilee weekend.

On the eve of the festival there was to be a special time of worship culminating in Holy Communion, with gentle songs and melodies celebrating Jesus as the Bridegroom of the soul. On Sunday the worship was to continue all day long as we lifted our hearts and voices, exalting the Lord for what He had done. For twenty-five years He had led and guided us, keeping us spiritually alive. He had revealed the treasure hidden in repentance and the sheer joy of loving Him.

Such a festival exalting Jesus in a world of growing darkness and blasphemy calls for a special cleansing beforehand. Satan is highly active when Christians want to celebrate. So when Mother Martyria and I sent out the invitations to the festival, we asked our friends to join us in seeking a new and deeper cleansing by the Lord:

A festival requires preparation. To quote Mother Martyria, your clothes need to be freshly washed and ironed and the house clean and tidy … So, dear friends, whether you're coming from this country or from overseas, across the English Channel or from Scandinavia, please join us during the coming weeks in preparing spiritually for the festival. In the face of troubles and hardship may our response be: "Thank You, Father. It's just what I need so that my clothes will be clean. Show me all the stains, so that I can bring them into the light and under the blood of Jesus. At all costs prepare me for the Love-Jesus Festival at Canaan."

… Let's pray, "Lord, I am determined. I won't let You go until You have prepared me for this festival. There's no other way I can come." God hears earnest prayer. Then our festal gathering will comfort and refresh the heart of Jesus, bringing Him joy. All the company of heaven will rejoice. The heavens will ring with the sound of angels singing the praises of Jesus, the loveliest, the purest, the most glorious of all, worthy of our love as none other, Lamb of God and heavenly Bridegroom … May 1972

Above all, God was speaking earnest words to us Mary Sisters as He led us through a new process of preparation. In His longing for the love of penitent sinners who weep over their sins, God spoke with unmistakable clarity so that we could all understand. Divine discipline leads to repentance, repentance to grace, and grace to bridal love for Jesus. Visibly and tangibly, this was our experience at Canaan.

That winter we had hardly any rain or snow; spring was very dry too, and the outlook for the coming months was bleak. Nationwide catastrophic drought conditions led to fears of large-scale insect plagues. As we don't use poisonous insecticides, Canaan's lawns, fields and orchards were particularly at risk. The trees and bushes were already showing signs of drought damage, and the fields were brown and parched. Over us the skies were shut even when it had started raining in other parts of the country. In late April severe frost struck. First the roses, the symbol of love, froze, then the blossoms in the orchards. In June, when sun was needed for haying, it poured for days on end. We sensed the Lord was grieved. He had to stand against us, as He was waiting for yet deeper repentance. Not until three days before the festival did things change.

The Bible verse I received from the Lord for those months was Isaiah 54:8. "With a little wrath I hid My face from you for a moment; but with everlasting kindness I will have mercy on you." (NKJV) Then the second half of the verse came true, and streams of grace and blessing flowed. The roses recovered and were in full bloom during the Love-Jesus Festival. The strawberry plants produced fresh buds and a bigger crop than ever. In the orchards some of the trees bore fruit after all. Due to the rain that finally fell, the grass grew high and dense, and at the last moment the hay was brought in completely dry. All the preparations were completed without a hitch. We couldn't help feeling awed at this proof of God's favour.

Over 1500 guests arrived from seventeen countries. Everything went smoothly, as if angels were working behind the scenes. Not a single bed too many or too few. The workmen finished their work in time. The PA system functioned. Everywhere the unity of love was evident. The spirit of joy, peace and love was poured out over our guests as they arrived. The weather on both days was a special token of God's grace, and during the celebrations we all sensed the presence of the Lord.

Guests wrote afterwards what an unforgettable occasion it had been, praising Jesus in song in ever new ways and experiencing His presence – truly a festival with a lasting impact. Holy Communion, as many said, was a foretaste of the Marriage Supper of the Lamb. For hours we celebrated together in the Herald Chapel, one in heart and soul, united in the desire that all our love would be His alone. During the mealtimes in the festive tent there was singing, and words of greeting were given by friends from around the world. We were like one big family. All day long the theme song resounded throughout Canaan:

O none can be loved as is Jesus.
None like Him is found anywhere.
It's He whom I love, whom I live for,
For no one with Him can compare.

O NONE CAN BE LOVED AS IS JESUS, no. 32

Was it any wonder that my heart overflowed with joy! My fervent prayers had been answered. Jesus had received the heartfelt love and worship of many souls.

THE EMMAUS SEASON – 1973

Night was rapidly descending upon our world. I couldn't shake off the sense of urgency. Somehow I had to find ways to call back all the sisters to the motherhouse the following year, this time for a more extensive time of preparation. Storm clouds were gathering on the political horizon and hatred of Jesus was flaring up globally. Inevitably Christians would be increasingly targeted. We stood on the brink of a new era. Worldwide persecution against Christians was impending.

At the same time moral depravity was becoming endemic. The crimes of humanity were crying out to heaven. All of this signalled that God's response would not be long in coming. His righteous judgment would fall, destroying those who destroy the earth (Revelation 11:18). I began to pray and plead that by then we would stand humbled and convicted in God's presence, not lashing out in rebellion when He executes judgment in His holy wrath. When that time comes, may we be so struck by God's grief over our sinful selves and this sin-laden world that we can only say, "Yes, Lord God Almighty, true and just are your judgments" (Revelation 16:7). Unless called by the Lord to suffer for Him, the humbled in spirit will know His protection in the age of wrath, just as a devoted son is spared by his father (Malachi 3:17).

I pleaded with the Lord to give me and Mother Martyria, along with our daughters, a time of spiritual training. We called it the Emmaus Season in memory of Jesus' conversation with the disciples on the road to Emmaus as He explained the scriptures to them. In prayer I appealed to Him who has all power and means and asked Him to raise up friends to stand in for the sisters serving abroad. In long discussions with sisters in charge of various work areas Mother Martyria and I drew up a plan for some of the work to be done in advance or postponed until after the first weeks of 1973. Our prayers were wonderfully heard.

When the Emmaus Season began, I was still recovering from a serious illness, but despite my physical frailty, I was able to deliver the talks for the sisters. Night after night God gave messages that reached their hearts, providing an abundance of spiritual sustenance for the times ahead. They received biblical teaching, in-depth study of God's prophetic Word about these dark days, as well as spiritual guidelines and encouragement to stand firm in suffering. Songs, prayers and watchwords for everyday situations completed the spiritual fare.

Though it was a constant battle to stem the tide of urgent work, most of the sisters had sufficient quiet time during the Emmaus Season to inwardly digest what they had heard. Already we were seeing a sharp increase in God's preliminary judgments as I spoke to the sisters about a coming time of disaster. That spring there was a rash of major crises ranging from natural disasters to uprisings, industrial action and acts of terrorism. The timing of our Emmaus Season was significant. It was as if God had set aside those weeks specifically in order to prepare us for a coming world disaster preceded by persecution of Christians.

On the night before sisters were due to return to the various countries, we met once more in the Motherhouse Chapel. Seldom had we experienced such an occasion in the holy presence of God as a community. After prayer, I felt led to speak to my daughters about Jesus calling us to His side as the hour of Gethsemane strikes for the whole world. What brought Him through in the garden long ago? His wrestling in prayer and His *yes* to the Father's will. For us, too, this is the way to victory in the times ahead.

I had written a prayer as an act of surrender to the Lord that we could personally make on that night. It was an opportunity to commit ourselves to the Lord no matter what suffering the future held. There was a sense that this might be the last time we could meet up in this way before the coming trials. So it was a deeply moving moment as we said goodbye to the sisters serving abroad, especially those in Jerusalem. Not long afterwards the latter received threatening calls and then the first anonymous letter demanding they leave the house and country within four weeks. As Christians they were being targeted by a secret terrorist organization.

If any of us had not yet known the Father-heart of God, we did now, as a fruit of the Emmaus Season. What loving-kindness of the Father to grant us this time together. How gracious, how amazingly kind and caring He is. Nowhere does the light shine so brightly as in the dark. Against the backdrop of the coming trials we had a unique glimpse of who our Lord and God is. He is eternal love. In times of distress He both can and will help those who belong to Him. Satanic powers and hostile forces must bow to the all-powerful God. Overwhelmed by His love, even the most fearful among us radiantly declared that fear could no longer dominate them. At the thought of future suffering they had learnt to put their trust in His ever-loving heart.

Other believers, hearing of our Emmaus Season, were keen to learn more. I myself had a burning desire to help prepare people, whether they knew the Lord personally or not, for the hard times ahead, which will bring death to millions. I gave the Lord no peace until He gave me another message in booklet and newspaper form with a wide distribution. My prayer was that many would be alerted to the coming perils and respond with repentance, so that they might experience the grace of God's help and protection. God heard me, simultaneously granting me two booklets in our series on contemporary issues: Countdown to World Disaster: Hope and Protection for the Future and The Eve of Persecution.

There was a real sense of urgency. At all costs we needed to get this message out. With the advance of the atheist left, the mounting threat of war, and the smear campaign against our sisterhood in full swing, it was a race with time. Night was falling rapidly.

BECOMING LIKE HIM IN HIS DEATH

AT THE SIDE OF MY DESPISED LORD

To love Jesus is our calling. My greatest desire for my spiritual daughters was that they would live up to their vocation. Love for Jesus was the pearl of great price I had found by searching, and all the more valuable because I had searched so long. I found complete happiness in this bridal, first love for Jesus – the answer to all my questions and problems, and fulfilment for my life. Ever since He sought me and set my heart aflame, my thoughts and emotions have revolved round Him. Jesus was the centre of my whole life. "Jesus, Jesus, Jesus" was the name ringing in my heart.

Jesus evoked from me words of adoration, songs of praise. He accomplished what no human love could ever have achieved. No one but Jesus could have induced me to choose a way of life contrary to my nature with the call to seclusion. Only Jesus could have prompted me to take up my much-disputed ministry of warning in a world torn by conflicting opinions.

In this love for Jesus I was completely united with Him. His pathway was mine. His sorrows were mine. What grieved Him grieved me. Wherever He was not loved, wherever He was rejected, even hated, I longed all the more to comfort and refresh His heart.

My grief for Jesus' sake intensified as we entered the 1970s. The permissive sixties had led to widespread immorality and glorification of sin. Now a tidal wave of blasphemy was rising against God and His Son Jesus Christ. For the first time in history there was an officially registered Church of Satan and high priest in

America with thousands of Satanic priests, innumerable Satan worshippers, sordid rituals, Satanic cults involving human sacrifice, and a Satanic Bible. An entire movement had sprung up, fuelled by hatred of Jesus.

Not content with his success, Satan was trying to invade every part of society, including the church, with blasphemy. From America to Australia irreverent rock operas denigrating Jesus were performed live to full houses, with the screen versions reaching global audiences. The controversial shows ran for years, in some towns with multiple performances on a single day and tickets sold out weeks in advance. Viewers, including churchgoers, schoolchildren and Christian youth groups, applauded while Jesus, the Son of God, was portrayed as a clown or a simpleton. Worse still, a film director tenaciously clung to his plans for an obscene film about the "sex life of Jesus Christ". It was advertised as "blasphemous, pornographic and sadistic".

I was sickened to read or hear about these horrendous blasphemies. If you love someone, you can't bear to see them so degraded. For me, Jesus is the purest, the noblest, most wonderful and winsome, awesome in majesty, high and exalted. He is the King of Love and Maker of all worlds and peoples. It broke my heart to think of Him reduced to a spectacle for millions worldwide, an object of shame and ridicule.

A lament rose from the depths of my heart. Long ago our thorn-crowned Saviour was mocked and profaned by His contemporaries, Jewish and Roman, in just one country. Today He is mocked and profaned in nearly every nation, especially in the so-called Christian West. Among the applauding crowds are some who know of Jesus as the Son of God and even those who call Him their Saviour.

In spirit I saw Pilate presenting Jesus to the howling mob. What an image of shame and degradation. There He stood, disfigured by the blows and scourging, mocked and profaned, His garments in tatters. You could almost hear the scornful cry, "Is this supposed to be the Son of God?" It was a moment of utter humiliation. Yet what must He endure today? Sometimes I felt it was more than my heart could take. On stage and screen He is portrayed as a fool, a loser, surrounded by capering clowns and scantily clad women. The Judge of the world is caricatured and His Passion mocked, His farewell discourses parodied and reduced to narrative jokes. In spirit I would weep at the feet of my Lord, whose dignity as King remains intact despite all the shame. I worshipped Him for His humility in allowing it to happen, deferring judgment in His yearning for more souls to be saved. In His amazing love He is willing to endure such abhorrent blasphemy if only some might yet find their way to heaven's glory. The shame He suffers is our opportunity to let Him know how much we care. We are called not just to believe in Jesus but willingly to suffer for His name's sake out of love and thanksgiving.

My one longing was to stand at the side of my degraded Lord and Saviour. Over the years I wrote against such productions. To my relief, some did heed the warning and experience a change of heart. They went on to warn others, passing on literature and at times even succeeding in stopping further performances.

Yet for me it was all too little in view of the rising tide of blasphemy. New screen and stage productions emerged, attributing even more shocking perversions to God the Father and our Lord Jesus. How often we have sung the verse:

> Love, to You our love we offer,
> Such as we would give no other,
> Love and comfort without end.

God was speaking to us at an even deeper level about ministering to His heart. It was all about feeling the pain with Him and refreshing Him. No one anywhere is so publicly defamed and mocked as Jesus, yet no one is more worthy of our love. In what way could I practically offer Him "love and comfort without end"? He knew.

In 1970, while I was away for a quiet time of prayer, a sister drove over from the motherhouse expressly to deliver a letter with deeply serious implications. It was a circular letter sent to the director of a gospel literature service, demanding that he sever connections with us. He was urged to stop promoting my books or else risk action being taken against his own organization. The letter further stated that if he continued to distribute my writings, he was endorsing the message of a dangerous, demonically-inspired false teacher and would come under this evil influence himself.

In a flash I realized that this was not an isolated incident. It was a systematic attack on my character and our ministry by the evil one. The intention was to destroy. What I then experienced in the way of shame and disgrace was an answer to my prayer to stand at the side of my mocked and despised Lord, only I didn't realize the full extent at the time. Because the circular letter arrived shortly after my birthday, I took it as a sign that in this new year of my life Jesus was calling me at a deeper level to walk the path of shame with Him.

With this circular letter a campaign had been launched, and soon darts were flying at me from all sides. In the following weeks letters arrived from further Christian organizations which had received the circular letter. These were well-known, influential ministries in our country, and their opinion was respected among committed Christians. They, too, had been threatened, and some were asking for clarification. Behind it all was Friedrich Wilhelm Ringsdorff, a spiritual son of Richard Ising, author of the 1965 book on powerful delusions. After the latter's death, he adopted Ising's legacy and resumed the attack, regarding it as his life's mission to destroy our ministry.

He seemed to be driven by the task. By his own admission in a letter, it consumed his time and energy, stretching him to the limit. Convinced he was acting on God's behalf, he appealed to many Christian leaders, visiting some in person, to supply him with incriminating evidence for his campaign against our ministry and my person. He also approached leading men in the evangelical movement and arranged for meetings to present his distortions and false allegations in order to galvanize them into action. He travelled throughout the country, holding lectures and recruiting allies. He succeeded in finding supporters, some perhaps motivated by envy of our extensive literature ministry.

In Christian circles it was common knowledge that Ringsdorff operated in lies and that his allegations against us were untrue. Still the defamation continued. Even Christian leaders with a neutral stance passed on the libel or did nothing to stop it spreading. The seeds of poison now sown had far more devastating effects than in the first twenty years of our sisterhood.

Negative reports came thick and fast during the next two years, from 1970 to 1972. At a youth gathering for Bible-believing Christians a well-known minister publicly warned against us. "War on two fronts" read the flyer for a workshop conference organized by an evangelical group. Believers were challenged to take up the fight not just against liberal theology but against over-enthusiastic Christianity (i.e. religious fanaticism), by which we were chiefly meant.

The main base of operations was in north-west Germany, but there were strongholds in southern Germany too. A major Christian organization influential in Pietistic circles became a further base of operations after being contacted by Ringsdorff.

In the Christian world, organizations, churches and fellowships were being systematically poisoned with allegations that the Sisterhood of Mary was demonic and occult. Catholic tendencies, the gifts of the Spirit, religious plays, the call to repentance, etc., were cited as evidence. Fictitious events were presented as facts. It was claimed, for instance, that a sister had died in Israel from fasting, another of appendicitis, as we wouldn't let her have an operation. Nothing of the kind happened. If Christians wondered why we should be considered dangerous, they were told, "Haven't you heard? The devil has infiltrated the Sisterhood of Mary."

Each fresh report was like a stab in the heart. The "war on two fronts" was raging, but in my heart burned another fire – the fire of love and faith. For over twenty years I had lived for the healing of the divisions within the broken Body of Christ and for the end of strife and jealousy among believers. And now, much to my grief, I and my ministry were at the heart of a major conflict. We had always been at the centre of controversy but never publicly on such a scale. And the campaign was spreading.

So why did the Lord allow Satan such a free hand? Why else unless to stretch our love and faith so that it would all end in a triumph of His love? So I reasoned at the time. I firmly believed He wanted the world to see a true body of believers emerge at a time when so many were falling away. One in the Lord, one in Christian love – what a witness they would be!

In April 1971 the Lord granted me a special moment of grace. The spirit of faith, which only God can give, came over me. I had been agonizing: *Surely God won't let lies win in the end! Surely Satan won't prevail and succeed in destroying the Body of Christ! It just can't happen!* At this point God graciously stepped in. A new era of faith dawned for us all. Mother Martyria in particular grieved with me for the Lord's sake and was very supportive, as were all the sisters. In the evenings we met to battle in faith and during the day we included extra prayer slots. I was gripped with the triumphant assurance that God would not fail to stand by His Word. I told myself, "Just keep on believing and persevering in faith. Just be patient and you will see victory. A body of believers will rise, united in the Lord, as an oasis for Jesus and a bastion against the evil one in a world permeated with his influence." My faith was strengthened by promises in His Word. "Is anything too hard for the LORD?" (Genesis 18:14) "With God nothing shall be impossible." (Luke 1:37 KJV)

In retrospect I can't thank the Lord enough for giving me love for those who opposed us. Again and again I would lift them up in prayer. For hours at a time I would sing songs of faith for them and their ministries, asking God to bless them and their church fellowships. As I prayed for them, I praised the blood of Jesus, looking ahead in faith to the day when Jesus would prove Himself greater still and remove the hatred from their hearts.

Not long afterwards various incidents bolstered our faith. Victory seemed imminent. A few Christian brothers decided to take action. For Jesus' sake they felt they couldn't stand by while havoc was being wreaked. Karl Beck, a businessman and Canaan Friend, felt led to write an open letter addressing "the sad state of affairs among Bible-believing Christians". Signed by prominent Christian brothers, it was distributed by the thousand.

District Judge Friedrich Stephan, who also headed up the Darmstadt City Mission, issued a statement in our favour. Shocked by the slanderous attacks, he spoke appreciatively of ministering together with us for over ten years in the City Mission in a deprived area. In his words it was "a God-given unity, marked by mutual love and respect, without which the task could not have been accomplished". The local and regional evangelical leadership, he stressed, had established that they had no grounds to warn against us. As a lawyer he observed that the libel published against us "would have long since been confiscated by the court, and the making of such assertions prohibited, if the Mary Sisters had taken the appropriate measures and filed a suit. In the world people tread more carefully than in Christian circles where there is considerably less hesitation in defaming other groups. For financial reasons people in the world are more cautious, not wishing to risk liability for untrue, unproven assertions ..."

Other Christian leaders, some of whom we didn't really know, also felt called to act for love of the truth. Through clarifying talks they sought to bring their influence to bear upon the leadership of evangelical fellowships affected by the controversy.

The Lord really seemed to be answering. At a conference for Bible-believing Christians the leadership publicly distanced themselves from Ringsdorff, "who has already caused so much harm", and a motion was passed to exclude him from the organization. Ising's book, which he had distributed extensively, was no longer to be recommended, but instead warned against. The majority of participants, including many ministers, declared themselves in favour of the Sisterhood of Mary. After receiving numerous requests, a Christian radio station in our country expressed interest in airing our programmes.

The joy was as great as the pain before. One night in particular stands out in my memory. We had just received a further piece of good news. Unable to contain our joy, we ended our evening meeting with a procession through the motherhouse, singing songs of praise. To all appearances, the love of Christ had triumphed over strife, slander and hatred. The body of true believers, distinguished by the unity of love, was beginning to materialize. This was the fellowship of those who love the Lord. Our fervent prayers had been heard.

Then it all backfired. The initiator of the slander campaign was not excluded from the movement after all. No one, it seemed, had the courage to take action against him. Thus the landscape changed entirely. Circulars intended to establish the truth had little influence. The Christian radio station soon pulled back due to the many letters from our opponents urging them to exclude us from the programming or else risk losing practical and financial assistance.

Not even the publication of a pastoral word about our sisterhood changed the atmosphere. Troubled by the effects of the slander campaign among Bible-believing Christians, a small group of brothers took action. Out of a sense of responsibility, they decided to publish *A Pastoral Word About the Evangelical Sisterhood of Mary in Darmstadt-Eberstadt* as the outcome of their personal investigation. They hoped it would help many confused by the toxic seeds sown. They wrote, for instance:

> Speaking from personal observation and experience, we can state that many have become free and happy children of God through a sound proclamation of the Word. Through the ministry of the Mary Sisters, especially through their literature, many have come to a living faith in Jesus Christ and have become active members of their churches. Others have grown spiritually and then shared the blessings in their churches.

> We have ascertained that the Bible in its entirety is the sole foundation and guiding principle of the life, faith and teaching of the Sisterhood of Mary.

This pastoral word, distributed by the thousand in our country, was liberating for some who were confused. But overall no real change was evident. Thanks to an iron blockade erected by our opponents, little filtered through to those circles mainly affected by the slander. If anything, the antagonism increased. The very fact that the paper was signed by over a hundred clergy and lay people, including well-known Christian leaders within their own ranks, spurred our opponents on to intensify their efforts in destroying our ministry.

People we had counted among our friends now distanced themselves and eventually took sides against us. At various places Christian leaders convened meetings where we were the topic of discussion. This happened even while we were celebrating our twenty-fifth anniversary with a Love-Jesus Festival. A furious controversy raged each time. No one was a match for the intense fanaticism of our opponents – neither those who were supportive of us nor those merely neutral.

One day a Dutch couple by the name of van der Kolk came to me in dismay. As Canaan Friends they had been distributing our literature in their homeland for years. Many requests came for them to show our sound-slide-series, and large numbers of Dutch Christians attended retreats at Canaan. The van der Kolks spent their retirement serving the Lord, keen to spread the Canaan message. There was such a hunger in their country for the message of repentance as the way to first love for Jesus and a joy-filled life. Now it all collapsed. Waves of slander had crossed the border, and blight had settled on many Christians in the Netherlands. No one wanted to have anything to do with sisters labelled as occult, spiritistic and demonic.

What hit even harder was the news that a major evangelical missionary radio station that had been transmitting our programmes for some time suddenly discontinued them. This change in policy could be traced to the same source. I knew how great the demand was for spiritual nourishment. Now with this blow the evil one succeeded in depriving millions, including our brothers and sisters behind the Iron Curtain, for whom programmes had just been prepared.

All this was a Mount Moriah experience on a massive scale, bringing me immeasurable grief. Had the evil one succeeded in his plan to destroy our ministry and rupture the Body of Christ? What about God's promises? Had they failed? Was all our praying and believing in vain? Again and again I surrendered to God's incomprehensible will. Yet for a long time I still agonized in my heart, *Why, Lord, why?*

This slander campaign began in the same year that God showed me I was approaching the end of my life. It was years since God had first given me a mandate to help build up the fellowship of those who love the Lord. This was His main call on my life. Was I to go home with the task unfinished? Was I to end my days labelled by my opponents and critics as "a demonically inspired false teacher"? What was God's purpose in all this? Why did He permit the evil one to cause such havoc and disunity in the Body of Christ?

FOLLOWING THE LAMB OF GOD

Into the darkness of this night a ray of light shone from above. I was reminded of Grünewald's Lamb of God in the Isenheim Altarpiece at Colmar. Deeper and deeper God burned in my heart the image of Jesus on the way to Calvary. He went like a lamb, enduring the cruel blows, hatred, lies and slander. Resolutely He moved forward, step by step, to meet His death, firmly clasping His cross. Blood trickled down from the wounds inflicted by malice, derision and mockery. In Grünewald's painting the drops of blood are gathered in a chalice, from which others would drink for their salvation and the building up of the true body of believers. It was like a divine summons to follow Jesus. With the Lamb of God leading the way, His little lambs follow step by step. They too embrace their cross and, as with Him, it often stands for shame, contempt and injustice. Nothing could be dearer to me than the Lamb of God, whom Paul Gerhardt acclaims in song:

> The Lamb of God goes forth to die,
> The sins of all men bearing…
> Led to the slaughter like a lamb
> Without resistance or complaint…

No longer did I need to ask, "What about justice? When will the truth triumph? When will believers finally see the truth and accept one another in love? Why haven't my prayers been heard?" Deep down inside I knew that I was on the right track. Where He goes, we go. His path is ours. Amid the pain, joy welled up within. What a privilege to walk with Him – mocked, despised, defamed as He was. Not for all the world would I have given up the honour of walking in His footsteps and sharing in His life.

In this picture of the Lamb of God I found the answer to my questions. Now I knew why the truth did not triumph in spite of all my praying and believing. It was the same for Jesus when He walked this earth. The truth did not triumph, but rather the lies of His enemies. The seeds sown by Jesus were poisoned by the Pharisees. In the end His people turned on Him; even His disciples deserted Him. The lies triumphed. Jesus was regarded by the religious world of His time as a false teacher, imposter, criminal – demon-possessed and a political agitator.

In His followers Jesus longs to see His own image reflected: the image of the Lamb, silent and uncomplaining in the face of disgrace, injustice and slander. He longs to find us following Him in love, thankful for the privilege of walking His path. This is where the greatest things are accomplished for His kingdom. After dying there is a resurrection – not for ourselves alone, but for the whole Body of Christ. How grateful I was for the long years of practice. Enduring slander had become second nature to me. Now my soul was still and I could love and bless our critics. But the Lord intended this love to crystallize into something even deeper – the kind of love expressed on the cross: "Father, forgive them; for they know not what they do" (Luke 23:34 KJV).

In all the pain I was comforted. The fellowship of His sufferings – what a privilege! Could there be a greater privilege than suffering pain and disgrace for Him who gave His life for us? He is our one true love, the Bridegroom of our souls, the King of kings, seated at the right hand of God's majesty, and one day He is coming again in glory. To be chosen to walk in His footsteps in some small measure – this was sheer grace. The disciple is not above the Master but is to become like Him, faring the same as He did (Matthew 10:24–25).

For me it was all about Jesus. Choosing the road He walked meant choosing Him, the Man of Sorrows. Years ago I had made the decision to put Jesus first in my life, and He took me up on that. At times He called me apart to be available for Him alone and to share in the fellowship of His sufferings. What I experienced privately in my prayer life was also played out in real-life situations – and now very publicly.

After all the blows and disappointments, Mount Moriah experiences, and the unanswered prayers for love to triumph in the body of believers, God had comforted me by focusing my gaze on the Lamb of God. But now God was challenging me to go further. Was I prepared at all costs to choose Jesus as the One crowned with shame? Was I prepared to prove my love for Him by willingly enduring the greatest blow ever yet dealt to me and my entire life-work?

Despite all the attacks of the evil one, Canaan still drew crowds. It was a popular destination with well-attended international retreats, religious plays performed to a full house and hundreds going forward for Holy Communion at our Sunday services. Canaan was populated by young people from around the world. Orders kept pouring in to the publishing house. The radio and tape department had peak season all year round. Our printshop was unable to keep up with the demand and we had to have many jobs printed commercially. I was sick at heart to think that all this would be destroyed. All my life I had lived for the dawning of a fellowship of believers one in their love for Jesus and each other. Was this how it would end?

Surrendering my will to the Lord, I had to face daily the possible demise of our ministry. This would mean the loss of the friends we still had, the end of the spiritually active cell groups established in various countries, and the discrediting of the message spread internationally through my writings and radio programmes.

In my turmoil I asked the Lord for a word and received 1 Corinthians 4:9 (AMP):

> For, I think, God has exhibited us apostles at the end of the line, like men sentenced to death [and paraded as prisoners in a procession], because we have become a spectacle to the world [a show in the world's amphitheatre], both to angels and to men.

Could the Lord have spoken more distinctly or mercifully? At the same time my heart was pierced. Wasn't this a mirror image of Jesus today? Publicly abused on screen and stage in degrading shows. A spectacle to the world, paraded like a defeated captive in a triumphal procession. Before our very eyes Jesus is undergoing ridicule today. How often I had asked myself, *What can I do to refresh the heart of Jesus and bring Him joy in His pain today?* Now I had the answer. *Walk the walk of shame with Jesus. Take your place at the side of your mocked and despised Lord and Saviour. That will refresh and comfort Him in His pain. And on this path of suffering your prayer to help build His church and bear fruit for Him will come true.*

The question was: When it came to the crunch, was I really prepared to walk the walk of shame with Jesus? My commitment was soon put to the test through an incident on Ascension Day 1973. At a nationwide rally for 20,000 Bible-believing Christians, a voice suddenly came over the loudspeaker during an interval:

"The distribution of literature from the Sisterhood of Mary is not permitted and must cease instantly." Other pamphlets were also being handed out, but the warning was specifically against us. The announcement was repeated several times with a closing remark that they had nothing to do with us. Confusion broke out in the hall. There were indignant murmurs. What had happened? Prior to the event, a minister's wife from Westphalia had asked the leader of the convention if she and her ladies' group could hand out my latest number in the current issues series, as at other conferences. Permission was readily granted, and the pamphlets were generally well received. The situation changed as soon as our opponents realized what was happening. They forbade the distribution of our literature and spread the rumour that the Mary Sisters didn't even abide by the rules – a further argument against us.

I knew that this was just another step in following Jesus. It might even reach the point where my name would be blackened before many thousands who had heard our message and knew of me worldwide. To be persecuted by God-deniers, those who don't believe in God, nor want to, is an honour. Such persecution has its own reward, because it is suffering for Jesus' sake. But to be hated and persecuted by those who call Jesus their Lord cuts to the core, because it comes from fellow believers. In the Christian world there is nothing honourable about this kind of persecution – only shame. It means suffering outside the camp, expelled from the fellowship of believers.

With increasing clarity the Lord showed me that this was the very path He took. The way to victory and resurrection first led to crucifixion, burial, the ruin of His lifework. He builds up the fellowship of those who love the Lord, not primarily on the path of faith – although faith is essential – but on the path of disgrace, destruction and suffering. This is what gives faith its depth, for it means believing in spite of disappointment, destruction and death. It means bearing the pain when God seems to stand against Himself and His own promises.

WONDERFUL IN COUNSEL, EXCELLENT IN WISDOM

Before me I could see the unfolding of God's wonderful purposes. Growth, not destruction, would be the final outcome. God's commissions would come to fruition; so would the vision of believers united in love. Out of pain and raw wounds, something new would grow. A new shoot would spring up out of the soil of suffering: the true body of believers. Only when Jesus' disciples are prepared to die with Him, can the body of believers rise and thrive. So why should I be surprised that the other side was winning in this battle? I was on the right path. Eventually it would lead to a resurrection, and in His good time the blossoming of the fellowship of those who love Him – even if I didn't live to see it.

God blessed me with a faith that reached beyond the chasm of destruction opening up before me. In His grace, He gave me a glimpse into the far future. What God had in mind was something bigger than temporary victories creating a little more unity among believers in one country. The sifting and purifying of the church worldwide was His aim. He wanted to see the Bride of the Lamb prepared and reaching full maturity.

Before me I could see the ultimate goal of God's wonderful purposes, which He accomplishes as we become like Him in His death. "Behold, I make all things new." (Revelation 21:5 NKJV) How Jesus rejoices at the prospect of the Marriage Supper of the Lamb, when the Bride, complete in number and maturity, will be gathered in as the firstfruits of His salvation. Having His Bride with Him for all eternity will be Jesus' greatest reward for His suffering. These are souls who through His sacrificial death reflect His nature as the Lamb. Living and suffering for this goal gives our life its deepest meaning.

What greater privilege than to help prepare the Bride by taking my share of disgrace for His name's sake! Paul writes: "I endure everything for the sake of the elect" – "to complete in my own sufferings something of the untold pains for which Christ suffers on behalf of his body, the Church" (2 Timothy 2:10; Colossians 1:24 PHILLIPS). How could I possibly mind about my small life in view of God's far-reaching plans? His thoughts are always far higher and more glorious than we can possibly imagine. The more senseless the path we tread, when all our praying, waiting and suffering seems to be for nothing, the more glorious the resurrection we will experience.

As of 1973 one of my favourite songs was a Bible verse set to music, which I often sang to the accompaniment of the harmonium in the evening or during the course of the day. At a very dark moment God had given me this verse, which stirred my faith with joyful assurance.

> He is wonderful in counsel, and excellent in wisdom.
>
> Isaiah 28:29 RSV

Years earlier when illness brought me to death's door, my one plea was, "Give me the grace to fulfil the task You have given me. Only then call me home." He answered this prayer – differently than I expected, but far more wonderfully. He granted me the privilege, in Paul's words, to "share his sufferings, becoming like him in his death" (Philippians 3:10 RSV).

Looking back on my life, I am filled with gratitude that the Lord counted me worthy to share His path. In this fellowship with Him I have found deepest fulfilment, His YES AND AMEN.

Epilogue: Whatever Our God Does Is Good

Mother Basilea could little have realized that her memoirs, spanning seventy years, were incomplete. A long way still lay ahead – over twenty-five years. Lovingly, prayerfully she endured, unswerving to the end, until the race was finished. She was always singing of heaven and would gladly have laid down everything she had built up in order to be with the Lord. But God had different plans. As early as 1975, during a time of prayer on the island of Patmos, He showed her that she would remain on earth to an advanced age.

What marked these later years? A new epoch began in 1979 and 1980. New branches were started in Australia, Hong Kong (later Taiwan), Japan, Egypt, South America, Canada, France, Norway, the Netherlands and Switzerland – and in further countries during the following years. This wasn't easy, either for the sisters sent out or for Mother Basilea and Mother Martyria, who accompanied each of their daughters in spirit. Releasing sisters also meant drastically cutting back on our ministry at Canaan. This was especially challenging for our friends, and we would like to thank them for their faithfulness at that time.

Yet dying leads to resurrection, as Mother Basilea was once more to experience – along with us. During the very first visit to various branches a new and totally unexpected ministry was born that would shape the coming years. We had never owned a television, and yet we were asked to produce television programmes. The director of a video lending library in Phoenix, Arizona, begged for a Christmas programme with a deep message. For lack of suitable material, programmes were being transmitted that weren't glorifying to God. In every country Mother Basilea visited she encountered the same problem. As inhibition thresholds sank, promiscuity and violence increasingly dominated the media. Blasphemous productions had become mainstream. Deeply troubled, Mother Basilea spent hours interceding for the various countries that had grown dear to her through her visits and the letters from sisters serving abroad.

In the following years video programmes were produced at Canaan for the United States and other countries. They were carried by Christian stations and even well-known secular networks. For Mother Basilea, this meant doing video recordings, mainly in English – a daunting enterprise at her age. But in her burning desire to help others have a genuine God-encounter, she was willing to use every opportunity.

When natural disasters hit, her days were filled with prayer for the victims and the rescue workers in the affected countries. The sheer magnitude of human tragedy can be overwhelming, yet she never lost sight of the pain in God's heart. Just as the Old Testament prophets lamented when God had no option but to withdraw His blessing from His disobedient people, Mother Basilea drew a parallel with the decline in biblical values, particularly in nations with a Christian heritage. At Sinai in 1963 she had suffered as she foresaw the consequences of rejecting God's laws. Now that it was happening, she didn't stand idly by. True to her unpopular calling as a watchman, she continued to sound the alarm as well as seek practical ways of stemming the tide of lawlessness.

God also blessed us in His abundant goodness. New brothers and sisters from various countries joined our community. Mother Basilea's books and pamphlets were translated into more and more languages and even found their way to those persecuted for Jesus' sake.

At the same time Mother Martyria was being led by the Lord along a very special path. For decades she had actively helped bear the responsibility for the sisterhood and brotherhood. With the support of founding members she led our community during those times when Mother Basilea was in seclusion, alone with the Lord. Her heart was filled with love for Jesus and gratitude for His humiliation from the manger to the cross. Very consciously she made an act of dedication to lowliness. And the Lord honoured her dedication. With increasing loss of memory, she retired from active ministry.

A leadership team largely took over the day-to-day decisions, and once again Mother Basilea was able to spend more time in seclusion. Yet to the end she was mother of our community and a spiritual mother to each one of us. She supported us in her priestly prayers and she was sensitive to anything grieving the Lord in our community. With unshakeable faith she clung to the goal that He would be present among us because we walked in His light.

Right up to the end of her life, even in illness, her motto was, "Whatever our God does is good". How she loved to quote these words from Bach's famous chorale. They so perfectly expressed her positive attitude to life, her determination and confidence in God's wisdom.

On the morning of March 21, 2001, came the moment Mother Basilea had often sung of: the moment when she would go to be with Jesus for ever and see Him face to face.

She was laid to rest in our motherhouse prayer garden, next to Mother Martyria, who had passed away in 1999. The Bible verse she chose for the simple headstone reads: "For to me, to live is Christ and to die is gain" (Philippians 1:21).

As Mother Basilea's doctor said at the service of thanksgiving for her life, "In her suffering she glorified Jesus. What was her secret? With her engaging, childlike spirit she demonstrated faith, trust, love for Jesus, for the Father and the Holy Spirit. She radiated a holy cheerfulness and infectious joy even when in severe pain. She was singing right up to the end."

Mother Basilea left us an inexhaustible spiritual legacy and a wealth of memories, both shared and personal. We were loved with a love that led us to God.

Only the Lord knows how many readers were blessed by the testimony of her life. But letters from many different countries give us a hint. A pastor in Russia wrote: "I am rereading Mother

Basilea's book and give thanks to God for her example of faith and trust in the Lord. Such witnesses of the faith are like stars, and when a star dies, its light continues to shine, its rays piercing the darkness for years to come."

Evangelical Sisters of Mary
Darmstadt, autumn 2017

APPENDIX

Further literature by M. Basilea Schlink

SOWN IN WEAKNESS, RAISED IN GLORY
hardback, full colour, 168 pages

From the spiritual legacy of Mother Basilea Schlink

This book reached me in the depths of my darkness and suffering, forcing me to look at what God was doing in my life and why. I had prayed for transformation and He had taken me by my word. He stripped away everything in my life that was keeping me from giving Him first place. New Zealand

MY ALL FOR HIM 176 pages

Fall in love with Jesus all over again

One book which has changed me so much is MY ALL FOR HIM. I realized just how cold I was to Jesus – there was plenty of mental agreement to Him as a Saviour, but not a really loving relationship. That is changing. Australia

Every time I read it, my love for Jesus is kindled. India

PRAYING OUR WAY THROUGH LIFE 64 pages

I was someone who didn't have much time for prayer, but now I have a regular prayer time daily. Cuba

It was like talking to someone face to face. And it answered my hundreds of questions. Kenya

REALITIES OF FAITH 144 pages

The miracles of God experienced today

An ideal handbook for beginning prayer groups because it is such a good faith-builder. USA

BEHOLD HIS LOVE 216 pages

Devotions on the Passion of Jesus

Unseen, Jesus still walks this earth, seeking true disciples. Words are cheap. What the world needs to see is Jesus shining out of people.

RULED BY THE SPIRIT 128 pages

Only the life-giving Spirit can prepare the church for the return of Jesus. When the Holy Spirit comes, bringing His presence and gifts, spiritual life will gain momentum and the church will have an impact on a world of growing darkness.

REPENTANCE – THE JOY-FILLED LIFE 160 pages

While reading REPENTANCE, tears coming from nowhere started flowing from my eyes. I found myself prostrate on the ground repenting and confessing my sins. Fears that filled my life went. People I used to find difficult in our church and others, I found myself loving genuinely. Uganda

MORE PRECIOUS THAN GOLD 416 pages

Daily readings on God's rules for living

Excerpt: Never write off anyone ... Only if you continue to love your neighbour with patience, can you be sure of God's patient love towards you.

MARY, THE MOTHER OF JESUS 128 pages

Can't say how challenged I've been by Mary's life of obedience and discipleship. Mary said *yes* when God asked the impossible of her. She dared to go where no one else had ever gone before. She trusted God, and He trusted her to see it through to the end. And because she was true to God's calling on her life, others were blessed. New Zealand

She writes without regard to critical comment on the Gospel narrative, but with a deep spirit of prayer and sympathetic identification.

The Church Times

BUILDING A WALL OF PRAYER 96 pages

An intercessor's handbook

When the future of a nation is in the balance, when politics, economics and ethics fail, it is the intercessors who can make a difference.

This book has taught me what to do in this time of crisis for my country. It is a storehouse of God's truth. Japan

ISRAEL, MY CHOSEN PEOPLE 144 pages

A German confession before God and the Jews

In this day as nations are turning once again from the Jewish nation, Christians need to be reminded that the Jews are still chosen of God. USA

I WILL GIVE YOU THE TREASURES OF DARKNESS 48 pages

The night is a scary place to be. Now I know that even though the evil one can rob me of everything, he can't rob me of my soul – not if I have entrusted myself to Jesus. New Zealand